School Counseling and Athlete

School Counseling and the Student Athlete explores empirical, theoretical, and practice-based issues that demand consideration by school-based counseling and educational professionals working at the pre-collegiate level. In its pages clinicians and students will find insights into both why student athletes experience many of the issues they do as well as the steps that counselors can take to help these individuals and their families. Theories of motivation and theoretical approaches to counseling student athletes are covered in order to provide an orientation to working with this group, and the book also includes a thorough discussion of the most important elements of counseling the student athlete: the academic, career, personal, and social issues they face; consultations with coaches, teachers, and parents; commercialism and the student athlete's identity; and gender, sexual identity, and culture issues. Each chapter ends with discussion questions and available resources for counselors. Grounded in research and pioneering in its analysis of sports psychology for students in grades K-12, *School Counseling and the Student Athlete* is a must-have book for school counselors, clinicians, and other professionals who work with elementary and secondary students.

Adam Zagelbaum, PhD, is an associate professor at Sonoma State University in the department of counseling's pupil and personnel services track, where he also serves as PPS program coordinator. He has authored, co-authored, and edited textbooks, articles, training videos, book chapters, and workbooks on school counseling, career counseling, group work, child and adolescent counseling, and working with immigrant families. He also has presented at various international and national conferences. His work with student athletes includes counseling roles at the K-12 level and within university settings.

School Counseling and the Student Athlete

College, Careers, Identity, and Culture

Adam Zagelbaum

Routledge
Taylor & Francis Group

NEW YORK AND LONDON

First published 2014
by Routledge
711 Third Avenue, New York, NY 10017

and by Routledge
27 Church Road, Hove, East Sussex BN3 2FA

Routledge is an imprint of the Taylor & Francis Group, an informa business

© 2014 Taylor & Francis

Library of Congress Cataloging in Publication Data
Zagelbaum, Adam.
School counseling and the student athlete: college, careers, identity, and culture / Adam Zagelbaum.
pages cm
Includes bibliographical references and index.
1. High school athletes—Counseling of—United States. 2. High school athletes—Education—United States. I. Title.
LC2581.Z34 2014
373.18—dc23
2013038060

ISBN: 978-0-415-53621-9 (hbk)
ISBN: 978-0-415-53622-6 (pbk)
ISBN: 978-0-203-11175-8 (ebk)

Typeset in Minion
by Book Now Ltd, London

Contents

Contributors

Robyn Brammer, Ph.D. is the Associate Dean of Graduate Studies and Research at Central Washington University. She has a background in health psychology and has worked with groups like the Multiple Sclerosis Society in helping members integrate their physical and mental health. She has also published extensively in the diversity literature and provides international workshops on gender and sexual identity.

Michael P. Hagan, Ph.D. has worked as a psychologist for over three decades, primarily working in juvenile corrections. He has worked with juveniles and young adults on a wide variety of psychological concerns, which is reflected in his publications. He has long had an interest in the interface between school, psychology, and athletics.

Gregg Kuehl, Ph.D., NCC currently works at a Veterans Administration Hospital in Tomah, Wisconsin, and has previously worked with student-athletes at the collegiate level within counseling and educational settings.

Carmen Wandel, M.A. is a credentialed school counselor. Her experiences as a student-athlete, high school swim coach, mother of two student-athletes, team mom, and high school counselor working with student-athletes in the public school setting have given her the varied perspectives valuable in assessing their needs.

Adam Zagelbaum, Ph.D., NCC is an Associate Professor at Sonoma State University within the Department of Counseling Pupil and Personnel Services track (and serves as the PPS Program Coordinator). He has authored, co-authored, and edited textbooks, articles, training videos, book chapters, and workbooks regarding school counseling, career counseling, group work, child and adolescent counseling, and working with immigrant families. His work with student-athletes includes both educational and counseling roles at the K-12 level and within university settings.

Acknowledgements

I wish to acknowledge the team of people who helped with this project. From the student athletes and stakeholders I encountered during my time at the University of Florida, University of Southern Mississippi, and Ball State University, to my professional work venues and, of course, my family and friends who challenge and support me in ways that truly make me a well-rounded counselor and educator, thank you tremendously for your efforts. Also, thank you to those who have directly contributed to the construction of this text: Dr. Greg Kuehl (Ball State University), Dr. Michael Hagan (Department of Corrections, State of Wisconsin), Dr. Robyn Brammer (Central Washington University), and Ms. Carmen Wandel (school counselor and graduate of Sonoma State University). I believe our teamwork has produced a winning result!

1 Orientation to Working with Student Athletes

Mike[1] was a 16-year-old student in the Midwest who was rigorously playing on the high school football team's offensive line, and had shown a lot of talent in the eyes of his coaches. His father, Mike Sr. (age 46), had played football in his youth and had a position on his high school team in a similar capacity, and was highly supportive of his son's "ability to make it" and believed there could be "possibilities for the next level". Mike's mother, Linda (age 44), was not a student athlete herself, but had interest and passion for the game, and it also appeared that his sister, Lynn (age 15), was strongly bonded to his mother in this way. There were always concerns about Mike's potential for injury, as he appeared to be a bit of a risk-taker in terms of physical activities that he engaged in as early as age 9, where he would jump from high places into the local lake, or swim out as far as he could in order to "outdo" everyone else. He would engage in a lot of rough-and-tumble play with friends and family, and often engaged in competitive games that required endurance, strength, and dexterity. Local community residents and friends of the family saw this child's potential to use his talents on the football field, and he had it in his head early on that he would be able to go far with this pursuit. Mike believed that everyone would fully support him, even though there were other things he had to do to succeed along the way, such as attend school.

When he began his freshman year of high school, Mike started to recognize that the game was becoming more competitive, the stakes were higher, and the proportion of players trying to make the squad was greater than he had grown up with in his community. He had to dedicate a large amount of time to practice and training sessions, making his academic studies a little challenging for him to keep up with at times. Though he had many talents on the gridiron, Mike would often feel like his Math and English classes were too difficult to handle. Teachers were often frustrated by the amount of late, incomplete, or missing work that he would turn in, and parent–teacher conferences would often focus on issues of motivation and time management. Mike was not a disruptive student, but he did not appear to be focused enough on course material. Coaches would try to encourage Mike to work harder on keeping his academic pace up, but with the talents that had to be focused on for him to succeed as a football player, these messages were sometimes conflicting or mixed in terms of how

Mike was receiving them. A referral to the school counselor was suggested as a way to see if Mike could better address these needs.

Mike Sr. was not certain about this referral. He was used to his son being able to work through various challenges and expectations that others had for him. Also, Mike Sr., to the best of his recollection, had not used the services of a guidance counselor in his school days for anything more than scheduling of or transferring from classes, so the idea of seeking out this service seemed like a strange concept. Linda and Lynn, because of their relationship and ability to communicate about stresses and struggles they and their close friends had encountered with school-related issues, were able to suggest to Mike Sr. that he be more open to the idea of having Mike work with the school counselor, and helped to reduce some of Mike Sr.'s initial concerns.

Mike and his school counselor would meet about once or twice a month for the next few years. Plans were constructed to have him schedule his practices and homework, and the parents were able to get on board with these plans by way of weekly progress reports, feedback from teachers, and consultation with the school counselor. The improvement in his schoolwork was not nearly as remarkable as the amount of rapport and disclosure that Mike would make during the course of this relationship. Mike did not appear at any point in his meetings with the school counselor to be lacking in academic potential or educational talent; he did not appear to fit any stereotype of a "dumb jock" that society had prominently depicted by way of media and water-cooler discussion. There was no record of him requiring special accommodations for physical, mental, or emotional needs. He did not appear to have struggled with alcohol or drug abuse issues, and was not engaging in any sort of delinquent behaviors on or off of school grounds. Mike was a good player, and appeared to be meeting a lot of expectations. Ironically, it seems like this dynamic may have been part of the problem.

The messages that he had often been hearing were about the fact that he "wasn't into" doing the work. Father did not necessarily think that schoolwork was unimportant, but there did not appear to be a lot of emphasis being placed on it at home. Teachers, on the other hand, were expecting a level of academic performance that emphasized his schoolwork quite a bit. Coaches would try to bridge this gap in some ways, but with the emphasis they had on athletics, Mike was not always able to apply these principles to the classroom. His peers were not necessarily any more aware of these concerns than other people in his life. Though many of his friends were on the team as well, Mike was not a team captain or quarterback. He was an important part of the team, but not necessarily a prominent figure who garnered as much popularity as the other players. Part of him was happy that he did not have this kind of attention, but part of him would also be frustrated about the fact that he was not always a part of the same clique as other players were. He was able to express his concerns and vulnerabilities in ways that helped him eventually get on track academically, and mediate some of the social pressures he would face regarding friends and community issues. He would eventually attend his senior prom, and make a commitment to a state college in order to play football and study the professional field of education. Eventual discussions between Mike Sr. and the school counselor also took a more supportive and open discourse as well. Some of the skepticism that the father had expressed about whether or not a counseling professional would add any major benefit to Mike's plans appeared to give way to more encouragement and belief that school counseling helped to link some of the concepts that Mike needed to transfer into the classroom. One of the quotes shared by Mike Sr. would best sum up the relationship: "For someone who may not have played sports in school, I was impressed with the game plan. Thanks for being part of the team."

Before the school year ended, Mike would have one more meeting with the school counselor. There was a final check on academic requirements and eligibility status performed, and his folder was complete. Mike was appreciative of several things that had happened during the course of the counseling relationship, but it was the departing message that seemed to carry the most impact. "Thanks for understanding how serious I am about my stuff," he said. "Not everyone understands how much there is to do sometimes, and it's not that I don't want to do it, but it's hard to do it all when people don't necessarily know how much each thing adds up." I did not know exactly what happened to Mike once he entered college, but I like to think that he was able to face the next level with an understanding that he would be able to find someone to seriously help him focus on the next goal(s) he would have.

Unique Influences on the Client

Mike, though he was a silent student in many of his classes, had a lot of expectations on and off the field to live up to. There was also some apprehension about the fact that some of the more popular peers did not seem to struggle in the same way that he did with balancing his social, academic and athletic demands. He felt that something may have been wrong with him, in that he would take some of the academic demands seriously, but parents and coaches may not have been completely reinforcing of his same level of seriousness. Mike would distance himself from some of the work because he would sometimes question if it would really matter if he was destined to be a successful professional football player, but at the same time, recognize that he was able to meet the demands of his physical practices and training schedule: so why quit on the schoolwork? Sometimes he felt that teachers were looking at him as if to say, "you may be good on the field, but this is a different game." His father, in trying to be supportive, would send him messages like "well, as long as you do your best in class, that's all that really matters." Mike was most likely confused more than anything else, and probably did not want everyone else to know how confusing it all was to him.

I had encountered students who played recreational sports or had other extracurricular involvements before, and were used to "blowing off" assignments or having disagreements with the importance of needing to learn certain things. My work with Mike, though, helped open up a new angle on what many student athletes face: pressure and confusion about having to deal with so many expectations and not necessarily knowing how to process it all. I would also encounter numerous other school counselors, counseling professionals, and educators in the years to come that would indicate Mike was not an isolated case.

There have also been high-profile and quite dramatic cases that have involved far more dangerous and traumatic crimes involving student and/or professional athletes over the past few years. Rape and sexual assault cases, murder and manslaughter are just some of the matters that comprise this list. Sometimes, the perception and athletic culture associated with athletics has a significant impact on how the crime and the individuals involved are handled and valued by public and community stakeholders. Though this text explores some of these issues, it must be noted that the vast majority of student athletes and coaches who participate in K-12 sports and beyond do not become involved in crimes to this degree, and that it is important to work with athletic communities and cultures with this specific notion in mind.

There are communities that are said to have a "win-at-all costs" mentality, wherein issues and acts that occur off the playing field are sometimes given less emphasis because of the successes that take place on the field. Though legal aspects of law are to remain unchanged, moral aspects and conduct-based elements of one's off-the-field antics can be malleable. Media perceptions and community judgments can often portray individuals as people who should have known better, because they have unique talents and skills that would make them more likely to succeed in life and more people to support them in times of crisis or distress. However, with these talents often comes expectations and demands that can create conflict, confusion, and drama.

One important lesson I uncovered from working with Mike and his father was that athletic and academic expectations can have different meanings for different people who are all part of the same system: be it a family system or school system. Mike Sr. believed in his son's abilities, but did not necessarily define Mike's academic success in the same way that teachers, coaches, and even Mike himself were attempting to do. The school stakeholders also appeared to believe in what skills Mike possessed, but had different types of contact and context with him to harness his potential in the academic realm. The well-intentioned but cross-communicated perspectives which exposed an underperforming area for Mike in his schooling may have directed him to seek out additional help: something that may not have normally been expected of him when engaged in his athletic pursuits. However, it provided Mike with a different type of support which allowed him to refocus his energies and his family to feel better about the resources available to him if he were ever to struggle again.

Nothing can be more frustrating to a student athlete than an adult who does not understand the gravity of what it means to compete for a sports position at the next level. It hurts credibility, potential for empathy, and becomes more concerning about how they perceive authority figures in some cases. This principle is not unlike the concept of Amir's (1992) contact hypothesis, whereby a counseling professional who makes contact with a client is encouraged to start from the perspective of locating strengths and positive expectations of how these strengths can be applied to both the counseling relationship and the client's everyday life. This approach has been applied to clients who are culturally different (Zagelbaum & Carlson, 2011), but considering that student athletes are part of a unique school culture (Chandler & Goldberg, 1990), extending the contact hypothesis to include these individuals appears to be a plausible move. As a result, various other issues can be revealed in the working alliance between counselor and student athlete.

Considering all the pressures that are already associated with K-12 schooling, coupled with the attention that a student athlete has for his/her performance on the field, there are many reasons that a school counselor or other school-based counseling professional would be involved with a student of this type. Student athletes participate in sports for various reasons, all of which it is intended to explore throughout this text.

Types of Student Athlete

There are many ways that student athletes can be defined. The terminology used can be as varied as the number of positions on a team or the amount of sports that exist. There are over 50 types of sports officially recognized at the college level, which include team and individual versions, as well as those restricted to men and those restricted to women. From baseball to wrestling, these types of sports vary from college to college depending on various factors (College Board, 2006).

The term "student athlete" emphasizes the role of student first for reasons that are often debated: is it because the athletic participant is also a student or because the studies are to take priority as the athletics develop further? Regardless of what side of the debate one is on, there are consistent terms used to identify student athletes at the collegiate level with which counselors need to be familiar during the K-12 years. *Grayshirt* athletes refer to individuals recruited out of high school, but often delay their college enrollment for at least one term. *Redshirt* athletes are recruited to play National Collegiate Athletic Association (NCAA) sports, but are held out of competition for one season so they are available to play for a fifth year, even though they cannot play in any collegiate games or scrimmages during their red-shirted academic year. *Qualifier athletes* refer to prospective student athletes who meet NCAA eligibility requirements, and can therefore apply for practices, competitions and financial aid packages to assist at the collegiate level. *Partial qualifier athletes,* unlike the qualifiers, only meet some of the academic requirements and can only play in Division II sports, but not for one academic year. Lastly, *nonqualifier athletes* are individuals who do not meet NCAA Division I academic eligibility requirements, and cannot receive athletic financial aid for their first year in college, nor participate in athletic competitions or practices during the first year as well (College Board, 2006).

Also, there are ways that some researchers have classified students and student athletes based on their type of motivation toward success. Covington and Omelich (1991), as an extension of Atkinson's (1964) work on motivation, have described *success-oriented* students as those who are highly motivated to succeed without being afraid of failing; *failure-avoider* students who are negatively motivated by the fear of failure and the anticipation of shame in response to a given failed effort; *overstriver* students who usually avoid failure by succeeding in their endeavors; and *failure-acceptor* students who are not particularly attracted to success, but are also not overly concerned about failing. Simons, Van Rheenen, and Covington (1999) have taken these classifications several steps further and applied them to how student athletes approach academic issues at the collegiate level, which also appears to have implications for how school-based counseling professionals can work with these students. However, regardless of the way in which student athletes are classified, it is clear that various counseling and educational professionals need to be involved with these students during their pre-collegiate years in order to best prepare them for subsequent phases of development. Many professional organizations have engaged in this practice for several reasons related to academic and athletic purposes.

Organizational Movements

In terms of standards and practices, various school stakeholders have been getting significantly involved with student athletes' academic preparation in recent years. The National Association of Secondary School Principals (NAASP), for example, reached an agreement with the NCAA in order to establish specific guidelines making school principals responsible for identifying school courses that meet the NCAA's core curriculum requirements (Dickman & Lammel, 2000). The National Federation of State High School Associations (NFHS) engaged in similar discussion in order to back this decision and further assisted NAASP to support academic reform for student athletes in other ways. Incoming student athletes in 2000–2001 were allowed to use Internet-based courses in order to assist with establishing initial eligibility (Dickman & Lammel, 2000). At the administrative level, it seems that student athletes were being advocated for, in so much that nontraditional teaching methods were used to assist with the demands these students have in order to balance their academic and athletic pursuits.

The American School Counselor Association endorses the support of student athletes through its Mission Statement which "ensures success of all students" (ASCA, 2005). The College Board (2006) has long been a valuable resource for school counselors and school-based counseling professionals who work with student athletes. It has specifically defined the counselor's role with the following points (pp. 10–12):

- Make sure that student athletes understand that they must meet academic requirements to play intercollegiate sports.
- Know academic requirements and eligibility rules, being aware of the fact that these can often change.
- Maintain open lines of communication with coaches and athletic directors.
- Be sure that students know that college admissions decisions are not ultimately made by coaches, but rather, admissions committees.
- Remind students that the availability of sports is not the only factor to consider when applying for college.

The academic and college focus for the school counselor appears quite clear among these points, but the intricacies that athletic organizations have regarding the recruiting and eligibility process suggest that the school counselor may have other needs and functions to provide students as they venture into these processes.

The main athletic organizations that largely regulate student sports in our country are the National Collegiate Athletic Association (NCAA, 2010) National Junior College Athletic Association (NJCAA, 2011) and the National Association of Intercollegiate Athletics (NAIA, 2011). The former has greater prominence than the others. This is not to speak to issues of quality or prestige, but rather a matter of exposure and familiarity. All organizations intend to monitor, mold, and encourage student athletes to be successful professionals and citizens; off-the-field qualities are stressed as importantly as on-the-field skills. The available data regarding student athletics, however, demonstrates how competitive and stressful this venue can often be.

NCAA Probability Statistics

In 2000, the NCAA released estimated probabilities of students who compete at the collegiate level and beyond. The sports identified in this report were included because they all have a major professional league in the United States and were officially recognized by the National Federation of State High School Associations. For sports such as men's basketball, women's basketball, football, baseball, men's ice hockey and men's soccer, the proportion of students who go on to play at an NCAA member institution does not reach double-digit percentages. Furthermore, the percentages of NCAA students who are eventually drafted by American professional leagues do not reach single digits for any one of these aforementioned sports.

The pressures of athletic competition, and the desire to perform at the top of one's game, do not appear to be purely perception-driven. There are limited roster positions and many student athletes vying for these positions, arguably at all levels of education. Student athletes do not always have the opportunity to see the full picture of the collegiate landscape because they are often competing at local and state levels that may not extend into national realms. Though media coverage of sports, scouting visits from top organizations, and communication with coaches and athletic stakeholders is/are possible, these methods often occur in one-to-one conversations or small groups; the student athlete may not always recognize how many other competitors and candidates are pursuing the same roster spots. Previous research has indicated that these statistics do not deter the vast majority of student athletes who believe they will become professional athletes (Miller, Melnick, Barnes, Farrell, & Sabo, 2005; Simons, Van Rheenen, & Covington, 1999). However, the past decade has dramatically shifted in terms of economic matters, and the financial costs of attending college, coupled with one of the bleakest job markets since the Great Depression. The degree of sacrifice that student athletes and their families may face as a result of these funding issues may create a new set of challenges and stressors about how much time and availability they will have to dedicate to the academic and athletic demands of college. It also remains to be seen about how competitive the student athletic market will become, as colleges and universities face extensive budget cuts expected to reduce the size(s) of various athletic programs to a degree not seen by previous generations.

There are documented cases of students losing scholarships as well, because of confusion and lack of education regarding NCAA rules and provisions (Naughton, 1996). The school counselor is one important resource for the developing student athlete to have as (s)he takes up this challenging, though still rewarding, gauntlet. The school counselor serves in consultative roles as well (Dinkmeyer Jr., & Carlson, 2006; Dougherty, 2005), so that other resources can be available to the student athlete and forms of advocacy can occur.

Some Programs and Methods for Assisting the Student Athlete

There are programs and methods that have long been recommended for the school counselor to use when working with student athletes, especially at the high school level. Goldberg and Chandler (1995) have specifically called attention to the principle of "catching them being good" as a driving mechanism by which coaches and school counselors can work together in order to positively reinforce student athletes for handling challenging situations and circumstances with prosocial behaviors. This largely Adlerian concept has been used in school settings for many purposes. Albert (2003) proposed it as a manner by which classroom discipline and etiquette can be expected on the part of teachers and maintained on the part of students. Goldstein and McGinnis (1983) have used it as a modeling approach, called Skillstreaming, by which students, counselors, and teachers and coaches demonstrate prosocial behaviors to display when exposed to an ambiguous and/or stressful social situation. Practicing these social skills, similar to practicing the physical motions of sport plays, can result in a transferring of such skills into the student's greater social surround. There have been several studies that have showcased the effective outcomes of these approaches, not just in terms of the new skills that are learned, but also how students successfully implement these prosocial behaviors into their everyday interactions with peers and authority figures (Goldstein, 1995; Greenleaf, 1992). These approaches have also been made into school curricula that are often incorporated into whole-school approaches that address all students, not only the student athletes (Goldstein, 1981; Goldstein, 1988). Though many trainings and curricula are available, it is also important to note that, when it comes to college preparation and academic skill development, research is starting to address the importance of groups and support networks for assisting the student athlete (Ward Jr., 2008; Petrie & Stoever, 1997; Ting, 2009). Considering that many student athletes participate in team sports, it would seem logical that group approaches to counseling and school-based interventions would be plentiful in number and scope. However, the majority of approaches have traditionally focused on specialized, individual approaches because of the social capital and expected prosocial skills that develop from the natural interactions of playing competitive sports (Eccles, Barber, Stone, & Hunt, 2003; Fredricks & Eccles, 2005). Many universities, for example, rely on classes or seminars to orient student athletes to school environments. Team meetings and motivational orientations to academic duties help disseminate the information about available resources to student athletes, but whether or not the resources are sought largely depends on the individual (Simons, Van Rheenen, & Covington, 1999). School-based counseling professionals have the ability to draw from the power of groups and, with the use of other stakeholders, further engage support networks and group approaches to assist student athletes with motivational and transitional issues that can assist with decision-making and commitments to academic, personal/social, and career-oriented goals. Guidelines and suggestions about how to do this are provided in subsequent chapters.

There are programs that assist student athletes at the high school level. Most are based on the mission of fostering positive youth development in terms of personal identity, team building, and development as a productive citizen (Fraser-Thomas, Cote, & Deakin, 2005). The Play It Smart Program is one of the most prominent examples of these programs (Tinsley, 2008). This program is primarily based on athletic development of football players, but it has been developed for other athletes and related stakeholders. The emphasis not only on athletic skills but also life skills has made this particular resource invaluable for assisting student athletes during the pre-collegiate years (Petitpas, Van Raalte, Cornelius, & Presbrey, 2004). Certainly, the individual approaches and opportunities presented to student athletes through Play It Smart are effective and involve multiple types of professionals who can help these individuals achieve their scholastic and athletic goals.

There appears to be a shortage of approaches that stress the importance of the student athlete's family when it comes to striking a balance between academic and athletic pursuits. There are many student athletes who come from long lines of athletes within their families. The cases of Mike and others, presented throughout this text, are some examples of how the positive involvement of the family in the counseling process as well as the academic and athletic pursuits of the student athlete can have significant and long-lasting impacts that assist with decision-making, and further enhance the support network that they will likely rely on as they matriculate into the collegiate level and beyond. Previous research has strongly indicated that student athletes often struggle to find appropriate role models and mentors within their chosen academic fields (Watt & Moore III, 2001), yet the involvement of parents within a student's educational and social development is deemed a critical element for success (Brown, Mounts, Lamborn, & Steinberg, 1993; Szechter & Liben, 2004). There appears to be something of a gap between the counseling services student athletes can receive and the support that family can further enhance and provide, that makes the school-based counseling professional a necessary link when it comes to assisting the student athlete with resources and skills to assist with their issues. There are even questions raised by the academic preparation of athletic trainers when it comes to dealing with many personal issues and matters that often surface during the course of their relationships with student athletes (Misasi, Davis Jr., & Morin, & Stockman, 1996). Though there are time limits and budgetary constraints that can often limit the amount of contact parents can have with the school-based counseling professional, being able to engage in a productive dialogue with the student athlete's parental/family system can provide significant long-term benefits that enable greater depth and clarity of academic, career, and personal/social matters to occur. The later chapters of this text offer various ways of facilitating this dialogue and interaction.

School-Based and Related Counseling Professionals

There are many school-based and related counseling professionals who can impact the development of the student athlete. For school psychologists and sports psychologists, the American Psychological Association is their main professional organization, namely the American Psychological Association (APA) Division 47 – Exercise and Sports Psychology. Community and family counseling professionals are mostly identified through the American Counseling Association (ACA). A unique subset of ACA counseling members are sports and athletic counselors, who are professionally organized through the Sports Counseling Interest Network (SCIN). College representatives associated with student athletics are not only represented through the aforementioned National Collegiate Athletic Association (NCAA), but also through the National Junior College Athletic Association (NJCAA) and the National Association of Intercollegiate Athletics (NAIA). However, in terms of addressing the school system and various stakeholders associated with student athletes, the American School Counselor Association (ASCA) is one of the most important organizations available to assist school counselors.

This is not to say that there are no other professionals who can assist student athletes. Certainly teachers, coaches, and trainers are critical to these individuals' development as well. The purpose of supporting the student athlete is manifold, and knowing each professional comes from not only interpersonal contact, but also understanding the ethics and standards of practice that each professional is trained to do and able to follow.

Text Overview

As can hopefully be discerned from this chapter, this is a text meant to focus on supporting the needs of the student athlete when it comes to academic, career and personal/social matters. The identification of resources and organizations that can assist with these issues is also provided so that school-based counseling professionals can further prepare and advocate for more needs that student athletes and their families are expected to have. As such, this text aims to focus largely on how the school system can best engage with student athletes and their stakeholders, and uses specific models and techniques to guide and inspire the reader.

Conclusion

The popularity of sports, particularly at the collegiate level, is strong within American society. The majority of students will likely express interest in sport, either as spectators, participants, or both. Even with the likelihood of playing sports professionally being a statistically difficult task for some to accomplish, the pursuit of this goal, at least at the amateur level, is a significant and serious endeavor for many students to undergo, and one that requires a large and varied support system to exist along the way. School counselors and other school-based counseling professionals have interesting positions within the school system to assist student athletes, but may not always be the first ones to have contact with these individuals because of perceptions about what it may mean for a student athlete to need counseling services if athletics and academics are the primary tasks they need to accomplish. Furthermore, many studies and literature tend to focus on collegiate and post-collegiate years of the student athlete, and there are many implications that these findings have for professionals who work at the pre-collegiate level. The purpose of this text is to further articulate how student athletes can be served at this time in their lives, and it encourages the school-based counseling professional to generate further ideas about engaging others in this process, such as peers and family members. Considering the current state of the United State's economy and the ways in which families, communities, and schools are struggling to provide resources for the career, academic, and personal/social goals of students and student athletes, exploring other methods and approaches to working with such students is both a viable and necessary cause. As is the case with other texts that have addressed large populations of clients, readers are reminded that between-group and within-group differences exist when conceptualizing and working with student athletes, and the information in this text attempts to take this matter into account at all possible times. Individuals training to be professional counselors, as well as already established counselors, are given ultimate authority to decide what information can be readily applied to the student athletes they will one day serve. Even if personal interests in sports are not significantly strong, we hope that the readers can be fans of the content of this text, so that the most victories can be accomplished.

Questions to Consider

1. What does it mean to have athletic ability? Who primarily defines athletic ability? How would this impact a K-12 student?
2. What do you believe are the main reasons that individuals play sports? How does this impact the decision to play for an amateur or professional team or organization?
3. What is your understanding of the process by which one becomes a student athlete? What is your understanding of the process by which one becomes a professional athlete? How do you believe these processes impact the work of a school counselor and other school stakeholders?

Note

1 All names presented are pseudonyms.

References

Albert, L. (2003) *Cooperative Discipline*. Circle Pines, MN: AGS Publishing.

Amir, Y. (1992) Social assimilation or cultural mosaic? In J. Lynch, C. Modgil & S. Modgil (Eds.), *Cultural Diversity and the Schools. Vol. 1. Education for cultural diversity: Convergence and divergence* (pp. 23–36). London: Falmer Press.

ASCA (American School Counselor Association) (2005) *The American School Counselor Association National Model: A Framework for School Counseling Programs*. Alexandria, VA: Author.

Brown, B., Mounts, N., Lamborn, S., & Steinberg, L. (1993) Parenting practices and peer group affiliation in adolescence. *Child Development, 64*, 467–482.

Chandler, T., & Goldberg, A. (1990) The academic all-American as vaunted adolescent role-identity. *Sociology of Sport Journal, 7*, 287–293.

College Board (2006) *College Counseling Sourcebook* (3rd ed). New York: Author.

Covington, M., & Omelich, C. (1991) Need achievement revisited: Verification of Atkinson's original 2X2 model. In C. D. Spielberger, I. G. Saranson, Z. Kulscar, & G. L. Van Heck (Eds.), *Stress and Emotion: Anxiety, Anger, and Curiousity* (Vol. 14, pp. 85–105). San Francisco: Jossey-Bass.

Dickman, D., & Lammel, J. (2000) Getting to the core of student athletic standards. *Principal Leadership*, 30–33.

Dinkmeyer Jr., D., & Carlson, J. (2006) *Consultation: Creating School-Based Interventions*. New York: Routledge.

Dougherty, A. M. (2005) *Psychological Consultation and Collaboration in School and Community Settings* (5th ed.). Belmont, CA: Brooks/Cole.

Eccles, J. S., Barber, B. L., Stone, M., & Hunt, J. (2003) School district size and student performance. *Economics of Education Review, 22*, 193–201.

Fraser-Thomas, J. L., Cote, J., & Deakin, J. (2005) Youth sport programs: An avenue to foster positive youth development. *Physical Education and Sport Pedagogy, 10*, 19–40.

Fredricks, J. A., & Eccles, J. S. (2005) Developmental benefits of extracurricular involvement: Do peer characteristics mediate the link between activities and youth outcomes? *Journal of Youth and Adolescence, 34*, 507–520.

Goldberg, A., & Chandler, T. (1995) Sports counseling: Enhancing the development of the high school student athlete. *Journal of Counseling and Development, 74*, 39–44.

Goldstein, A. (1981) *Psychological Skills Training*. New York: Pergamon.

Goldstein, A. (1988) *The PREPARE Curriculum: Teaching Prosocial Competencies*. Champaign, IL: Research Press.

Goldstein, A. (1995) *Understanding and Managing Children's Classroom Behaviour*. New York: John Wiley & Sons.

Goldstein, A., & McGinnis, E. (1983) *Skillstreaming in Childhood: Teaching Prosocial Skills to the Secondary School Child*. New York: McNaughton & Gunn.

Greenleaf, D. (1992) The use of programmed transfer of training and Structured Learning Therapy with disruptive adolescents in a school setting. *Journal of School Psychology, 20*, 122–130.

Miller, K., Melnick, M., Barnes, G., Farrell, M., & Sabo, D. (2005) Untangling the links among athletic involvement, gender, race, and adolescent academic outcomes. *Sociology of Sports Journal, 22*, 178–193.

Misasi, S. P., Davis Jr., C. F., Morin, G. E., & Stockman, D. (1996) Academic preparation of athletic trainers as counselors. *Journal of Athletic Training, 31*, 29–42.

NAIA (National Association of Intercollegiate Athletics) (2011) History of the NIAA. Retrieved July 7, 2011 from http://naia.cstv.com/genrel/090905aai.html.

Naughton, J. (1996) Hundreds lose scholarships in confusion over NCAA rules. *The Chronicle of Higher Education, 43*, A49(2).

NCAA (National Collegiate Athletic Association) (2010) Estimated probability of competing in athletics beyond the high school interscholastic level. Retrieved June 7, 2011 from http://www.ncaa.org/wps/portal/ncaahome?WCM_GLOBAL_CONTEXT=/ncaa/ NCAA/Academics+and+Athletes/Education+and+Research/Probability+of+ Competing/Probability+of+Competing.

NJCAA (National Junior College Athletic Association) (2011) Mission Statement. Retrieved July 9, 2011 from http://www.njcaa.org/todaysNJCAA.cfm.

Petitpas, A. J., Van Raalte, J. L., Cornelius, A. E., & Presbrey, J. (2004) A life skills development program for high-school student athletes. *Journal of Primary Prevention, 24*, 325–334.

Petrie, T., & Stoever, S. (1997) Academic and nonacademic predictors of female student athletes' academic performances. *Journal of College Student Development, 38(6)*, 599–608.

Simons, H., Van Rheenen, D., & Covington, M. (1999) Academic motivation and the student athlete. *Journal of College Student Development, 40(2)*, 151–162.

Szechter, L., & Liben, L. (2004) Parental guidance in preschoolers' understanding of spatial-graphic representations. *Child Development, 75*, 869–885.

Ting, S. (2009) Impact of noncognitive factors on first-year academic performance and persistence of NCAA Division I student athletes. *Journal of Humanistic Counseling, Education and Development, 48*, 215–228.

Tinsley, T. M. (2008) Advising and counseling high school student athletes. In A. Leslie-Toogood & E. Gill (Eds.), *Advising Student Athletes: A Collaborative Approach to Success.* Monograph Series Number 18. Manhattan, KS: NACADA.

Ward Jr., R. (2008) Athletic expenditures and the academic mission of American schools: A group-level analysis. *Sociology of Sport Journal, 25,* 560–578.

Watt, S., & Moore, J. III (2001) Who are student athletes? In M. F. Howard-Hamilton & S. K. Watt (Eds.), *New Directions for Student Services: Vol. 93. Student services for athletes* (pp. 7–18). San Francisco: Jossey-Bass.

Zagelbaum, A., & Carlson, J. (2011) Orientation to working with immigrant families. In A. Zagelbaum & J. Carlson (Eds.), *Working with Immigrant Families: A Practical Guide for Counselors* (pp. 1–20). New York: Routledge.

2 Theories of Motivation and Student Development

When speaking about motivation and student development, there are various approaches to consider. Some approaches emphasize the use of stress and crisis to engage the individual in a process of change, while others speak about holistic concepts that do not necessarily view crisis as the main mechanism by which motivation occurs.

Given that many competitive factors and pressures are involved with sports and athletic pursuits, it is not easy to determine which approach would be best for a particular student athlete. Taking the stress into account may be viewed as a realistic and welcomed process by which rapport and goal-setting could be easily established, but an approach that mainly emphasizes optimism and problem-solving could be beneficial by allowing a student athlete to reframe his/her struggles in a way that does not give an extraordinary amount of power and attention to the otherwise stressful variables that may cause motivation to remain stagnant. The theories of motivation and development reviewed in this chapter are intended to encourage school counselors to consider the pros and cons of each approach, so that appropriate decisions can dictate the direction to proceed with a student athlete in need of motivation.

Also, it should be noted that many of these models are designed for uses beyond the role of a school counselor, such as an athletic consultant, but as can be seen from each overview, the school counselor is often in a position to make initial or eventual contact with a student athlete in need. Thus, these theories are useful from the standpoint of joining with the student athlete's family, coaching and school-related systems, and assisting with the establishment of goals and objectives that can lead the student athlete to a better outcome. Furthermore, the educational cornerstones upon which most of these theories are based make them highly appropriate for use by a school-based professional.

Mobilization Model

The Mobilization Model has the ultimate goal of using educational information and supportive interventions to help student athletes analyze their crises and coping mechanisms, by which transitions can be made (Stambulova, 2011). Stambulova has many excellent resources and detailed approaches by which this model has been applied to various types of athletes who are experiencing various types of crises, and readers are highly encouraged to seek out these materials for further information related to highly specific crises. The essentials of this model, however, boil down to six steps:

1. *Collecting and Sorting Out the Student Athlete's Information*
    Though the use of empathic listening, student athletes provide information about their personal and professional background, the events which have led them to a counseling service, and the expectations that they have with their future(s). Stambulova (2011) specifically organizes this information among six categories, which include: (1) client as a person; (2) client as an athlete; (3) client's social roles and environment; (4) client's near past; (5) client's present situation; and (6) client's perceived future

2. *Identifying, Prioritizing and Articulating the Problem Issues*
    The main purpose of this step is to detect the level of motivation that the student athlete has to solve his/her problem(s) and to assess the level of internal and external pressure (s)he has in his/her life at present. As is the case with any goal-related process, it is important for the school counselor to be clear and explicit about the ways in which goals and problems are defined (Greenberg, 2003; Reeves, 2011). Stambulova (2011) reminds professionals that health-related issues, such as injury or poor mental health, are recommended to have priority over issues such as frustration and anxiety.

3. *Analyzing the Current Status of the Student Athlete's Coping Resources and Barriers*
    In order to recognize and best articulate what a student athlete's coping resources are, a mapping approach is recommended, so that a visual display is included in this process (Stambulova, 2011). Though Stambulova uses a dichotomous listing of internal and external resources, other types of map can be applied to this approach. Youths who are well-connected to their community can benefit, for example, from a community geonogram where not only are the resources identified, but the physical location of people and places also provides a visual aid to where these individuals can go when they are in need of assistance (Ivey, Ivey, & Zalaquett, 2010; Ogbonnaya, 1994). Regardless of type of map, it is important for the counselor to help the student athlete identify the barriers to the resources as much as the resources themselves.

4. *Discussing the Transition Alternatives and Stimulating the Student Athlete to Make a Strategic Decision*
    The K-12 student athlete may not be in a position to make the strategic decision fully on his/her own. There may be confidential issues and consultation services that are best used to build a team- and systems-based approach toward helping the student athlete make the most effective strategic decision. The ability to have family, coaches and teachers involved with this process can be of significant benefit to the student athlete, but it is best to

keep these connections open and transparent (Donohue, Miller, Crammer, Cross, & Covassin, 2007; Dougherty, 2005). Stambulova (2011) notes three strategic decisions that can be made: (1) rejection, that is to continue in the sport or relationship associated with the traumatic situation; (2) acceptance by the student athlete to continue in his/her current situation but with different attitude(s) toward the people and variables involved in the situation; and (3) a fighting response, which involves an active procedure on the part of the student athlete to drastically change the situation for the better.

5. *Goal Setting and Planning in Regard to the Strategic Decision Made*

   This step will probably be undertaken in conjunction with other professionals. Depending on the decision made at Step 4, the student athlete must now take action(s) toward implementing the decision. Perhaps this can be best thought of in a fashion parallel to the Preparation and Action Stages of Prochaska and DiClemente's model of change (Prochaska, DiClemente, & Norcross, 1992). The student athlete has determined a need to change his/her situation, by either removing him/herself from a crisis or working through it in some fashion, and the counseling professional helps to encourage the student athlete to follow through on the decision(s) made. In this sense, the counseling professional takes on more of a coaching identity, in that less time is spent listening to the client's background story and more time is spent encouraging the client to take the initiative in creating change (Stambulova, 2011). Also, Stambulova notes that the counseling professional must carefully monitor the student athlete's attitude and mindset during this process, because student athletes may sometimes engage in revenge-seeking behaviors during this period of change. Levels of stress can be quite high for the student athlete during this step in the process (Wippert & Wippert, 2008) and, even when the initial decision is made and planned for, it does not mean that it is an easy process to facilitate at all times (Brown, Glastetter-Fender, & Shelton, 2000).

6. *Concluding and Providing Follow-Ups*

   Related to the points made in Step 5, counseling professionals must also follow-up and appropriately monitor the progress of the student athlete after the plans and goals are in place. Stambulova (2011) recommends a "phasing out" approach, whereby follow-up meetings are scheduled at greater distances between one another. The school setting, fortunately for most, allows for occasional contact between student athlete and counseling professional in a way that does not require termination to equate with no further contact, but it can be considered a difficult dynamic to handle if the counselor and client are not clear on the terms of termination.

The Mobilization Model has been mainly used on athletes who are transitioning out of a sports career (Stambulova, 2011), which does not necessarily apply to many student athletes at the pre-collegiate level. However, there are school-based studies which appear to lend support for the use of this model by school counselors. A counseling dialogue with mobilization toward goals and tasks has been viewed as an effective strategy to increase performance and self-regard among struggling student athletes (Yopyk & Prentice, 2005). Frequent communication between coaches and parents that follow this type of strategy also assist school and family systems with the stresses associated with performance and evaluation (Harwood, Drew, & Knight, 2010). Ryska (2002) also noted that the athletic identity of high school students influenced levels of non-sport-related competence as a function of the motivational goal perspectives adopted within sport. Mobilizing one's efforts and supports as a student athlete can prove to be a vital tool in the development of the student athlete as a citizen, as well as a participant in academics and sport.

Achievement Goal Theory

Achievement Goal Theory (AGT) is one of the more researched and established models used to aid student athletes' motivation and accomplishments of tasks (Morris & Kavussanu, 2009). It is similar to the Mobilization Model in that student athletes are motivated to accomplish or avoid tasks based on the resources and sense of agency that they have to attain these outcomes. However, instead of the mechanism of crisis driving the process, AGT uses success-drive for this purpose. This drive for success is mostly defined as a cognitive and behavioral balance between what an athlete wants to achieve, and what an athlete is able to demonstrate when performing (Dweck, 1986, 1999; Nicholls, 1984, 1989). It also relates to some of the perceptions of self that student athletes have when it comes to identifying their athletic and non-athletic competencies. Ryska (2002) conducted a study which concluded that high school students who identified with their athletic role in terms of its social and affective components was related to the social acceptance and behavioral conduct aspects of personal competence, while exclusive identification with the athletic role was related to scholastic and vocational competence perceptions. Thus, the way in which student athletes perform athletically can relate to the way they perform and perceive their performance academically. Considering the demands placed on student athletes to perform well in so many school-based aspects, it is important to help these individuals frame things in terms of manageable goals. Doing this can create a climate within which student athletes can adapt and adjust to the highs and lows they experience as a result of the tasks they must accomplish in order to reach their intended outcomes (Fry & Newton, 2003).

Also related to how students strive for success is the type of orientation they have toward approaching tasks in the first place. There are *task-oriented* individuals who feel successful because of the actions they take to learn, practice, improve, and master material, and are able to reference themselves and their efforts when reflecting on the notion of success (Nicholls, 1989). These individuals also tend to have higher levels of sportsmanship and more positively perceived relationships with coaches and other players because of their ability to focus mostly on aspects of their work that they can control and improve (Fry & Newton, 2003). Whether or not this type of orientation is learned or innate has been debated for significant periods of time, but it is clear that task-orientation is a desired approach toward helping student athletes develop various skills from athletics, to academics, and moral and prosocial actions (Sheilds & Bredemeier, 1995).

Ego-oriented individuals, however, perceive and define success primarily through the criteria presented by others, such as how well they perform in relation to the performance of others (Nicholls, 1989; Morris & Kavussanu, 2009). The competitive efforts exerted by these individuals can often be high, but the prospect of failure can be difficult for these individuals to handle and possibly lead to withdrawal from tasks and a loss of intrinsic motivation (Morris & Kavussanu, 2009). Such behaviors can also produce conflict within a school environment, especially when these individuals engage in poor self-regulation strategies (Gano-Overway, 2008).

Gano-Overway (2008) has specifically noted that student athletes identified as ego-oriented individuals tended to perceive their performance difficulties as direct implications that they are lacking abilities, primarily because of their comparisons to others. They expressed beliefs that these low ability levels were largely outside of their control, and were less likely than task-oriented individuals to monitor, evaluate, and strategically plan ways to better develop their skills and future approaches toward goals. However, when the conditions under which student athletes were given tasks to complete strongly emphasized involvement with the task itself (e.g., many people show slow reaction times at first, but with more practice, reaction time begins to improve), these individuals were more able and likely to use effective self-regulation strategies. Though this may not always be possible to do in the "real world," findings related to this use of task explanation are encouraging signs that there are effective ways to approach and encourage student athletes to construct goals and pursue outcomes in a manner that keeps motivation alive, even in the face of a threat or crisis. However, AGT does not necessarily take into account the notion of positive and negative thought processes when addressing motivation and development, and this is why school counselors should also consider the use of optimistic thinking and modeling as a way to connect with student athlete motivation.

Optimistic Thinking and Modeling

Though it is not a formal theory in some circles, optimistic thinking and modeling has been linked to several aspects of motivation and learning that also impact student athletes. As will be seen in subsequent chapters, student athletes not only struggle with their own senses of self and motivation to succeed, but also with other individuals' expectations and demands, such as parents (Harwood et al., 2010), coaches, teachers, peers (Donohue et al., 2007), and media. Also, because of the myriad of services regarded as effective psychological interventions for athletic performance issues (Maniar, Curry, Sommers-Flanagan, & Walsh, 2001; Watson, 2005), coupled with the need for brief counseling and therapy to occur in most school settings (Giges & Petitpas, 2000; Hoigaard & Johansen, 2004;

Stone & Dahir, 2006), the use of optimistic thinking and other such reframing approaches are seen as both essential and well-suited methods by which issues of motivation can be initially approached. Furthermore, they can also enable counseling professionals to establish effective rapport with student athletes, given that some of these clients are often guarded about seeking out such services because of concerns they may have about placing too much attention on problems and not solutions (Hoigaard & Johansen, 2004). The use of optimistic thinking mainly boils down to a problem-solving approach, and having an encouraging tone with student athletes that positively emphasizes the sense of personal agency they have to learn from and adapt to challenges that come their way (Vallaire-Thomas, Hicks, & Growe, 2011). This is not meant to oversimplify the problems and issues that the student athletes are experiencing, but rather, it is a way to initiate an approach by which a block to motivation and performance can be acknowledged, addressed, and eventually overcome.

Czech et al. (2006) cite twelve essential tips for professionals to bear in mind when attempting to encourage student athletes in both the classroom and on the playing field:

1. *[Articulate to student athletes that] Optimism is a choice, not an inheritance*
   There are difficult circumstances and results that will always be encountered on and off the field. The notion of choosing how to handle difficulties gives the student athlete more personal power to learn from and respond to such circumstances, as opposed to taking a passive and/or helpless stance (Czech et al., 2006; Seligman, 2006).

2. *[Remind yourself as a professional that] Student athletes are human beings*
   The ability for human beings to learn is one of the greatest talents possible. Some individuals may not view student athletes with this talent in mind (Kennedy & Dimick, 1987). The desire to succeed at sports can be misinterpreted and/or recognized in a manner that reduces the student athlete's identity to one who performs on the field but does not apply this characteristic to anything else (Pearson & Petitpas, 1990). By helping the student athlete establish short-term and long-term goals with the ability to commit and follow-through on reaching them, the counseling professional can view the student athlete in a more complete fashion, which in turn helps the student athlete believe in his/her ability to succeed.

3. *[Note that] Change is inevitable; even negative outcomes can lead to positive ones*
   Sometimes, adversity does not appear to be something that will pass. Helping student athletes understand that there are lessons to be learned from adversity can reduce some of this ever-lasting effect and encourage them not to take failures and shortcomings in too negative a fashion (Harwood et al., 2010). Modeling this type of optimism can also have a contagion effect on teammates and other stakeholders who can learn to support one another during times of loss or failure (Zagelbaum, 2011).

4. *Teach student athletes to look at what they have left—not at what they have lost*

It can be misleading to assume that the early stages of a game, or school year, can determine the entire outcome. There are several examples of underdogs and athletes who were not favored to win, but through will and determination were able to either defy odds or surprise their critics with a stronger than expected performance after a sluggish start. Helping the student athlete focus on the strong finish can reduce the negative power that an initial defeat or failure can otherwise have on subsequent performance, strategies and decision-making (Harwood et al., 2010; Zagelbaum, 2011).

5. *Teach student athletes to keep optimism growing by tapping into positive memories*

It can be easy to forget positive memories in the face of negative circumstances, but reminding oneself of prior successes can offset some of the difficult feelings and thoughts that are elicited in times of failure (Pancer, Hunsberger, Pratt, & Alisat, 2000). The use of positive memories is not meant to replace the negative circumstances altogether, but rather, aids the student athlete with his/her belief that (s)he can return to "winning ways" once again.

6. *[Remind clients that] It is important for a student athlete to take small steps at first but to never lose sight of the end result they want*

The goals set by a student athlete should be a mix of short-term and long-term ones, enabling progress to be seen incrementally and with a larger outcome in mind. This way, challenges serve as motivators without becoming desensitizing instruments that can cause a student athlete to become too complacent with small accomplishments and/or too impatient with the need for larger ones (Pancer et al., 2000). Counselors and other stakeholders should revisit this concept often as the student athlete continues this process.

7. *Help student athletes develop alternative, more optimistic explanations for the same events*

Student athletes can often view the outcome of an event in terms of all-or-nothing mentality, coupled with best and worst case scenarios for future plans. Sometimes this form of thinking can place too much blame on the student athlete, and can also be used to diffuse responsibility away from the student athlete (Czech et al., 2006). An appropriate balance of internal, stable, and global thinking (Seligman, 2006), with a positive belief system about enacting future planning and strategy, can go a long way toward positively motivating a student athlete to change and continue work toward meeting his/her expected goals.

8. *Challenge your student athletes' pessimistic thinking*

Paying close attention to words and phrases that the student athlete uses to describe him/herself and his/her beliefs about self and others is an important way to notice the degree to which a student athlete's pessimistic thinking can be reframed (Czech et al., 2006; Seligman, 2006). Sometimes phrases such as "I am just no good" or "I can never" can be uttered in the heat of a competitive defeat, but during the process of practice and training, these phrases can give important insight into the mentality of the student athlete. It is recommended that student athletes be helped to reflect on the meaning of these statements regardless of when they arise. By actively rephrasing the words into more optimistic phrases such as "I need more practice" or "I may have missed this detail", the helplessness and hopelessness factors that may otherwise derail the motivation level of the student athlete can be decreased.

9. *Provide encouragement to student athletes*
   Given that student athletes can themselves be role models for others, they often heed the words that closely regarded adults have for them as role models themselves (Lubker, Visek, Geer, & Wastson II, 2008). Student athletes may not readily internalize messages of encouragement, but over time, consistent and appropriate levels of praise and encouragement from adults and other support systems can be converted into self-talk, and enable further motivation and accomplishment to occur.

10. *Model [and serve as a role model for] optimistic thinking within the sport culture*
    Similar to the notion described in Tip 9, the counselor and/or school stake-holder is advised to model optimism and optimistic thinking for the student athlete by also referencing this form of cognition and behavior from sources specific to the world of sport. Student athletes who have graduated from the same school, professional athletes, and coaches can all be sources of optimistic thinking and encouragement, but because of their unique link to the student athlete in terms of expertise and understanding of the firsthand demands of being a student athlete, they offer a level of credibility and empathy that may reach the struggling student athlete in a deeper and more personal manner (Lubker et al., 2008). A counselor or stakeholder who is not an athlete can still reach a level of credibility for the struggling student athlete (Maniar et al., 2001): if their actions and presence at the school and at sporting events displays a level of sincerity, support, and encouragement, they can enhance the optimistic thinking style of this individual. The ability to step outside of the office (Stone & Dahir, 2006) and into the sports arena can be a small gesture that goes a long way toward the support of a struggling student athlete.

11. *Use stories that promote persistence and optimism*
    The use of narratives can often be viewed as a valuable tool in counseling and, for some student athletes, they can be seen as invaluable. Whether or not a counselor should use self-disclosure as part of this process is left up to the professional to ultimately decide. Some student athletes may appreciate the trust and personable nature by which self-disclosure can serve as a vehicle to enhance rapport between counselor and student. However, too much self-disclosure in terms of depth or frequency, can disrupt the encouraging nature of this tool and end up discrediting the professional in the eyes of the student athlete or damage the working relationship. In order to best promote persistence and optimism, stories are recommended to be brief in nature (so as not to dominate the entire session's time),

positively focused (to ensure the optimistic message is as clear as possible), and appropriately related to the struggle(s) presented by the student athlete (to best establish a link between the story and the motivational issue in question) (Young, 1998; Ivey, Ivey, & Zalaquett, 2010).

12. *Emphasize strengths and acknowledge success*

This may sound like a simplistic tip, but school professionals can often overlook certain aspects of this idea, even when they have good intentions. It is important, for example, to comment on strengths and accomplishments in a consistent manner and not only after a mistake has been made (Albert, 1996). Even though professionals can view this act as a positive one, it could be indirectly reinforcing the idea that one must struggle in order to be successful. Also, it can stigmatize the role of the counselor within the eyes of the student athlete and create the expectation that the professional is looking for the problem more than the solution (Maniar et al., 2001). This is not to say that a counselor or school stakeholder should only be looking for a student athletes strengths and accomplishments at all times, but rather, that striking a balance of praise and challenge can better motivate and encourage the student athlete to accomplish more. Even in times of failure, acknowledging the strengths and successes of the student athlete can indicate that (s)he has experienced a setback, but not necessarily an obstacle that can no longer be overcome. One final note about this tip is that acknowledging strengths and successes can also have a contagion effect, meaning that student athletes who consistently receive this type of treatment can model it for other student athletes, especially their teammates. Thus, the motivation is not only modeled and passed on to one student athlete, but also to a group, which is a critical factor when dealing with the competitive nature of some sports.

Summary

The concept of motivation can take on different meanings for people, but for the student athlete, it has the ability to help or harm various types of performance. Though the school counselor is not usually the first school-based professional to address issues of athletic performance with a student athlete, knowledge of theories of motivation and student development allow an important in-road to be established within the counselor-client relationship. Coaches and trainers may have explicit goals and objectives established for the student athlete within their established system and relationship, but when struggles persist and motivation remains in a fairly elongated slump, a school counselor can effectively join with this system to assist the student athlete by possibly exploring other reasons behind why the performance is in need of improvement. The three theoretical models provided in this chapter can assist with this exploration.

The Mobilization Model may be effective if the student athlete is encountering a crisis or major crossroad that requires significant re-evaluation of his/her ability to continue with athletic pursuits. It also takes into account the student athlete's perceived and available resources that enable him/her to cope with decisions that require support and adjustment to a new way of approaching athletic and academic tasks. By recognizing the student athlete's beliefs and choices, along with the present and missing parts of his/her school, community, and family support systems, the school counselor can more readily take on the role of advocate as well, should the need arise.

Achievement Goal Theory may be effective if the student athlete is struggling in some aspects of his/her athletic and/or academic goals, which do not necessarily need to be crises. It also takes into account the personal style of how the individual approaches tasks, so that appropriate goals can be reframed or newly constructed in cases where motivation may be suffering. By recognizing the student athlete's understanding of the goals and his/her perceived ability to accomplish them, the school counselor can more readily take on the role of a consultant as well, should the need arise.

Optimistic modeling and thinking may be effective if the student athlete is dealing with a poor sense of self or conflict between his/her desired outcomes and actual achievements. It takes into account the brief nature of time and availability that can often dictate the pace of a counseling relationship within the school system, so that problem solving approaches can be more readily acknowledged and applied. By helping the student athlete reframe and rethink his/her attributions of their results, the school counselor can more readily take on an advising role, should the need arise.

In conclusion, these theories are not limited to the uses and concepts presented in this summary alone. They can be complements to each other, or possibly an eclectic mix that the school counselor may need to use with a student athlete as the counseling relationship progresses and uncovers issues beyond those that the initial presenting problem suggests. Regardless, the ability to understand motivation and the goals designed to monitor and improve the athletic performance of a student athlete is an invaluable tool for the school counselor to have. It provides a form of system support in that it uses the same language and concepts that other school stakeholders have (Stone & Dahir, 2006), such as coaches and athletic directors. It also helps to link the goals of counseling with the goals that the student athlete has for him/her self outside of the counseling relationship. As a result, it can serve as a form of encouragement and motivation for the student athlete to believe in the counseling relationship and also lead to change.

Questions for Discussion

1. What are the pros and cons associated with the Mobilization Model? The AGT Model? The Model of Optimistic Thinking?
2. How much influence do you believe motivation has with respect to athletic performance? To academic performance? How much emphasis would you place on each type of performance in a counseling relationship with a struggling student athlete?

3. How do you encourage task-orientation? What characteristics do you look for to determine that a task-oriented approach has been taken?
4. How do you draw a line between counseling and education when it comes to dealing with a student athlete who must find the motivation to change/readjust his/her goals?

References

Albert, L. (1996) *Cooperative Discipline.* Circle Pines, MN: AGS Publishing.

Brown, C., Glastetter-Fender, C., & Shelton, M. (2000) Psychosocial identity and career control in college student athletes. *Journal of Vocational Behavior, 56,* 53–62.

Czech, D. R., Whalen, S. J., Burdette, G. P., Metzler, J. N., & Zwald, D. (2006) Optimism and pessimism in sport and in the classroom: Applied tips for teacher-coaches. *Georgia Association for Health, Physical Education, Recreation and Dance Journal, 39(3),* 15–17.

Donohue, B., Miller, A., Crammer, L., Cross, C., & Covassin, T. (2007) A standardized method of assessing sport specific problems in the relationships of athletes with their coaches, teammates, family and peers. *Journal of Sport Behavior, 30(4),* 375–397.

Dougherty, A. M. (2005) *Psychological Consultation and Collaboration in School and Community Settings* (5th ed.). Belmont, CA: Brooks/Cole.

Dweck, C. S. (1986) Motivational processes affecting learning. *American Psychologist, 41,* 1040–1048.

Dweck, C. S. (1999) *Self-Theories: Their Role in Motivation, Personality, and Development.* Philadelphia: Psychology Press.

Fry, M. D., & Newton, M. (2003) Application of Achievement Goal Theory in an urban youth tennis setting. *Journal of Applied Sport Psychology, 15,* 50–66.

Gano-Overway, L. A. (2008) The effect of goal involvement on self-regulatory processes. *International Journal of Sport and Exercise Psychology, 6,* 132–156.

Giges, B., & Petitpas, A. (2000) Brief contact interventions in Sport Psychology. *The Sport Psychologist, 14,* 176–187.

Greenberg, K. R. (2003) *Group Counseling in K-12 Schools: A Handbook for School Counselors.* Boston: Pearson Education.

Harwood, C., Drew, A., & Knight, C. J. (2010) Parental stressors in professional youth football academies: A qualitative investigation of specializing stage parents. *Qualitative Research in Sport and Exercise, 2(1),* 39–55.

Hoigaard, R., & Johansen, B. T. (2004) The solution-focused approach in Sport Psychology. *The Sport Psychologist, 18,* 218–228.

Ivey, A. E., Ivey, M. B., & Zalaquett, C. P. (2010) *Intentional Interviewing and Counseling: Facilitating Client Development in a Multicultural Society* (7th ed.). Belmont, CA: Brooks/Cole.

Kennedy, S. R., & Dimmick, K. M. (1987) Career maturity and professional sports expectations of college football and basketball players. *Journal of College Student Personnel, 6,* 293–297.

Lubker, J. R., Visek, A. J., Geer, J. R., & Watson II, J. C. (2008) Characteristics of an effective Sport Psychology consultant: Perspectives from athletes and consultants. *Journal of Sport Behavior, 31(2),* 147–165.

Maniar, S. D., Curry, L. A., Sommers-Flanagan, J., & Walsh, J. A. (2001) Student athlete preferences in seeking help when confronted with sport performance problems. *The Sport Psychologist, 15*, 205–223.

Morris, R. L., & Kavussanu, M. (2009) The role of approach-avoidance versus task and ego goals in enjoyment and cognitive anxiety in youth sport. *International Journal of Sport and Exercise Psychology, 7*, 185–202.

Nicholls, J. G. (1984) Achievement motivation: Conceptions of ability, subjective experience, task choice, and performance. *Psychological Review, 91*, 328–346.

Nicholls, J. G. (1989) *The Competitive Ethos and Democratic Education.* Cambridge, MA: Harvard University Press.

Ogbonnaya, O. (1994) Person as community: An African understanding of the person as an intrapsychic community. *Journal of Black Psychology, 20*, 75–87.

Pancer, S. M., Hunsberger, B., Pratt, M. W., & Alisat, S. (2000) Cognitive complexity of expectations and adjustment to university in the first year. *Journal of Adolescent Research, 15*, 38–57.

Pearson, R., & Petitpas, A. (1990) Transitions of athletes: Pitfalls and prevention. *Journal of Counseling and Development, 69*, 7–10.

Prochaska, J. O., DiClemente, C. C., & Norcross, J. C. (1992) In search of how people change: Applications to addictive behaviors. *American Psychologist, 47(9)*, 1102–1114.

Reeves, A. R. (2011) *Where Great Teaching Begins: Planning for Student Thinking and Learning.* Alexandria, VA: Association for Supervision and Curriculum Development.

Ryska, T. A. (2002) The effects of athletic identity and motivation goals on global competence perceptions of student athletes. *Child Study Journal, 32(2)*, 109–129.

Seligman, M. E. P. (2006) *Learned Optimism: How to Change your Mind and Life.* New York: Vintage.

Sheilds, D., & Bredemeier, B. L. S. (1995) *Character Development and Physical Activity.* Champaign, IL: Human Kinetics.

Stambulova, N. (2011) The Mobilization Model of counseling athletes in crisis-transitions: An educational intervention tool. *Journal of Sport Psychology in Action, 2*, 156–170.

Stone, C. B., & Dahir, C. A. (2006) *The Transformed School Counselor.* Boston: Lahaska Press.

Vallaire-Thomas, L., Hicks, J., & Growe, R. (2011) Solution-focused brief therapy: An interventional approach to improving negative student behaviors. *Journal of Instructional Psychology, 38(4)*, 224–234.

Watson, J. C. (2005) College student athletes' attitudes toward help-seeking behavior and expectations of counseling services. *Journal of College Student Development, 46*, 442–449.

Wippert, P. M., & Wippert, J. (2008) Perceived stress and prevalence of traumatic stress symptoms following athletic career transition. *Journal of Clinical Sport Psychology, 2*, 1–16.

Yopyk, D. J. A., & Prentice, D. A. (2005) Am I an athlete or a student? Identity salience and stereotype threat in student athletes. *Basic and Applied Social Psychology, 27(4)*, 329–336.

Young, M. E. (1998) *Learning the Art of Helping: Building Blocks and Techniques.* Upper Saddle River, NJ: Merrill.

Zagelbaum, A. (2011) *Counseling the Student athlete.* Alexandria, VA: Alexander Street Press.

3   Commercialism and the Identity of the Student Athlete

There is undeniable popularity and attention given to sports and athletic competition within our society, from both a social and financial perspective. Socially, the drama of competition and excitement of victory and accomplishment can captivate an audience, and create a sense of bonding and identification among individuals who find parallel processes between themselves and an athlete or his/ her team. Even in moments of defeat or setback, individuals and groups can feel connected to an athlete's emotions or motivation to overcome these trials and tribulations when the next opportunity presents itself. Also, even if individuals are not connecting to athletes in such a fashion, the discussion of competition(s), outcome(s), and/or human interest stories associated with sports in some ways appears to often be a valuable outlet by which some people bond and link interests. This can be in the form of "water cooler" discussion at the office, online communications through blogs, fantasy leagues and/or social media venues, and for some children and young adults, during social periods which occur within their communities and schools.

It seems that even non-athletes—at least in the physical sense of one who plays sports—parallel the social and emotional energy associated with athletics when one considers the notion that competitions such as the National Spelling Bee and the World Series of Poker are televised on channels such as the Entertainment and Sports Programming Network (ESPN). There are also slang terms within our society, such as "mathletes," which are used to identify individuals who academically compete among other individuals for awards and recognized accomplishments for their abilities within the field of mathematics and empirically related sciences (Lord, 2001). It is also clear that non-athletes who play sports, either recreationally or in other non-organized fashions such as with friends and family only, are captivated by sports and the athletes who play them. Some of this may be due to media attention, while some can be due to the attraction of athletic competition in and of itself. There are controversial reasons, such as the attraction of gambling and sports betting, that have been woven into this web, though the use of fantasy leagues and simulation games that are often not involved with such profit-making schemes also garner significant levels of attention from athletes and non-athletes alike (Anderson, Blackshaw, Siekmann, & Soek, 2011). Nearly all individuals seem to appreciate the drive, story behind, and outcomes of sport, whether as spectators or individuals who fantasize or mirror the athletes and sports themselves. If imitation truly is one of the sincerest forms of flattery, though, there appears to be a significant level of appreciation for sports throughout the world.

Financial Elements

The other side of attention paid to many sports and related organizations is clearly the financial one. However, there is some debate as to what types of financial variables contribute to a sport program's commercial success. For example, Scott-Clayton (2012) reported that about 25% of the 120 colleges associated with the National Collegiate Athletic Association's Football Bowl Subdivision (which used to be known as Division I-A) yielded a minimum of $14.4 million anually from their men's athletic programs. These numbers may seem promising, but statistics from a few years back show an interesting comparison and contrast. In 2007, the University of Georgia, Ohio State, and Auburn University yielded a minimum of $45 million dollars each for their football programs alone; *Forbes Magazine* also rated the private University of Notre Dame that year as the most valuable team in college football, with an estimated worth of $101 million (Schwartz, 2007). However, when taking into consideration overall athletic departments—all men's programs and women's sports—the net revenues become considerably less; it is also estimated that an average university with approximately 12,000 students would spend over $440 million annually with respect to its overall budget (Scott-Clayton, 2012). There are many places that the money can go, and no shortage of perceived pros and cons for each location. Student athletes at the college level continue to question and advocate for financial compensation regarding the use of their likenesses on various forms of merchandise. Controversies arise when college-level student athletes become allegedly associated with sports agents (Vergara, 2013) and possible memorabilia sales that are not permitted while these athletes are enrolled in school (Uthman, 2013). Television broadcasts and programming contracts, stadium construction, management and upgrades, and contributions to academics and other university-related programs are all involved in this mix (Schwartz, 2007). However, when it comes to discussing the money within the field of sports, people often comment on the salaries and contracts of professional players and coaches, and some of the more dramatic salaries can be found among college-level head football and head basketball coaches.

The salaries that several college-level coaches earn grab significant attention within media and popular culture. For example, ESPN (2011) compiled College Athletics Revenues and Expenses for the fiscal year that ended in 2011 by examining documents that colleges and universities are required to file with the National Collegiate Athletic Association (NCAA). The top 40 NCAA Division I men's football programs show a range of coaches' salaries and benefits which starts at $7,881,848 (University of Memphis) and extends to $17,810,365

(University of Texas). Though these figures do not indicate how the money is specifically divided among coaching staff and/or at each institution, they are still indicators of how much revenue sport can provide. It also provides further frustration as to why scandals associated with coaching staff and college athletic programs seem to be difficult to monitor. Clearly, the most significant coaching-related scandal of 2011–2012 was that of Jerry Sandusky of Penn State, who was found guilty of sexually assaulting and abusing numerous underage boys over a 14-year period while serving in the role of Defensive Coordinator of its football team (Drehs, 2011). The release of the subsequent Freeh Report upon the investigative conclusion of this scandal provided scathing criticism mainly centered around the fact that top university officials, extending all the way to its President (Graham Spanier), Vice President (Gary Schultz), Athletic Director (Tim Curley), and Head Football Coach (Joe Paterno), failed to take any steps toward protecting the victims; among many positive motives attributed to these decisions, one of the most significant ones cited by the Freeh Report was an attempt to "avoid bad publicity" (Muskal, 2012). Civil lawsuits and investigations that are likely to follow for the next few years in the wake of this scandal may shed additional light on this subject, but the notion of protecting potential recruits and sponsorship over the welfare and safety of Sandusky's victims will cast a considerable shadow over much of the Penn State football program and the leadership of Penn State University. At this time, all aforementioned figures are either on administrative leave from or no longer at Penn State University, and the university culture and community will have to find ways by which to adjust and heal. This is clearly an extreme case, but it was not the only nationally covered scandal in college athletics during the academic/athletic year of its uncovering.

There were other scandals that also surfaced regarding improper use of funds and standards that grabbed national attention as well. Rutgers University fired head basketball coach Mike Rice after video evidence surfaced showing him being physical with players during practices and using homophobic slurs (Norlander, 2013). Within the 2010–2011 academic year alone, numerous college and basketball programs were involved in several types of scandal and violation of NCAA rules regarding the recruiting and eligibility of players that placed coaches and coaching staff at the center of these events. At least eleven colleges and universities were punished because of their football and/or basketball programs' involvement with some form of impropriety, ranging from inappropriate contacts with recruits to impermissible receiving of benefits, playing of ineligible players, and other forms of unethical conduct (McGee, 2011); these cases did not even include the more prominent ones involving Head Football Coach Jim Tressel of Ohio State and Head Basketball Coach Bruce Pearl at the University of Tennessee (Lesmerises, 2012; Parrish, 2011). Nearly every one of these cases involved some exposure of the fact that coaches knew these improprieties were going on in some way, and that significant actions to stop such acts were avoided or not performed with enough consistency to control the behavior(s). The full impact these cases have on the next generation of athlete and/or coach to participate in these sports may not be realized for a long period of time, but the mixed messages that many individuals have already seen and heard with respect to how long and often these behaviors were allowed to occur suggests that it can be very difficult for some individuals to be attracted to collegiate and professional level sports simply for a love of the game. Commercialism may not be the direct cause of these controversies, but it can be part of some discussions as to why some pressures and decisions become intensified for some associated with sports (Brewer, 2002). Benford (2007) provides a comprehensive and detailed review of commercialism and college athletics that showcases many ways in which academic integrity can be undermined as a result.

Commercialism in Sports

Benford (2007) calls attention to the fact that commercialism within college sports is certainly not a new phenomenon, and that its origins can be traced back to the late 1800s. Though college sports were initially organized and presided over by students, administrative influences did not take long to intervene and regulate. However, in order to maintain effective control and build a league for many sports, financial support and backing from other organizations was needed. This process (which was largely initiated by Harvard University in order to gain support from other surrounding universities at the time) became one of many movements that likely had good intentions of providing academic and athletic support along with regulations to appropriately maintain order among students, staff, and community, but could not gain wide enough support to consistently strike this balance (Craughron, 2001). Benford (2007) further notes how social influences have also fed into this process. Values that concentrate on the entertainment value of sport—as exciting and motivating as they can be—can sometimes blend into school and university academic culture and present a mixed message or distorted view to stakeholders about what the main mission of the scholastic institution can or should be. Though some form of entertainment within educational media and related scholastic applications has been found to provide some value and benefit to schools and its stakeholders (Killeen, 2007), college athletics has often been criticized for how far it sometimes takes this value. Benford (2007) cites the construction of various stadiums and complexes as one example, especially when one considers the fact that student fees are often one form of revenue that fuels this process. The pursuit of championships is also seen as one process by which these values become complicated; being able to compete with "power conferences" that often compete for such titles often requires finances and incentives like media coverage, apparel endorsement, and other compensation packages that blur the balance between athletic and academic importance (Benford, 2007; Sharp & Sheilley, 2008). There are many cases of contracts that provide coaches with salary bonuses and other forms of payment when such tasks are accomplished; other university professors do not receive similar forms of profit for parallel processes (Benford,

2007; Duderstadt, 2000). When one also takes into consideration how other forms of media, such as video games, are produced and distributed with university names and logos regarding sport and athletic competitions, these figures can reach even higher levels. It remains both a concern and a mystery as to why college and university coaches are usually the only staff members who are allowed to profit from these images and accomplishments, and it will not likely make the controversy associated with commercialism and college sports any less significant. While it is clear that not all colleges and universities follow this perceived pattern, its prominence has prompted several NCAA Presidents, including current President Mark Emmert, to make public statements and missions to reform this aspect of college athletics (Associated Press, 2012). There are also several organizations, such as the Drake Group and the Knight Commission on Intercollegiate Athletics, that act to inform the public and champion reform movements within college athletics (Benford, 2007; Killeen, 2007), so the issue of commercialism will not likely fade from public consciousness any time soon.

Commercialism in Schools

It is also important to bear in mind that commercialism exists in American schools and related athletic programs as well, and that the college level does not always parallel the K-12 level or vice-versa. There are many reports about how some companies advertise within school settings, either on posters, through media such as the Internet and television in the classrooms, or in some of the more controversial forms such as textbooks (Daily, Swain, Huysman, & Tarrant, 2010). An estimated 80% of elementary, middle, and high schools within the United States have some connection with corporate advertising (Moore, 2007). It is clear that some of these partnerships between schools and companies can be beneficial to a degree. Killeen (2007) details several examples of how certain school districts, in partnership with banking and credit unions, help to assist families with sport participation fees and other related services and activities that appeared to some stakeholders to be an effective way of dealing with budgetary concerns. Though not always the norm or preferred way by which some budgetary issues are addressed within school settings, such partnerships do exist and are approved by voting members of school boards and community stakeholder agencies. There are also mixed reports as to how effective some advertisements reach their target audiences, which are primarily the students. Reports from children themselves often indicate that, although some of the ads and commercials they see in the classroom are "dumb" or "stupid", even criticism of these campaigns or messages can still allow for the product's name to remain in one's head (Carby, Hutchinson, & Solow, 2001). Children and their families still buy the products, and many do not think about the fact that advertising and commercialism within the school is being supported through these actions. Particular concern has been raised at the way some products that have been linked to childhood obesity and diabetes are marketed within schools, and appear to be having a disproportionate effect on Latino/a and African American children (Molnar, 2003). These issues are not necessarily new to the field of advertising and/or public health, but the involvement of professional athletes in some of these campaigns, combined with the role-model status that schoolchildren often gravitate toward with respect to these individuals, makes these issues quite prominent within American culture. There are also interesting perceptions that students have of athletes who participate in some of these school-based and school-related advertising campaigns.

In a study of 200 teenagers within grades 6–12 living in rural Missouri, Roy F. Fox (1995) reported some interesting themes among students who, over a two-year period, watched a newsroom broadcast called *Channel One*. The program is a mixture of current event news stories and public service announcements that include a series of advertisements for products endorsed, in some cases, by professional athletes. When conducting a focus group just regarding the ads featuring the professional athletes, their responses hardly ever recognized the fact that the ads were for products or services. Instead, they were viewed as ad campaigns for the athletes, which were being used to help promote themselves or their teams. In other words, they appeared to attribute the athletes' role in the commercial with their perceived role as an athlete. Some of the stated reasons they gave when asked why professional athletes make commercials for products included: athletes are sponsored by different companies; it elevates their status and reputation; and it motivates them to play better (Fox, 1995). While these findings cannot be generalized to all American teenagers, they provide some insight as to how they may perceive what the profession of athletics can offer them. However, none of the students in Fox's study were identified as student athletes, so perhaps individuals with a more specific drive towards athletics and the sporting profession(s) would have a different perspective as to why athletes are involved with media campaigns and sponsorship.

It is highly recommended for coaches and school staff to have discussions about commercialism and media images, if only just to strike a balance between perception and reality when it comes to making sense of personal and professional motives. Academic motivation and the ability to develop professional skills are important variables in these discussions (Sharp & Sheilley, 2008). Such discussions can also help illuminate important comparisons and contrasts that can be uncovered when processing media and commercial images that athletes and student athletes can sometimes encounter.

One of the more significant issues regarding media images of athletes has long been gender. There have been numerous reports about how female athletes are often depicted and/or perceived within media images and commercial campaigns as sex objects more than athletically inclined individuals (Aamidor, 2003; Daniels, 2009; Daniels & Wartena, 2011). Certainly, this can also depend on viewing audience and the type of advertisement depicted. For girl viewers, media depictions involving sexualized images have been associated with issues related to body image and beauty ideals (Daniels, 2009). Boy viewers have also demonstrated some concerns regarding body image, but this effect has not been established with the same amount of research to date as it has been for girl viewers (Pope Jr., Phillips, & Olivardia, 2000; Daniels & Wartena, 2011). However, some research has shown that, regardless of an athlete's gender, those who are portrayed more for their physical attractiveness as opposed to their athletic ability are rated by viewers as less skilled and talented at their sport than athletes who are portrayed more for their athletic ability (Knight & Guiliano, 2001). Thus, if greater attention is given to skill and ability, it appears that children, adolescent and the majority of adult viewers will objectify athletes less (Daniels, 2009). There are certain movements within media coverage that appear to be moving in this direction, including greater coverage of women's sports and sport leagues, such as the Women's National Basketball Association which has been enjoying some commercial success for more than a decade (Daniels & Wartena, 2011). There are still differences in terms of audience size and popularity, but the amount of sport-focused coverage appears to be increasing for many female athletic sports. Also, because of advances in technology and coverage, the majority of sports (including those with more modest commercial success as compared to football and basketball) are reaching global audiences (Stokvis, 2000). What this ultimately means for men's and women's sport leagues it is too early to say, but it is hoped that, as part of this greater coverage, the audiences that follow such sports will be properly aided by a focus on athletic talents and positive role-models that extol the virtues of academic and athletic preparation in order to pursue such a career.

Changes in Technology

Considering the ways in which media and its related technology has changed over time also sheds light on the ways in which students and student athletes within the K-12 school system are being affected by commercialism. Print media, radio and television, which were once the only significant forms of advertising within American homes, are now complemented and supplemented by Internet media, such as social networking sites and video sharing forums like YouTube. Just as the forms by which media are transmitted have increased in number, so has the amount of coverage of sports and sport-related events. Multiple sport networks exist and are broadcasting more forms of sporting event than ever before. Twenty-four hours per day, seven days per week, it is possible to be exposed to some kind of athletic competition or news story; thus, it is also possible to have similar exposure to sport-related commercials and advertisements (McClellan, King, & Rockey, 2012; Pegoraro, 2010). While broader exposure and coverage can help to bring sports to more people than was the case in previous decades and generations, it has also provided greater and faster exposure of many student athletes within K-12 settings than ever before. Some student athletes already have high expectations of turning pro when they start playing at the K-12 or university level (Kennedy & Dimmick, 1987). Student athletes who make game-winning plays may not just gain local attention, but also national and international exposure. The fact that we are already a society that thrives on competition can become even more concerning for a student athlete who is not only becoming a talent, but also having to carry the extra attention of the media spotlight; in other words, early success may equate in some people's minds to "superstardom" (Kartakoullis, 2009). However, just as one game-winning moment can become an instant grabber of positive attention, a lackluster play or game-losing moment can become a magnet for criticism. Thus, the social support system of a student athlete becomes a critical variable with respect to assisting him/her with the necessary perspectives of personal and professional identity. One must also bear in mind the use of some social network forums like Twitter. Their use by significant numbers of professional athletes to communicate with fans and student athletes is reformatting the way in which social networks and supports are established and grown (Pegoraro, 2010). These forums allow role-models to communicate with up-and-coming athletes in ways that were almost impossible in generations past. Getting an instant message from one's idol can help inspire a student athlete toward accomplishing further goals. However, the fine line between personal lives and professional identity can become blurred when online communications can be followed on a round-the-clock, day-by-day basis. More research will likely be needed to determine what appropriate limits and benefits these media have when it comes to motivating and distracting a student athlete, but for now, they remain a powerful tool by which fan bases and commercial interests can be energized regarding sport and sport enthusiasts. It is also important to understand that the virtual and/or commercialized world of online exposure does not always mirror the face-to-face world of school and local community. Being able to handle the pressures of criticism after a loss, the importance of sportsmanship, and the understanding of how to regain focus after the newfound attention are just some of the important topics that coaches and parents are highly recommended to discuss and monitor with student athletes (Kartakoullis, 2009; Nash, Sproule, & Horton, 2008; Stokvis, 2000). These approaches also parallel ways to deal with other forms of pressure that student athletes experience, such as academic/scholastic ones.

The pressure to earn sport scholarships and the competition associated with earning a spot on a college team can sometimes lead pre-collegiate student athletes into difficult spaces whereby the pursuit of academic accomplishment can sometimes be challenging to balance with the demands of athletics (Ginsburg, 2007; Kennedy & Dimmick, 1987). Even though it has been shown that scholarship support by itself is not a significant predictor of whether or not a student athlete at the college level remains with a sport or athletic program

(Le Crom, Warren, Clark, Marolla, & Gerber, 2009), for many student athletes attempting to gain admission in the first place, it can be one of their most critical goals. It can lead some to view their role of a student athlete almost as if they are being paid as skilled workers for providing sport services (Riemer, Beal, & Schroeder, 2000). Individual students who play sports can sometimes experience greater academic outcomes than students who do not (Kremer-Sadlick & Kim, 2007), but when viewed through a district-level analysis, such positive correlations do not always exist between athletic expenditure and the development of academic skills that are found to be important for college preparation (Ward Jr., 2008). There is a significant need to involve parents, coaches and student athletes in discussions about academic and athletic expectations, so that pressures to succeed can be handled effectively within the student athlete's support network (Kremer-Sadlick & Kim, 2007). It is important for school counselors and coaches to gain a strong sense of school climate and sport culture within their respective campuses as well, in order to best address the academic and athletic values of each student athlete. The more transparent school support agents can be about expectations for success and strategies that can be adopted when student athletes are veering off course from meeting these conditions, the less likelihood exists for a student athlete to hear mixed messages about the importance of sports versus academics or vice-versa.

Stopping the Mixed Messages

One specific recommendation for school districts, coaches, and athletic departments to consider when it comes to striking the balance of academic and athletic importance for student athletes is to consider travel limitations on sport competitions (Roberts, 2007). Though this is ultimately up to school boards as well as other state and national associations to decide, some states like Michigan have utilized this rule as a way to not only reduce expenses but also to inspire and encourage local competitions in ways that enable athletics to appropriately balance with academic focus (Roberts, 2007). Without the distraction of national competition pressure, it is argued that middle and high school students may have more ability to maintain appropriate athletic and academic responsibilities along with a schedule that does not likely result in fatigue from long-distance travel. School counselors and teachers may be able to support the school and the concerns of family and community stakeholders regarding this issue by articulating the known points about child and social development in order to temper concerns that may otherwise exist about devaluing the importance of athletics. This is not to say that opposition is likely, or that coaches and administration do not understand the developmental needs of students, but rather that, since school counselors and teachers are not meant to be in positions to regulate sport and athletic competition, articulating the benefits that come from striking the academic and athletic balance is more likely to support the school and its related systems when addressing issues that limit the time and schedule that school sports have.

Parents and other family members are also encouraged to engage in healthy discussions about sports, sport competition, and media coverage, so that student athletes keep certain athletic, social, and academic goals in perspective. Though this may go without saying, there are families where open dialogues and narratives may be missing because of assumptions that can be made about what sport means for the student athlete. Such patterns of behavior can be found in families where parents were once athletes and/or student athletes, and/or ones where parents are so encouraging of their child's athletic talent that they do not wish to "get in the way" (Ginsburg, 2007; Kremer-Sadlik & Kim, 2007). We will detail more about how to consult with parents and coaches in subsequent chapters, but in terms of what school counselors can generally attempt to do for families that may be struggling with this type of communication, it is recommended that at the start of sport season(s), arranging formal and informal contact with coaching staff, players, and parent sponsors can initiate important discussions about the academic and athletic missions of the school. Establishing a theme early and often about what it means to be a student athlete can help all stakeholders stay on the same page about what goals and pursuits are most necessary and valuable (Burnett, 2010); it also enables the school counselor to make him/herself available as a resource, should conflicts or difficulties arise and discussion with coaches, staff and/or teammates difficult to initiate. Just as commercialism can serve as effective publicity for products and companies, initial dialogue about the values of education and student role-modeling can be an effective agent of support and motivation for student athletes to succeed beyond the scope of a game or competition.

Another way of helping to establish clearer messages about athletic and academic missions is to call greater attention to the non-athletic accomplishments of student athletes. Within the business and professional sport(s) world(s), the notion of *corporate social responsibility* (CSR) is sometimes used to refer to ethical practices and related functions that companies use to further interests outside of the main realm of finance (Sheth & Babiak, 2010). Whether they are used for public relations, philanthropic pursuits, or ways of establishing one's self as a leader and/or role model within a community, the mechanism of CSR is designed to help establish healthy partnerships that can be used to balance the financial side of business with the humanitarian side of community support and engagement. Though these methods cannot override all forms of skepticism that may exist among consumers and businesses, they can serve as functions by which charitable organizations and other stakeholders can receive some benefit from working with organizations that must also rely on profits from consumers. It is possible that student athletes and school-based sport teams can also benefit from similar approaches by promoting their community service efforts. One example of this is happening within the Chicago area, whereby Sprite rewards the efforts of African American male Most Valuable Players (MVPs) who meet academic, community service, and essay-writing criteria while also participating in their school sport programs (Chicago Public

Schools, 2012). Recipients of this honor not only are able to meet members of the Chicago Bulls basketball team, but also become recognized within their school and local community for skills that extend beyond their athletic talents. Ms. Chantelle Peterson, serving in the role of Tilden Career Community Academy School Counselor, was credited by student Devonte Sims as being the catalyst who made this "once-in-a-lifetime experience possible" when receiving this award (Chicago Public Schools, 2012). When interviewed about what led him to such an accomplishment, this student athlete who plays both football and basketball stated, "Academics are very important to me. It's a number-one priority. I study really hard and get good grades. My mom tells me often that if I want better for myself, I have to work hard and do well in school." (Chicago Public Schools, 2012). One can only imagine the positive impact such a statement can have on a school, school system, and school counselor when it comes to assisting student athletes who are struggling with the balance between academics and athletics. It can also be argued that the CSR efforts of the Sprite Corporation and the Chicago Bulls to assist with such a pursuit help to put a positive light on the otherwise financially focused motives of commercialism. Perhaps some schools may not have such access to this type of resource, but the ability to honor academic and social service accomplishments is always possible, and in so doing, help the school and community rally behind educational missions more than would be the case if focus were only given to the winning of a sports championship.

Summary

The effects of commercialism with respect to sports and pursuit of sport-related competition are as deep and profound as they are diverse and complicated. Rightly or wrongly, K-12 schools use media and commercialism for sources of support and, in the current climate of budgetary concern for American school systems, there is no indication that such usage will cease any time soon. Developmentally, schoolchildren have different levels of connection to advertising and sport. Younger children, especially at the elementary level, may have no understanding of competition and simply model the media and sport-related images they see. Older children, from middle school age on, may be drawn to different elements associated with sport and competition, and discussing what they value can help to decipher their goals and interests that can set the stage for future pursuits, athletic or otherwise. Parents, coaches and teachers must also be aware of how to discuss media images effectively and how student athletes use them for motivation and/or further interest regarding academic, personal/social, and career development. The school counselor may be one of the more effective stakeholders to engage these individuals in such dialogues because of their non-direct affiliation with sport programs, understanding of childhood development issues, and responsibility regarding academic tracking and matriculation of all students. Coverage of college and professional level sports have lately been shedding light on several forms of scandal and questionable decision-making on the part of student athletes, coaches, and administrative staff, so it is not clear what messages are being sent or understood regarding the importance of balancing academic and athletic roles among schoolchildren who are seeking to play sports at the next level. This appears to necessitate more discussion and availability of K-12 level adults to assist student athletes who are engaged in this process.

Furthermore, with the advent of faster and more mobile technologies by which media coverage of sport exists, it appears that such discussions are going to be more necessary in terms of frequency and depth. Gender differences and racial/ethnic differences regarding media coverage and commercial depiction of athletes also add to the details of discussions. Images which objectify women and men are not new to the phenomenon of commercialism, but the frequency and accessibility by which media are available to schoolchildren are creating greater needs to make them aware of what goals and characteristics are most meaningful for them to value as they become more interested in athletic participation. Along with these values comes the need to organize and implement practices that allow for appropriate scheduling and travel commitments, plus appropriate recognition for student athletes who are able to portray the values and skills associated with the school mission and athletic program's goals. School counselors are strong resources for allowing such messages to spread, and reinforce the school climate to react accordingly. Ironically, some of these messages are also carried by corporate agencies and individuals who are attempting to at least exemplify corporate social responsibility and, by using this type of media and publicity, many of the otherwise controversial messages can possibly be tempered and tamed. This explanation is not meant to oversimplify the nature of commercialism and sports, but it hopefully provides a strong foundation upon which strategies and techniques regarding the needs of student athletes can be further developed, understood, and explored as we will do for the remainder of this text.

Questions for Discussion

1. What place does sport-related media have within the classroom? What part should the school counselor play when it comes to addressing media images related to sport and commercialism?
2. What approaches come to mind when addressing media images with elementary, middle/junior high, and high school students? Should these be school-wide, classroom specific, or some other form? What are the advantages and disadvantages of each?
3. How should school counselors interface with coaching staff, administration, and parents to address issues concerning commercialism and school-related sport?

References

Aamidor, A. (2003) *Real Sports Reporting*. Bloomington, IN: Indiana University Press.

Anderson, P. M., Blackshaw, I. S., Siekman, R. C. R., & Soek, J. (2011) *Sports Betting: Law and Policy*. The Hague, The Netherlands: Asser Press.

Associated Press (2012) NCAA President Pushes to Clean Up College Sports. *January 12, 2012*.

Benford, R. D. (2007) The college sports reform movement: Reframing the "edutainment" industry. *The Sociological Quarterly, 48*, 1–28.

Brewer, B. D. (2002) Commercialization in professional cycling 1950–2001: Institutional transformations and the rationalization of "doping". *Sociology of Sport Journal, 19*, 276–301.

Burnett, C. (2010) Student versus athlete: Professional socialization influx. *African Journal for Physical, Health Education, Recreation and Dance, 16(4)*, 193–203.

Carby, C., Hutchinson, K., & Solow, J. (2001) Coca-Cola high school. *The New York Amsterdam News: Children's Express, June 7–13, 2001*.

Chicago Public Schools (2012) An "MVP" in his school and community: Tilden senior recognized for his work in and out of the classroom. *Chicago Public Schools Spotlight, 305*, 1–2. Retrieved July 16, 2012 from http://www.cps.edu/Spotlight/Pages/Spotlight305.aspx.

Craughron, R. L. (2001) An historical perspective of reform in intercollegiate athletics. *International Sports Journal, 5*, 1–16.

Daily, N. L., Swain, L. P., Huysman, M., & Tarrant, C. (2010) America's consumerocracy: No safe haven. *English Journal, 99(3)*, 37–41.

Daniels, E. A. (2009) Sex objects, athletes, and sexy athletes: How media representations of women athletes can impact adolescent girls and college women. *Journal of Adolescent Research, 24*, 399–422.

Daniels, E. A., & Wartena, H. (2011) Athlete or sex symbol: What boys think of media representations of female athletes. *Sex Roles, 65*, 566–579.

Drehs, W. (2011) Not my coach, not my town, not anymore. *ESPN The Magazine, December 26, 2011*, 42–47.

Duderstadt, J. J. (2000) *Intercollegiate Athletics and the American University: A University President's Perspective*. Ann Arbor: University of Michigan Press.

ESPN (Entertainment and Sports Programming Network) (2011) *College Athletics Revenues and Expenses – 2011*. Retrieved July 10, 2012 from http://espn.go.com/ncaa/revenue/_/year/2009/type/expenses/sort/coach_pay.

Fox, R. F. (1995) Manipulated kids: Teens tell how ads influence them. *Educational Leadership, 53(1)*, 77–79.

Ginsburg, R. D. (2007) Winning at what? *Independent School, 66(4)*, 18–28.

Kartakoullis, N. (2009) Ethical considerations in sports management: The involvement of children in competitive sport. *International Journal of Sport Management, Recreation, & Tourism, 3*, 1–17.

Kennedy, S. R., & Dimmick, K. M. (1987) Career maturity and professional sports expectations of college football and basketball players. *Journal of College Student Personnel, 6*, 293–297.

Killeen, K. (2007) How the media misleads the story of school consumerism: A perspective from school finance. *Peabody Journal of Education, 82(1)*, 32–62.

Knight, J. L., & Guiliano, T. A. (2001) He's a Laker: She's a "Looker": The consequences of gender-stereotypical portrayals of male and female athletes by the print media. *Sex Roles, 45*, 217–229.

Kremer-Sadlik, T., & Kim, J. L. (2007) Lessons from sports: Children's socialization to values through family interaction during sports activities. *Discourse & Society, 18(1)*, 35–52.

Le Crom, C. L., Warren, B. J., Clark, H. T., Marolla, J., & Gerber, P. (2009) Factors contributing to student athlete retention. *Journal of Issues in Intercollegiate Athletics, 2*, 14–24.

Lesmerises, D. (2012) A year after his departure, Jim Tressel carries no regrets from his time with Ohio State. *The Cleveland Plain Dealer, May 29, 2012*. Retrieved July 12, 2012 from http://www.cleveland.com/osu/index.ssf/2012/05/a_year_after_his_departure_jim.html.

Lord, M. (2001) Michael Jordans of math: U.S. Student whizzes stun the cipher world. *U.S. News & World Report, 131(3)*, 26.

McClelland, G. S., King, C., & Rockey, R. L. (2012) *The Handbook of College Athletics and Recreation Administration*. San Francisco: Wiley.

McGee, R. (2011) The most scandalous year ever in college sports…until next year. *ESPN The Magazine, May 30, 2011*, 52–58.

Molnar, A. (2003) School commercialism hurts all children, ethnic minority group children most of all. *Journal of Negro Education, 72(4)*, 371–378.

Moore, A. (2007) A balancing act. *American School Board Journal, 194(5)*, 28–30.

Muskal, M. (2012) Sandusky scandal: Freeh report condemns top Penn State officials. *Los Angeles Times, July 12, 2012*. Retrieved July 12, 2012 from http://www.latimes.com/news/nation/nationnow/la-na-nn-penn-state-freeh-report-released-20120712,0,519370.story.

Nash, C. S., Sproule, J., & Horton, P. (2008) Sport coaches' perceived role frames and philosophies. *International Journal of Sports Science & Coaching, 3(4)*, 539–554.

Norlander, M. (2013) After firing, Rutgers settles with Mike Rice for $475K. *CBSSports.com Eye on College Basketball*. Retrieved June 3, 2013 from www.cbssports.com/collegebasketball/blog/eye-on-college-basketball/22105338/after-firing-rutgers-settles-with-mike-rice-for-475k.

Parrish, G. (2011) While Pearl lives in luxury, his ex-assistants go through upheaval. *CBS Sports.com Basketball Insider*. Retrieved July 12, 2012 from: http://www.cbssports.com/collegebasketball/story/15650956/while-pearl-lives-in-luxury-his-exassistants-go-through-upheaval.

Pegoraro, A. (2010) Look who's talking – Athletes on Twitter: A case study. *International Journal of Sport Communication, 3*, 501–514.

Pope Jr., H. G., Phillips, K. A., & Olivardia, R. (2000) *The Adonis Complex: The Secret Crisis of Male Body Obsession*. New York: The Free Press.

Riemer, B. A., Beal, B., & Schroeder, P. (2000) The influences of peer and university culture on female student athletes' perceptions of career termination, professionalization, and social isolation. *Journal of Sport Behavior, 23(4)*, 364–378.

Roberts, J. (2007) A sane island surrounded: How can school sports programs stave off the negative effects of the combined pressure of commercialism and professionalism? *Phi Delta Kappan, 89*, 61–66.

Schwartz, P. J. (2007) The most valuable college football teams. *Forbes.com, November 20, 2007*. Retrieved June 19, 2012 from http://www.forbes.com/2007/11/20/most-vaulable-college-football-teams-business-sports-college-football.html.

Scott-Clayton, J. (2012) Do big-time sports mean big-time support for universities? *The New York Times, January 27, 2012*. Retrieved June 19, 2012 from http://economix.blogs.nytimes.com/2012/01/27/do-big-time-sports-mean-big-time-support-for-universities/.

Sharp, L. A., & Sheilley, H. K. (2008) The institution's obligations to athletes. *New Directions for Higher Education, 142,* 103–113.

Sheth, H., & Babiak, K. M. (2010) Beyond the game: Perceptions and practices of corporate social responsibility in the professional sport industry. *Journal of Business Ethics, 91,* 433–450.

Stokvis, R. (2000) Globalization, commercialization and individualization: Conflicts and changes in elite athletes. *Culture, Sport, & Society, 3(1),* 22–34.

Uthman, D. (2013) Report: Johnny Manziel accepted money for autographs. *USA Today Sports, August 5, 2013.* Retrieved August 7, 2013 from http://www.usatoday.com/story/sports/ncaaf/sec/2013/08/04/texas-am-aggies-johnny-manziel-money-for-autographs/2617413/.

Vergara, A. (2013) Carter shows Buckeye love in speech. *Fox Sports, August 4, 2013.* Retrieved August 7, 2013 from http://msn.foxsports.com/nfl/story/cris-carter-hall-of-fame-speech-apology-ohio-state-buckeyes-minnesota-vikings-philadelphia-eagles-080313.

Ward Jr., R. E. (2008) Athletic expenditures and the academic mission of American schools: A group-level analysis. *Sociology of Sport Journal, 25,* 560–578.

4 Theoretical Approaches to Counseling the Student Athlete

The theories contained in this chapter are intended to complement the theories of motivation discussed previously. Unlike the previous chapter, the theories are viewed from the broader perspective of life skill development and issues that can be extended beyond academic and athletic motivation. Though motivation is certainly an important part of development, the theories in this chapter are presented to address the needs of the student athlete as one who exists within a system and has internal and external influences which allow him/her to achieve possible goals. The school counselor is likely to use these theories and related techniques because they are largely viewed to be effective but brief, in terms of the usual amount of time available for implementation within a counseling relationship; thus, they are believed to be beneficial within the school setting, where schedules and responsibilities of both student athlete and school counselor can be difficult to maintain for extremely long periods of time. Furthermore, since coaches and other athletic professionals use these theories when building team mentality, sport culture, and player mindsets, they also provide a common ground by which school counselors can join with the support network of the student athlete. The main theories which serve this purpose are Social Learning/Social Development Theory, Cognitive Behavioral Therapy/Rational Emotive Behavior Therapy, Reality Therapy/Choice Theory, and Solution Focused Brief Therapy. It must also be noted that, in order to establish effective rapport with the student athlete, a school counselor should at least initially lead with a style that encourages the student athlete to be open and feel secure within the counseling environment. Certainly, a humanistic approach that uses microskills, such as open-ended questions and paraphrasing statements, can be of tremendous advantage (Ivey, Ivey, & Zalaquett, 2010). However, with the often concrete expectations that student athletes encounter due to the requirements of athletics and academics, one of the four theories mentioned above will likely enter the counseling relationship at some point. Thus, examining the major tenets and approaches of each theory is expected to provide not only an effective foundation for the remainder of this text, but also a concrete understanding for counseling professionals to adapt and apply a style that can work for the student athletes they are likely to one day encounter.

Social Learning/Development Theory

Originally created by Bandura (1977), Social Learning Theory mostly refers to the use of modeling approaches designed to assist individuals who are attempting to make behavioral changes, which can also lead to changes in an individual's motivation, beliefs about him/her self, and the possible capacity to do more. It is through the concept of *self-efficacy*, or the individual's beliefs about his/her likelihood to reach a goal, that people are inclined to approach, attempt, and complete tasks that are available to them. An individual tends to avoid tasks and challenges where self-efficacy is perceived to be low, and thus (s)he tend to take on tasks where self-efficacy is perceived to be high. Bandura's concepts are also linked to the work of Vygotsky (1978), who emphasized Social Development Theory as a way to assist individuals learn skills and perform tasks through the use of adult guidance and peer collaboration. The concept of the *zone of proximal development* is hypothetically used to explain how much space there is between an individual's need to rely on the support of others in order to complete a task and his/her ability to complete tasks on his/her own. The "ideal" position within the zone can be dependent on numerous factors and variables, but it is usually hoped that an individual's total dependence on others is not what is always required. Regardless of whether Social Development or Social Learning Theory is being applied, theorists assume that individuals are responsible for reflecting on their learning experiences and the shaping of their environment (Gilson, Chow, & Feltz, 2012). Thus, even though other agents can assist an individual by serving as models and teachers, it is the learner's ultimate responsibility to gain the sense of meaning and purpose that comes from the task or challenge itself.

When applied to the field of athletics, Christensen, Laursen, and Sorensen (2011) have used three social learning principles to engage student athletes in the learning process. Adapted from Wenger's (1998) models of learning communities, they include mutual engagement, joint enterprise, and a shared repertoire. *Mutual engagement* refers to the idea that, even though a team or community is comprised of different players in terms of demographics and levels of learning and skill development, learners and learning agents can come together and focus on the goals that need to be accomplished. In other words, teammates and coaches recognize their roles and responsibilities to themselves and others in order to set, meet, and address challenges. Every team member carries this engagement with them into other relationships within their larger community, agreeing to be responsible for setting and reaching related goals appropriately. *Joint enterprise* refers to the creation of a developmentally progressive context within which skills and accomplishments are minimally considered to be at a strong level, and maximally considered to be at a level of elite accomplishment(s). In other words, people jointly expect to work together toward achieving short-term and long-term goals that appropriately reflect the sport culture and personal values that are involved with the team and its supporters. This refers to concepts of professionalism and sportsmanship in addition to the skills required to play the game. A *shared repertoire* refers to the specific skills and details needed to excel at the sport in question; it can contain sports jargon, symbols such as team logos and chants, skills and playing strategies designed for practice and/or game time play, and anecdotal stories and legends designed to inspire further success(es). This repertoire can be quite complex, but it is not necessarily meant to be secretive to others within the community. Thus, school counselors attempting to assist student athletes who are struggling with issues outside of the athletic realm are recommended to connect with some of this repertoire so that appropriate rapport and respect can first be established. It represents a way of showing a learner that the model attempting to assist and guide him/her is a credible and open agent who is trying to appropriately understand where (s)he is coming from (Long, Pantaleon, Bruant, & d'Arripe-Longueville, 2006).

There are also indirect ways of bringing about self-efficacy and other forms of social learning, such as the use of imagery and metaphor (Munroe-Chandler, Hall, & Fishburne, 2008; Short, Tenute, & Feltz, 2005). By using one's mind and perception to create images that represent symbols of success and desired outcome, it is believed that some individuals create a hybrid of positive self-talk and modeling which allows feelings of self-efficacy to increase. As a result, student athletes can transfer these inner models to the real world and mediate stresses and conflicts that can sometimes interfere with performance. These are not the same concepts as dreams, because they involve deliberate, conscious strategies by which participants are learning to find symbols and images that can help them focus and develop a sense of confidence to take on the next challenge that comes their way. Though not every student athlete may respond to guided imagery exercises with the same level of motivation, using such approaches can be helpful especially when: live models are not available; the student athlete may have a skills set that allows for imagery and metaphoric exercises to be used with some effectiveness; and/or the messages from external sources, such as coaches and teammates, have become stale or desensitized for a period of time (Short et al., 2005). Given that sports can often be a metaphor for other life events and lessons, having a student athlete make these links through narrative exercises can also be of benefit. For example, if a student athlete has experienced a string of low grades on course assignments, engaging him/her in a discussion about a time when (s)he experienced a losing streak or sport slump and overcame this situation may help him/her refocus his/her energy toward academic improvement. While it may not be the exact solution to the problem, the constructed narrative can disrupt the negative self-talk and thoughts (s)he may have about his/her academic ability (Munroe-Chandler et al., 2008). However, it is important to be aware of the general language and details of the student athlete's sport when engaging in such dialogue, because it can be taken as a sign of disrespect or disconnection within a counseling relationship (Martin, 2005). It can also confuse the learning process if terminology is applied inappropriately, but most student athletes tend to appreciate the efforts that people make when trying to assist them in a counseling or consultative relationship if this is done in a sincere manner (Goldberg & Chandler, 1995; Martin, 2005).

Strengths and Limitations

Among other purposes, social learning and social development theories have been applied to student athlete populations in order to address issues of moral reasoning and decision-making (Long et al., 2006), motivation to excel during practices and preparation for games (Gilson et al., 2012), and academic/educational lessons learned from athletic experiences (Christensen et al., 2011). They also apply to individual student athletes when used for the purposes of stress management (Humphrey, Yow, & Bowden, 2000), career counseling (Brown, Glastetter-Fender, & Shelton, 2000; McQuown-Linnemeyer & Brown, 2010; Shurts & Shoffner, 2004), and self-esteem development (Jowett & Lavallee, 2007). The main reasons for this appear to be because of the reliance on team and social support, which one can argue is a natural part of the student-athletic experience in the first place. Many sports that take place in K-12 settings are team sports, which initially require student athletes to develop a group identity as well as an understanding of the positions and roles they have within the team and designated groups used for practices and other preparatory purposes. Thus, using theories that have a social element to address more personal issues may be seen by the student athlete and counselor as comfortable and familiar approaches that align with the typical manners in which on-the-field matters are addressed. Also, these theories are rather concrete in nature. In other words, they focus specifically on the steps and strategies that are to be taken by an individual who needs to accomplish a particular task or goal. A model, be it a live human, recorded agent, or narrative set of instructions, provides sensory data to enhance the otherwise abstract nature of constructing a goal and the path one must travel to reach it. This can be of tremendous benefit to a client who is a visual and/or auditory learner, and considering the performance-based nature that most student athletes are accustomed to, it may also be seen as a less intrusive way of tapping into issues (s)he may be dealing with off-the-field. The use of an additional model who is not the teacher may help the student athlete, because it mirrors the process by which (s)he may practice with his/her teammates, and allows the learning to occur with a greater sense of efficacy because of the perceived credibility of a peer who is able to provide a concrete demonstration of the skill(s) needed. Teachers may also benefit from this type of experience because it creates a collaborative learning approach that allows diverse classrooms to exist and differentiated levels of instruction to be used in a manner that does not alienate or isolate students who are either struggling to learn or so far ahead of their peers that they become disengaged from the classroom environment (Tomlinson & Imbeau, 2010). It can also be implemented in a relatively short period of time because of the use of lesson planning and measurable outcomes.

However, with its major emphasis on learning and cognition, Social Learning and Social Development Theory do(es) not always tap into an individual's feelings and emotions, which can also be factors that impact motivation and goal attainment (Crain, 1992; Magen, 1998; Palmer-Cleveland, 2011). Student athletes who are not performing well in school can be experiencing emotional blocks they are not comfortable sharing with others out of fear or concern about being viewed as weak or crazy; using a learning or social modeling approach will not readily be able to facilitate discussion about such blocks. Also, it is not always the case that models and team approaches are readily available for all types of tasks that can occur during the course of a school day, week, semester, or year. The over-reliance on social models and the under-use of independent work can lead some individuals toward a pattern of learned helplessness or stagnation if taken to excess levels (Seligman, 2006). Though it is expected that individuals are to be accountable for the lessons they learn and reflect on as they progress toward their goal(s), the use of a model or team effort can also provide some individuals with an opportunity to engage in social loafing and/or shift this responsibility away from themselves when faced with elements of failure or non-clarity (Thompson, 2003). Counselors, just like coaches, must be aware of these pitfalls when working with student athletes, and use I-messages, along with other self-reflective statements, to balance this perspective. Even in moments of loss or failure, personal learning and responsibility can be found and reframed as strengths.

Cognitive Behavioral Therapy/Rational Emotive Behavior Therapy

One of the more empirically based theories that has been applied to school settings as well as work with student athletes is that of Cognitive Behavioral Therapy (CBT)/Rational Emotive Behavior Therapy (REBT). Albert Ellis (2004) served as one of the key founders of the former and was the main proponent of the latter. Similar to social learning, CBT and REBT largely view the individual as the one responsible for how they view the world and create the meaning(s) behind which lessons are learned when events are encountered. This process unfolds in a model described through an A-B-C cycle. The *activating event*, or part A, is the occurrence that a student athlete experiences, and triggers certain perceptions and beliefs as a result. Often, these events are some kind of adversity, failure or setback. This is not to say that positive events do not fit such a model, but in terms of what is likely to be part of a counseling process, most student athletes would initially attempt to seek help because of a negative event. As a result of the event, the individual registers *beliefs*, or part B, which can be based on rational or irrational ideas. For example, a student athlete who serves as the goalie of his soccer team can miss a block that enables the other team to score a game-winning goal. He may believe, because of his perspective on this event, that it was completely his fault that the game was lost. It may be an accurate reflection of the situation, but not necessarily the full explanation, as it can also be possible that his teammates were unable to keep control and possession of the ball, or the player who aimed the ball was particularly adept at scoring, among other contributory factors. As a result of these beliefs, there are emotional and/or behavioral *consequences*, which reflect part C. The goalie may: feel depressed; withdraw from or avoid contact with others because of concern about embarrassment; overcompensate for the outcome by practicing more; and/or shrug it off and pretend that the event was not a big deal. There are numerous actions and inactions that can be taken as a result, and not all may be appropriate in terms of the climate and system within which (s)he exists. Thus, a coach or counseling professional must be available to help the student athlete recognize the options available to him/her and which ones are most likely to lead to positive, healthy outcomes.

Some strategies that are used to encourage change in thoughts and behaviors often involve role-playing and practice. With respect to teens, adolescents and preadolescents, "Skillstreaming" is one program where social skills and behavioral training are used to assist them in dealing with negative activating events (Goldstein & McGinnis, 1997; McGinnis & Goldstein, 2003; McGinnis & Goldstein, 1990). Usually conducted in a group setting with a counselor, teacher, or coach as a facilitator, participants are presented with descriptive information about a particular prosocial skill, exposed to the application of such a skill in a hypothetical situation, and asked to practice the skill in the presence of others who can provide feedback and further discussion about how to use the skill in future encounters. A student athlete lamenting about his inability to stop the game-winning goal may be able to practice I-statements and messages that can allow him to develop a sense of coping strategy and ability to gradually move past this difficult activating event (e.g., "It was one missed goal, and I can block more with more practice."). Other strategies that can be used without the use of a group include scale-based journaling techniques and worksheets that individuals can use to monitor their progress toward goals and the use of skills that can better enhance future approaches toward activating events they may next encounter; such approaches can assist individuals deal with issues related to self-esteem, depression, anxiety, and motivation (Christodoulou, Jorge, & Mezzich, 2009). As long as the individual is able to recognize the gradual progress required of him/her during the process, such techniques are able to help him/her reach an effective outcome.

Strengths and Limitations

Similar to social learning, CBT and REBT are rather concrete approaches that are specific and detailed in terms of defining problems and outlining steps that one can take toward improvement. Also, because of the use of modeling and practice, visual and auditory data help individuals feel better able to see the change and progress they wish to make. For student athletes who are visual and auditory learners, these theories are of significant benefit, especially as they can tap into more abstract concepts, like emotions and feelings of self-worth, which may not be as easy to disclose during the early stages of counseling and therapy (Storch, Storch, Killiany, & Roberti, 2005). Also, these theories emphasize here-and-now approaches which allow individuals to actively and proactively involve themselves in the process of change. Since student athletes are often encouraged to prepare for their next challenge, practice, and/or competition even in the face of adversity, such a parallel process within the counseling relationship may be seen as a non-threatening and common procedure allowing effective discussion about personal issues to occur.

The drawbacks associated with such theories can be related to the fact that they are so individually focused that the student athlete's relationships to others can be under-emphasized. Coaches, parents, teammates, and others have significant connections to student athletes, which can also impact the ways that they perceive themselves and their abilities. Though great respect and power is given to the independent choices that an individual can make through CBT and REBT, some individuals do not define themselves separately from the beliefs and opinions of others. Certain cultural differences and communalistic values reflect this type of individual who may not be best suited for approaches that ask for such an amount of independent action (Ogbonnaya, 1994). Though group work and dyadic interaction can be a part of the process, certain individuals have a connection to others that extends beyond the school-based or classroom-based connections; for this purpose, a more socially integrated perspective may be more beneficial. It is also important to note that while numerous types of problems can be addressed through CBT and REBT approaches, they are not necessarily brief or short-term in nature. Issues such as depression and addiction, for example, are not necessarily dealt with in a series of simple steps, and school-based counseling professionals need to collaborate with other professionals who are able to provide individuals struggling with these types of issues greater and deeper levels of therapeutic support in order to more comprehensively address these matters. However, when used in conjunction with the work of other therapeutic professionals, CBT and REBT can themselves provide deeper and greater levels of support than several counseling approaches that are used within school settings.

Reality Therapy/Choice Theory

Reality Therapy and Choice Theory were developed by William Glasser. They revolve around the idea that individuals are in control of their actions, and they use their actions, thoughts, and physiological impulses and feelings to best relate to the world around them (Glasser, 1980). Though individuals can only control their thoughts and actions, their total behavior(s) are used to fully orient themselves to those around them and the events that occur. Similar to the fore-going in this chapter, Reality Therapy and Choice Theory also take a here-and-now approach toward understanding one's self, one's situation, and in what direction(s) (s)he is able to head as a result of making plans and goals to get there (Corey, 2005; Stone & Dahir, 2006). However, some of the unique aspects of Reality Therapy and Choice Theory revolve around the idea that people need to be consciously focused on what behaviors they need to use for survival, connections to others, and positive outcomes; to do this, counselors sometimes rely on confrontation and challenging clients to see the realistic criteria that they need to have for themselves. Coaches often apply this concept through the tone and relationships they form with players within their athletic programs, which make Reality Therapy and Choice Theory strong options for use with student athlete populations (Klug, 2006). These theories have been applied to work with athletic motivation (Parish & Williams, 2007), parental involvement (Pound, 2009), and transitioning athletes who are retiring or deciding to leave sports (Stankovich, Meeker, & Henderson, 2001). They have also been applied to how physical exercises and training can assist individuals develop better self-esteem and aggression management (Law, 2004), which showcases the range that the empirical support of these theories have. One popular model that connects the various applications of these theories is the *want-direction-evaluation-plan* (WDEP) system (Wubbolding, 2000).

When using WDEP, counselors and clients first examine what each *want* the outcome of counseling to be, and try to understand the perceptions associated with the things stated as being wanted (Wubbolding, 2000). Regarding the case of Mike, for example, he may state to his counselor that he wants to improve his grades in Math so he can continue to play football. In order to further assist Mike, the school counselor may also express a wanted action of having Mike better balance his academic and athletic time, so that future dilemmas like the one that brought him to the counseling office are minimized.

The second part of the system examines the *direction* in which Mike is headed as a result of what he is currently doing and what steps he may choose to next take. Examining Mike's athletic schedule, homework schedule, and other responsibilities may be such a way of getting this information, but it is also important to uncover what Mike thinks and feels about these tasks and schedules, so that effective determinations can be made about where his performance is lacking and what relevance this lack of performance has for his counseling goal(s). If Mike does not have an appreciation of Math, he may need to further explore and address this topic, so that a more effective action plan can be formed—one that does not merely involve him "going through the motions" so he can play, but rather, one that helps him not view academics and athletics as mutually exclusive duties.

The next part of the model involves Mike's *evaluation* of how effective his current actions are when it comes to helping him achieve his wants. As previously noted, this is not only about Mike's feelings, but also his thoughts and actions that carry him toward or away from the desired goal.

After such an evaluation has been discussed, counselor and client develop a *plan* to allow positive change(s) to occur. The range of planning options should fit with the school, family, and social systems in which the student athlete exists, and allow for a realistic expectation of success. In the main, this means the actions must be followed through and taken in reasonable increments.

Mike may be able to devote more study time to Math class, but expecting one assignment to completely achieve the goal that he wants may not be a realistic expectation. However, building on the initial success can get him significantly closer until the outcome is ultimately reached.

The use of the WDEP model may occur in several aspects of a student athlete's life without the aid of a counselor, teacher, peer, or coach, but it may be due to a lack of conscious attention about these occurrences that student athletes may need a professional's perspective in order to learn more about it. This is also why Reality Therapy and Choice Theory are often used for the purposes of psycho-education and classroom guidance within many school systems (Stone & Dahir, 2006).

Strengths and Limitations

One of the more significant strengths of Reality Therapy and Choice Theory is that they provide the individual with a strong sense of control. Clients are not passively engaged in the change process, and being able to decide how to take action can be an empowering and encouraging motivator for them to work toward their goal(s). For student athletes who are normally accustomed to practicing and demonstrating their talents and abilities, these theoretical approaches may be natural fits, or in cases where student athletes are not accustomed to having choices available to them, they can also be exciting and novel approaches to facilitating change. Also, just as is the case for the theories discussed previously, Reality Therapy and Choice Theory are concrete and detailed in nature. The specific steps and descriptions required of counselor and client help ensure clarity and assist with the tracking of progress toward the ultimate goal(s). The direct nature of conveying thoughts, feelings, and perceptions can also be appreciated by both counselor and client, because it places a level of authenticity onto the therapeutic relationship, where honesty and clear communication serve as the backdrop to how goals and plans are constructed. The collaborative nature of the counselor–client relationship can also be considered a strength because it can parallel the relationships that are familiar to student athletes outside of the counseling realm, such as their connections to coaches and teammates.

One drawback of Reality Therapy and Choice Theory is that they can be difficult for student athletes who are not particularly adept at articulating their thoughts and feelings in a concrete fashion. Since emotions are complex matters for some individuals, asking for concrete descriptions about their wants and evaluations of their perceived effectiveness may create more of a problem than a solution. Some student athletes are guarded about emotional disclosure in the first place, so taking such an approach may not be the most effective starting point within a counseling relationship. Also, it is difficult to determine the exact length of time required for a client to reach his/her desired goal. Though Reality Therapy and Choice Theory use concrete language and description to define and outline the actions needed for change, the process does not necessarily keep such a specific form. It is also important to bear in mind that Reality Therapy and Choice Theory do not place strong emphasis on the biological and physiological roots of problems. Clients who are clinically diagnosed with certain issues are likely to need interventions and treatments that are not directly addressed through these theoretical approaches. Counseling professionals must be able to work in cooperation with clinical professionals when such cases exist, and ensure that treatment plans are compatible with all parties involved. Bearing these factors in mind can enable more effective results to occur.

Solution Focused Brief Therapy

Solution focused brief therapy (SFBT) is a social constructivist approach that emphasizes client perception as a way of bringing about progress toward goal(s) (Berg, 1994; de Shazer, 1991). Unlike the fore-going theories of this chapter, however, the core of SFBT centers on the notion that focusing on problems and reasons as to why help is needed is not a productive way of bringing about change. Thus, it is not only a theory that emphasizes here-and-now perspective(s), but also a future-oriented style that requires clients to create steps toward forward movement and accomplishments. In order to accomplish these tasks, counselors provide specific language and questions to clients, so that a solution-focused dialogue becomes the norm of counseling sessions (Corey, 2005). Such questions include:

1. *The miracle question*
    A client is asked: if a miracle were to happen overnight, resolving any issues related to a perceived problem, but you were unaware that this had occurred, what would be some of the first things you notice that would indicate the problem has gone? If applied to the case of Mike, for example, his miracle may include the notion that his struggles in Math have vanished. One thing he may notice is that his Math teacher praises his work more often, which constitutes a marker for change and improvement that, in addition to his ability to remain on the sports team, allows him to feel better about the work he is able to do. Uncovering this indicator of change can assist Mike in creating an action plan to, for example, check in with his Math teacher more often so that he can be better assured that his work is on the right track, and with some encouragement from his teacher, that his perceived fear of failure or lack of support from his classroom environment are not accurate (Corey, 2005). As a result, Mike may be more able to improve his work and feel better about how he has been able to do so.
2. *Exception and/or coping questions*
    These are approaches whereby a client is asked to essentially answer "What are things like when the problem is not occurring?" and "How do you handle that?" and, in so doing, provide insights as to how (s)he can function under perceived circumstances of difficulty and stress. Asking Mike,

for example, "How are you able to go to class even though the subject material is difficult and/or stressful for you?" can help him find strengths and skills that may not otherwise be noticeable to him, and allow him to feel better about the steps he can take to improve his situation. When looking for the exceptions to the problem, Mike could be asked "What do you do when you are not struggling with the material?" and report how he engages in other behaviors that are likely to be of benefit to his everyday functioning. There are several individuals who may, in the face of difficult work, quit or act in ways that disturb the classroom setting; considering that Mike is not doing this shows that he can handle some of the stress involved with his current situation, and that taking a slightly further step in speaking with his teacher or trusted classmate about how to get additional help can lead him to a more favorable outcome.

3. *Scaling questions*

   These numerically identify where a client is currently at in terms of dealing with their perceived issues and what steps are needed in order to reach a higher level of effectiveness (Corey, 2005). Mike, for example, may identify his struggles in Math at a level of 4 on a scale where 1 represents an unbearable level of concern and 10 represents no concern whatsoever. The counselor would be wise to encourage Mike that he is not at a level of 1, and ask Mike what it would take to get to a level of 5. It is this incremental shift that makes the notion of finding a solution more bearable and realistic for Mike. Though a level of 10 may be ultimately desired, attempting to reach it early on in the counseling relationship may not be an approach that can be easily done or realistically accomplished immediately. According to SFBT, building on small successes on the way to the major accomplishments is more likely to assist Mike (Berg, 1994; de Shazer, 1991).

With respect to school settings and student athletes, SFBT is often used to improve classroom behaviors (Vallaire-Thomas, Hicks, & Growe, 2011) and assist with athletic performance issues and the personal impacts they can have on other forms of school-based performance (Hoigaard & Johansen, 2004). The use of positive terminology and action-focused strategies is what seems to make it an effective match for K-12 students, while the brief time frame and structure of interaction is what makes the theory effective for many school counselors and school settings. This is not to say that SFBT is not used for other purposes, but its general style and focus on future accomplishments tends to make it of particular benefit to student athletes who are struggling with performance-based issues either on or off the field.

Strengths and Limitations

Clearly, SFBT has a strong advantage in terms of its brief nature. The amount of contact time that school counselors have with many individual students can be quite limited, so the use of SFBT can assist both counselor and student athlete with respect to their schedules and needs. Its here-and-now approach, along with its emphasis on action, can also be of particular benefit because student athletes who are accustomed to playing and practice efforts are often able to view solutions in terms of skills and steps required to reach the desired outcome. Also, given that SFBT prefers to view matters in terms of positive wording and expectations, it can be considered an advantage to student athletes who are often encouraged to not dwell on failures and negative outcomes for inordinate periods of time. Though there is value in dealing with a loss or setback, dwelling on it may not prove to be a useful strength or strategy in terms of reaching certain goals. The use of SFBT can also be advantageous because of its premise of encouragement, which does not feel as intrusive as some theories and approaches that initially start with an analysis of emotional issues or blocks that a client may be facing. The work involved with finding a solution can be difficult for some, but with the ability to focus on strengths and what has worked in the past for a client, (s)he may not find this work as difficult or taxing as would be the case with more emotionally driven theories that emphasize a description of the problem.

However, it is still important to recognize that short-term approaches do not always lead to long-term gains. Though SFBT is able to accomplish these goals, there are counseling professionals who note that only focusing on solutions and steps toward improvement may not be addressing deeper concerns that may underlie the matters being addressed in brief counseling sessions. Also, some student athletes may need emotional space to address some of the perspectives and points that have brought them to the counseling office. Therefore, SFBT may not be an initially strong match for clients who have a strong connection to their feelings and emotions and view these factors as important ones which link to their issues. It is also important to note that SFBT tends to be an individual approach, and that extending it to the group- or team-level may not be done as easily as is the case with other theories. Certainly, there are group counseling approaches that are based on SFBT principles, but outside of the counseling office, individuals are often the ones responsible for following through on their efforts toward change.

Summary

The theories reviewed in this chapter are meant to provide an overview for the future sections of this text by showcasing the general themes and approaches that can be used when school counselors work with student athletes. As can be discerned from these overviews, many constructivist themes and strategies appear to be often applied to the counseling work of student athlete populations. Some of the reason for this may be due to the fact that student athletes are often expected to perform in concrete ways that allow the breakdown and practice of skills to be both detailed and regimented in terms of how learning is done and improvement is made. It can also be due to the fact that many student athletes are reinforced for their active participation within sports and within their team meetings, and theories which actively involve clients making plans and taking steps toward reaching their ultimate goals naturally fit with these behaviors. Whether a counselor uses a narrative construction with a social learning focus, scaling strategy with a solution-focused perspective, planning method with a Reality Therapy emphasis, assessment strategy with a cognitive behavioral framework, or analysis of emotional responses with the use of Rational Emotive Behavior Therapy, the use of concrete and direct language to communicate the ideas and goals to student athletes is what appears to bind these theories together. This not only helps establish strong rapport with the student athlete, but also assists with tracking the progress and outcome of his/her work. Readers are encouraged to develop a style that pulls from the elements of theories that they deem effective for reaching the student athlete populations they will be exposed to one day, but to recognize that there is no universal approach free of drawbacks or exceptions. It is hoped that future chapters addressing the range of academic, personal/social, and career-based issues associated with student athletes will help with this notion of style development as well.

Questions for Discussion

1. How clear is your style of counseling in terms of theory? How many theoretical approaches do you use in your counseling work? How do you convey this to a student athlete; a student athlete who may not normally seek counseling services?
2. How similar should the school counselor's style be to a student athlete's coach? What are the advantages and disadvantages of being similar to this style? Different from this style?
3. When creating plans with a student athlete, who should be responsible for their outcome? How do you address this when an outcome falls short of expectation?

References

Bandura, A. (1977) Self-efficacy: Toward a unifying theory of behavioral change. *Psychological Review, 84*, 191–215.

Berg, I. K. (1994) *Family Based Services: A Solution Focused Approach.* New York: Norton.

Brown, C., Glastetter-Fender, C., & Shelton, M. (2000) Psychosocial identity and career control in college student athletes. *Journal of Vocational Behavior, 56*, 53–62.

Christensen, M. K., Laursen, D. N., & Sorensen, J. K. (2011) Situated learning in youth elite football: A Danish case study among talented male under-18 football players. *Physical Education and Sport Pedagogy, 16(2)*, 163–178.

Christodoulou, G., Jorge, M., & Mezzich, J. (2009) *Advances in psychiatry: Third volume.* Athens, Greece: BETA Medical Publishers.

Corey, G. (2005) *Theory and Practice of Counseling & Psychotherapy* (7th ed.). Belmont, CA: Brooks/Cole.

Crain, W. (1992) *Theories of Development: Concepts and Applications.* Englewood Cliffs, NJ: Prentice-Hall.

de Shazer, S. (1991) *Putting Difference to Work.* New York: Norton.

Ellis, A. (2004) *Rational Emotive Behavior Therapy: It Works for Me – It Can Work for You.* Buffalo, NY: Prometheus Books.

Gilson, T. A., Chow, G. M., & Feltz, D. L. (2012) Self-efficacy and athletic squat performance: Positive or negative influences at the within- and between-levels of analysis. *Journal of Applied Social Psychology, 42,* 1467–1485.

Glasser, N. (1980) *What are You Doing?: How People are Helped Through Reality Therapy.* New York: Harper & Row.

Goldberg, A. D., & Chandler, T. (1995) Sports counseling: Enhancing the development of the high school student athlete. *Journal of Counseling & Development, 74,* 39–44.

Goldstein, A., & McGinnis, E. (1997) *Skillstreaming the Adolescent: New Strategies and Perspectives for Teaching Prosocial Skills.* Champaign, IL: Research Press.

Hoigaard, R., & Johansen, B. T. (2004) The solution-focused approach in sport psychology. *The Sport Psychologist, 18,* 218–228.

Humphrey, J. H., Yow, D. A., & Bowden, W. W. (2000) *Stress in College Athletics: Causes, Consequences, Coping.* Binghamton, NY: Haworth Press.

Ivey, A. E., Ivey, M. B., & Zalaquett, C. P. (2010) *Intentional Interviewing and Counseling: Facilitating Client Development in a Multicultural Society* (7th ed.). Belmont, CA: Brooks/Cole.

Jowett, S., & Lavallee, D. (2007) *Social Psychology in Sport.* Champaign, IL: Human Kinetics, Inc.

Klug, K. (2006) Applying Choice Theory and Reality Therapy to coaching athletes. *International Journal of Reality Therapy, 25(2),* 36–39.

Law, D. R. (2004) A Choice Theory perspective on children's Taekwondo. *International Journal of Reality Therapy, 24(1),* 13–18.

Long, T., Pantaleon, N., Bruant, G., & d'Arripe-Longueville, F. (2006) A qualitative study of moral reasoning of young elite athletes. *The Sport Psychologist, 20,* 330–347.

McGinnis, E., & Goldstein, A. (1990) *Skillstreaming in Early Childhood: Teaching Prosocial Skills to the Preschool and Kindergarten Child.* Champaign, IL: Research Press.

McGinnis, E., & Goldstein, A. (2003) *Skillstreaming in Early Childhood: New Strategies and Perspectives for Teaching Prosocial Skills.* Champaign, IL: Research Press.

McQuown-Linnemeyer, R., & Brown, C. (2010) Career maturity and foreclosure in student athletes, fine arts students, and general college students. *Journal of Career Development, 37(3),* 616–634.

Magen, Z. (1998) *Exploring Adolescent Happiness: Commitment, Purpose and Fulfillment.* Thousand Oaks, CA: Sage.

Martin, S. B. (2005) High school and college athletes' attitudes toward sport psychology consulting. *Journal of Applied Sport Psychology, 17,* 127–139.

Munroe-Chandler, K., Hall, C., & Fishburne, G. (2008) Playing with confidence: The relationship between imagery use and self-confidence and self-efficacy in youth soccer players. *Journal of Sports Sciences, 26(14),* 1539–1546.

Ogbonnaya, A. O. (1994) Person as community: An African understanding of the person as an intrapsychic community. *Journal of Black Psychology, 20,* 75–87.

Palmer-Cleveland, K. (2011) *Teaching Boys who Struggle in School: Strategies that Turn Underachievers into Successful Learners.* Alexandria, VA: Association for Supervision and Curriculum Development.

Parish, T. S., & Williams, D. (2007) Some tips regarding how to motivate athletes. *International Journal of Reality Therapy, 26(2),* 39–40.

Pound, P. (2009) Choice Theory and psychoeducation for parents of out-of-competition adolescent athletes. *International Journal of Reality Therapy, 29(1),* 34–37.

Seligman, M. E. P. (2006) *Learned Optimism: How to Change Your Mind and Life.* New York: Vintage.

Short, S. E., Tenute, A., & Feltz, D. L. (2005) Imagery use in sport: Mediational effects for efficacy. *Journal of Sports Sciences, 23(9),* 951–960.

Shurts, W. M., & Shoffner, M. F. (2004) Providing career counseling for collegiate student athletes: A learning theory approach. *Journal of Career Development, 31(2),* 95–109.

Stankovich, C. E., Meeker, D. J., & Henderson, J. L. (2001) The Positive Transition Model for sport retirement. *Journal of College Counseling, 4,* 81–105.

Stone, C. B., & Dahir, C. A. (2006) *The Transformed School Counselor.* Boston: Lahaska Press.

Storch, E. A., Storch, J. B., Killiany, E. M., & Roberti, J. W. (2005) Self-reported psychopathology in athletes: A comparison of intercollegiate student athletes and non-athletes. *Journal of Sport Behavior, 28(1),* 86–98.

Thompson, L. L. (2003) *Making the Team: A Guide for Managers.* Saddle River, NJ: Pearson/Prentice Hall.

Tomlinson, C. A., & Imbeau, M. B. (2010) *Learning and Managing a Differentiated Classroom.* Alexandria, VA: Association for Supervision and Curriculum Development.

Vallaire-Thomas, L., Hicks, J., & Growe, R. (2011) Solution-focused Brief Therapy: An interventional approach to improving negative student behaviors. *Journal of Instructional Psychology, 38(4),* 224–234.

Vygotsky, L. S. (1978) *Mind and Society: The Development of Higher Mental Processes.* Cambridge, MA: Harvard University Press.

Wenger, E. (1998) *Communities of Practice: Learning, Meaning, and Identity.* Cambridge: Cambridge University Press.

Wubbolding, R. (2000) *Reality Therapy for the 21st Century.* Bristol, PA: Accelerated Development.

5 Family Approaches to Counseling the Student Athlete

Michael P. Hagan

There is a wide range of interests and purpose amongst student athletes and their families. A large number of students have no interest in athletics and a large number of students who have an interest in athletics go it alone, as their families have no interest or are unable for other reasons to follow their sports activities. Students' interests vary from enjoying a sport and having fun, to making new friends, moving towards self-actualization, finding fulfillment, and staying in shape. For other students and their families, the purpose of sports in school is to provide a pathway to college sports and hopefully a partial or full scholarship.

In the interest of full disclosure, I played three sports in grade school: football, basketball, and baseball. It was likely the highlight of grade school and, in addition to learning about discipline, making a commitment to a team, making new friends, and enhancing friendship with others, it also provided valuable life lessons. One of these life lessons was that there was absolutely no future—even at the high school level—in any of these sports, in no small part because you had to be somewhat good at it. Not discouraged, high school athletics included cross country and track, which included distance running and the high jump. I would describe myself as somewhat above average in high school sports, attaining varsity team membership and varsity letters, including one divisional championship in track. I considered it a completely satisfactory athletic career.

Antshel and Anderman (2000) describe many reasons why sports are popular and why students want to participate. Being involved in something that challenges mind and body is helpful to one's development. Being involved in sports provides competition, the chance to keep in shape physically, and the chance to learn hard lessons about winning and losing, both as part of a team and as an individual. Some sports, such as soccer, have literally exploded in popularity in the past 30 years. Others, such as basketball, have become all-consuming for some students and their families.

It was not that long ago that minority families saw athletics not as a way to pay for college, but as a way to get into college in the first place. Integration of college sports, particularly but not only in the South, came very slowly, aided more by a desire to win than a desire to do what was right. Halberstam wrote about the integration of football at the University of Alabama (Halberstam, 2002, p. 12). He wrote about Sam

"Bam" Cunningham, an African American football player from the University of Southern California. The University of Alabama played the University of Southern California at Birmingham's Legion Field 1970, and it was the first time a fully integrated team played against Alabama in Birmingham. They handed the Crimson Tide of Alabama a 42–21 defeat. Southern Cal had several African American players on the team, including Sam Cunningham, a sophomore back-up, who scored two touchdowns in the first half. The next year, Alabama integrated their varsity football team; they already had an African American on the freshman football team, and the joke was that Sam Cunningham did more to integrate Alabama football in 30 minutes than anyone else did in 50 years. Today, one of the questions that will challenge the school counselor in working with families is being able to understand the myriad of motivations and agendas for the student athlete and their family. This writer believes that this is a key to successful work with families.

Role of the Counseling Professional

Defining the role of the counselor is always an important topic when considering any type of counseling. It is likely that, prior to the commencement of school counseling with families of student athletes, the school counselor will have to think about what his/her role will be in counseling, and this starts with identifying and defining the client. When working with families, it is the whole family that is the client and the counselor's role is to help the family resolve issues and work together to improve their lives, both as a family and as individuals. There are several factors to look at in helping to define the role of the counseling professional. They include the following:

• Who made the referral?
• What is the objective of the referral?
• How is the role of the counselor viewed by the family?

Students and families come to see counselors with a perception of what the role of counseling is, and what the role of the counselor is going to be. This can vary from seeing him/her as an arbitrator, to seeing him/her as someone who will hear a reasonable concern and advocate for it amongst the other family members.

While not in any way a comprehensive list, thinking about what role the school counselor will play is essential prior to the start of counseling. The counselor must be prepared to deal with different agendas, and also must be prepared to accept a wide range of affective responses to family counseling based on them. As a School Psychologist, I ran a Multidisciplinary Team meeting many years ago while in juvenile corrections. Approximately 20 people attended the meeting, including numerous staff from the school system to where these youths were returning. Everyone had an agenda for the meeting and primary concerns were related to: what was going to be recommended? and what possible programming was the school he was returning to going to be saddled with? The parents, and the youth—not someone who shied away from confrontation—looked lost in that room full of people. When I made it clear that the purpose of the meeting was to decide on the best programming for the youth while he was incarcerated, and not to dictate what should happen when he returned to the public schools, the tension in the room lifted immediately. The perceived agenda, which was not the agenda, brought out several interested parties all concerned with how decisions that day would impact on their own work, and what may be expected of them in the future.

Issues for Counseling

Parental vs. Student Expectations

The school counselor may have some confidence that a willingness to participate as a family in counseling is taking the first, and possibly the most important, step. The expectations of parents and children often differ. This can be true both for parents who want to see more and better athletic participation, and those who want to focus more on academics and less on athletics. Exploring the future goals and how they relate to athletics is important. Finding out how academic progress has been affected by sports is a way to find out more about the student's and the parents' perspective. It is not unusual, nor should it be thought of as problematic, if this is the case. Using the cognitive approach of reframing provides a good opportunity for the school counselor to point out that it is good that there is such interest and importance placed on these issues. Another example of this would be using Solution-Focused therapy, which does not avoid the problem but works with a positive, forward-looking approach in resolving them.

Athletics is seen by some families as a means to secure funding for college. Athletic participation in college is at a very different, and far more intense, level. Individuals in NCAA Division III athletics can expect a large part of their time to be taken up with weight training throughout the year, being on the road for athletic events, and involvement in academic study programs to keep them on track. This is even more of a factor for students in Division I or II. The same applies to students who go to NAIA schools. Athletics is not a particularly good way of funding college, except for the most disciplined student or motivated or gifted athlete. There are still ways to make college affordable. One can go to a community or technical college, or two-year university for two years and live at home, and then go on to a four-year university to save money. One can join the armed services and receive benefits from the GI Bill after serving, or join the Reserve Officer Training Corps and have tuition paid by the armed services. One can go to one of the military academies, focus on school and winning an academic scholarship. There are many ways to fund college if one wants to go, and athletic scholarships are a wonderful way to go to college, but carry with them the need for a high level of commitment and discipline. Wolverton (2007) points out that many college athletes choose not to pursue their desired major due to the pressures of college athletics but, interestingly, most of them do not regret it.

School vs. Club Sport Participation

Hensch (2006) discusses the challenge of dealing with youth who perceive focusing on one sport as necessary for athletic success. This is in no small part because many sports are now year-round. Once the sports year has ended for a sport, student athletes merely change leagues and continue to participate. In other words, kids often specialize in sports at too early an age. If you want to get offered a college scholarship in hockey, the likelihood of getting one out of high school is low. Actually, the likelihood of being the one of approximately 200 Americans who get a hockey scholarship each year is low at any point, but for those who get one, most have played junior hockey and are more likely to be 19 to 21 years old (American Hockey Center, 2013).

Participating in school athletics has, for some youth, become either a minor supplement to their club sports activities, or not a part of their athletic interests at all. Club sports, the Amateur Athletic Union (AAU, 2013), junior sports, and traveling teams have all amped up the need to push hard for more and more athletic dedication earlier and earlier in a student athlete's life. The results of soccer games for third graders show up in local newspapers. In many areas the model for soccer, which is one that is gaining popularity, is to have youth involved in a particular program or team from age 5 through age 19. The season will sometimes not correspond with school sports so a youth can play in both, but at times they do. In addition, the belief is that to get the very best of competition you need to travel, often to very distant states, and at times for national tournaments. In Wisconsin, there was also a recent fight between parents, schools, and the Wisconsin Interscholastic Athletic Association about who held the television rights to high school basketball games (Han, 2011).

The school counselor has to help families and the student athlete keep everything in perspective. This must be done carefully, because a direct approach is going to be rebuffed. The family and student athlete must be guided to explore these issues on their own. The role of the counselor is to help people resolve their own problems and to learn how to resolve other problems in a similar manner. Using Socratic dialogue, one is able to help the family focus on the presenting concerns without giving advice, and to work collaboratively to understand thinking and how it relates to feeling and behavior.

Retaining Students to Enhance Athletic Performance

Students are retained in school, but generally it is not particularly helpful. Some students are not started in school when they are eligible to start due to their age. The reason for the delay can vary, often it is seen as the fact that they are immature emotionally, not ready for school academically, and at times it is an attempt to give them a leg up on other kids later on in athletics. The latter can be done prior to the start of school or later in school, such as the start of middle school or just prior to high school. The greatest concern in dealing with this issue with families is that sometimes it works. Clay Matthews, an All-Pro linebacker from the University of Southern California who presently is the top defensive back for the Green Bay Packers is something of a case in point. He had been redshirted as a freshman, and turned down the opportunity to go into a game as a freshman in order to maintain his four years of eligibility. At the time, his coach thought it was funny because he did not think Matthews was going to be an important part of the team in the future (Merril, 2010). The history is still being written on him, but thus far, it looks like he made the right choice.

For most students, purposefully retaining them in school to boost their athletic achievements is not a good idea. The counselor has the job, however, to remain neutral in their own views. For some students, the decision will have already been made for them before they enter first grade, and it will often be only part of the decision-making process on the part of the parents. We will also see later that some sports may not allow for all student athletes to gain equal playing time, which can also impact decision-making processes and family dynamics.

Stress and Student Athletics

There has always been stress for athletes, and in fact, this can be one of the benefits of it. One can learn to deal with stress by being exposed to it and coping with it, developing strategies that generalize to other areas of their life. Few people who have participated in sports have been immune to having "butterflies" before an athletic event. Adrenaline starts flowing into the blood system in response to one's fight-or-flight response to an anxiety-provoking situation (Sonstroem, 2009). Once the game begins, the anxiety quickly dissipates because the body is using the adrenaline by extending oneself physically. This phenomenon is temporary, however, and the primary concern for student athletes has to be the long-term issues with stress that may occur. In 1986, a young star athlete named Kathy Love Ormsby set the record for the women's 10,000 meter run at the Penn Relays in April. She was a premed student at North Carolina State University and hoped to become a medical missionary. She routinely made the Dean's list and was one of those rare individuals who combined athletic and academic excellence. She balanced her life with deep religious convictions. But on June 4th of that year, while competing in a 10k meter event in Indianapolis Stadium, she ran off the track and out of the stadium, ran to a nearby 50 foot bridge over the White River and jumped off (Litsky, 1986). She did not die, but was paralyzed from the waist down. Her parents were considered to be warm and not pushy. Her father had reservations about her competing at that level (Heisler, 1986). There were some signs she was under stress in that she had previously dropped out of races, but no one could have predicted what happened. Even in hindsight, it is impossible to know the true combination of factors that precipitated this tragic event (Fleischman, 1986). Looking at many tragedies, such as completed suicides, it is easy to see factors that may have contributed to the death. It is harder, however to tell why these factors affected one particular person. The difficulty is distinguishing between the bad outcome and the usual outcome which is good or at worst benign, even under the same set of stressors. Ms. Ormsby was under severe stress, but so are many athletes at that level. She was driven and likely a perfectionist, but again so are many young people. Additionally, we all want to figure out what happened, and do not want to think that maybe there were uncontrollable variables that factored in. What if she had caught a second wind and had started to move up instead of becoming convinced she was going to fail? It may have been just another collegiate race and she may have finished her career and become a medical doctor. Permanently paralyzed from the waist down, she is now a very skilled and highly successful occupational therapist.

Stress is also a great motivator, it is like having a tiger by the tail, so to speak. It helps you to push yourself harder, to do more, and to become motivated when you do not succeed. It can be internal or external stress that motivates one. Lufi and Parish-Plass (2011) found improvement over several areas for kids with emotional and behavioral concerns, using a sport-based group therapy program for one year. They found improvements in several areas for both the children and their parents, particularly in the reduction of anxiety. The school counselor has to help families first recognize the nature of stress, and help them find the causes of it and the impact it is having. The student athlete always has to feel that there are resources available and people available that (s)he can talk to when feeling that stress is getting out of control. These resources need to be nurtured by the school counselor.

The Unreality of Athletic Exceptionality

The school counselor needs to recognize that many young athletes today are treated differently from their non-athletic counterparts, and the better they are the more they are experiencing a reality that is going to last only as long as their success continues to propel them to the top. There are exceptions. William Henderson, a fullback for the Green Bay Packers started planning his transition from football before he left. He developed solid business interests back home in North Carolina. He said that he had older brothers who were exceptional athletes, but who, due to injuries or other reasons, never made it to the big time. Henderson feels he learned from his brothers' mistake of not planning ahead, and while he did make it in a big way as a professional athlete, he recognized he had to start planning for the day he was no longer going to be playing football. He began developing his business interests in the off-season, well before his playing days were over.

It is likely too much to think that in these unusual situations a school counselor is going to help a family recognize the limitations of the future, but the limitations are there. Few high school athletes make it to college, and few college athletes make it to a professional career. Attempts should be made to look for a fallback position. Beale and Jacobs (2004) wanted to take a positive approach to helping students who were interested in sports expand their thinking about what constitutes a career in sports. Specifically, they wanted to expand students' thinking to include the many additional jobs there are related to sports besides being an athlete. This includes coaching, teaching, television and radio production, financial representatives, and many other areas. Their idea was that kids can pursue a career as an athlete on the field while pursuing a career for afterward off the field. Most people can recognize that injury or other circumstances can change things quickly, so helping the family help the athlete prepare for a path inside and outside of athletics is a worthwhile goal, not only because injury can derail a career, but because very few outstanding athletes—even outstanding college athletes—will be able to become professional athletes.

The Purpose of Athletics

School counselors also have to be aware of some of the problems associated with student athletics. These problems include the formation of cliques, egocentrism, and aggression. Snow (2010) overviews the long relationship between aggression and athletics. Several sports (hockey, football and wrestling come immediately to mind) have aggression as an inherent part of the sport. Hitting others, hard, and wrestling around with them with the intention of pinning them to the mat are aggressive behaviors. The question for many is how much of this makes its way into the everyday life of the student athlete. There are many anecdotal instances of excessive aggression on the part of student athletes, often correlated with alcohol, outside of their athletic lives, often ending tragically. There are two views, one that athletics can be cathartic and the other that the modeling of violence can generalize to the athlete's family or community. It is important for the school counselor to be aware of this debate and to seek out answers as to whether the student athlete is aggressive and if this is due to their involvement in sport.

Family stress can be a significant factor for the school counselor to consider. For some families, the athlete is a person who can bring better things to the family, such as a first time college graduate, or perhaps at some point a professional contract. Ferguson (2008) discusses many of the stressors families of athletes face. There is the stress of the athlete to keep up with school and athletics which can now be year-round, and there is also the stress to the parents of making sure their child is not over-extended, or that they are not increasing the pressure on their child to succeed beyond their skill or their interest. Ferguson writes that surveys have found at times a majority of parents get "out of control" at their children's sporting events at one time or another. It is up to the school counselor to probe the dynamics of the family they are working with to see if this is a problem for counseling.

So again, what are the purposes of athletics? There are many purposes and the goals of the student, the family, the coaches, and the school all vary. Some coaches are trying to instill values, some are trying to promote a lifelong interest in staying in shape, some are trying to be successful so they can move up in the coaching world, and their own success depends on the success of the student athlete. The goals for parents vary: some want their kids to have fun, some want them to develop an interest in working out and staying healthy, some think it teaches discipline, some want to see college scholarships, and some just want to experience the enjoyment of watching their kid(s) compete—which is significantly enhanced when they compete successfully. The same is true for student athletes: some really just love to play sports, some like the recognition and the sense of belonging, and some hope it will lead to bigger and better things down the road. Athletics can encourage a natural peer group. In working with families, the school counselor—like anyone working with families and groups—recognizes the wide variety of goals amongst the family members, and needs to remain neutral, particularly sensitive to whether the issue of athletics is an opportunity on the part of the family to seek out help for more serious problems by focusing on something that appears by comparison relatively safe. For example, parents may have major disagreements about child rearing, issues related to divorce, and issues related to their own concerns that can coalesce around a safer issue such as their child's participation in athletics. For the purpose of elaboration, there is a parallel when it comes to working with violent youth. Most delinquents are wary of talking about the real reasons for their problems because they are protective of their families, and feel threatened by the idea of exposing themselves to a counselor. They want to hide what they are really thinking and feeling in order to protect themselves from further hurt. They do not want to talk about problems they had growing up, nor do they want to talk about being neglected or abused. But what they will talk about is their problem with anger, which for someone who is violent is somewhat obvious. This is because to a large extent, it is a badge of honor to have problems with anger and violence. They are willing to say that this is something they need help with. This can effectively be used as a segue into work on more personal and challenging issues. The same holds true for the school counselor, in that a hidden agenda for family counseling may result in a more positive outcome when the more problematic issues are able to surface.

Family Counseling

There is nothing inherently different about working with families of student athletes from working with families on other issues. Making people aware of this service and having confidence in its usefulness are often important. Gee (2010) found that coaches, athletes, and administrators are reluctant to seek professional help on issues dealing with athletic success, even though there is evidence it helps. Because these issues are less likely to be brought to the school counselor's attention, it is reassuring to know that the skills acquired in learning to facilitate family counseling in other areas translate quite nicely to work with families of student athletes. One of the first issues that must be decided is who in the family should be included in the counseling. Part of this decision should be based on the age of the child involved. This writer suggests that under age 12, the primary people involved in family counseling are going to be the parents, and this is because a Social Learning approach (Patterson & Stouthamer-Loeber, 1984) is recommended. When kids are over 12, a Cognitive Behavioral approach (Dattilio, 2007) is suggested. This is not a hard and fast suggestion because, for kids between the ages of 10 and 12, it would depend on the readiness and ability of the child to participate as one of the primary family members in counseling. Once a child has reached age 12, it is likely their peer group rather than their parents are going to play a more important role. Certainly, the counselor will want to use his/her own discretion. If there is no conflict, there is less of a need for a social learning approach. This is also not to say that these are the only approaches that may be useful for family counseling with student athletes. School counselors may use any approach in which they are trained and comfortable with the earlier areas of focus in mind.

Cognitive Behavioral Approach

Dattilio (2007) does an excellent job of describing the basics of cognitive-behavioral intervention as applied to couples and families. In addition, it is an approach that works well for school counselors because it can be done in a reasonable amount of time. In working with families instead of individuals, we are interested in the cognitions, schemas, and distorted thinking patterns, and work to change the thinking and cognitions to ones that are more helpful. The two primary alliance dynamics will be between either the student athlete with one parent against the other parent, or one or two parents against the student athlete. A mother and daughter, for example, may be highly supportive of athletic experiences even if they impact on academic performance, allied against a father who believes the opposite. This may be complicated by the involvement of step-parents, although they may at times also play a role of being a more objective observer. The first area to be concerned about is the variability of thinking on the importance of athletics. Exploring the thinking behind this is a good way to get the family talking about the value they attach to it. Some questions that can be used to gain a better understanding in this area include: How important does each of you feel athletics are at this point? And: Where do you hope your athletic path will lead in the near, middle and distant future?

Social Learning Approach

One Social Learning Approach from the Oregon Social Learning Center (Patterson & Stouthamer-Loeber, 1984) is particularly useful when there is underlying conflict between the parents and the child. For example, the child is not doing adequately in school and instead wants to join a traveling team for basketball. It is very often applied to work with children who are behaviorally problematic, but the same underlying tools are applicable elsewhere. The focus should be on the parents getting together and making a plan that uses positive rewards, particularly praise and encouragement, while decreasing the behaviors that are problematic. So, in the case of a child who is not doing what (s)he should be in school, the focus would initially be on monitoring their school progress, developing a method of monitoring their school progress, and rewarding positive changes. Obviously, just monitoring academic progress in a formal way is positive. This approach also is helpful to the parents because they find tools and strategies that help them feel they have a better pathway for dealing with the concerns of their child.

Summary

For the school counselor, working with families of student athletes can be a rewarding but challenging endeavor. It is important to see the whole family as the client, but to keep in mind that the student athlete is the focal point of counseling, and helping the family help them is going to be worthwhile for the whole family. It is important to welcome the opportunity to work with these families, but it is also important to remember one's limitations, particularly in knowing that there needs to be motivation to change on the part of the individuals in the family and within the student athlete. It is also important to recognize that the make-up of families varies greatly as does the relationship between the student athlete and his/her family. One must also be cognizant of issues related to diversity, and to see them as strengths to be utilized in family work. Finally, it is worth repeating that the school counselor will succeed when using strategies that have worked for them in the past, and have been proven effective in working with families.

Questions for Discussion

1. Education and athletics are closely combined in the United States. Does it make sense to separate the two, and have athletic programs be provided exclusively through other recreation and club sports programs? What are the pros and cons for families when using these models?
2. What role does gender and family play in the development of interest in participation in school athletics? What about sibling roles?
3. How well trained should school counselors be in providing family counseling to the families of student athletes?
4. What are the pros and cons of working with parents who are former student athletes with respect to children who are student athletes? How can a school counselor best approach these family dynamics?

References

AAU (Amateur Athletic Union) (2013) AAU Athletics. Retrieved December 10, 2013 from http://www.aauathletics.org/.

American Hockey Center (2013) *College Hockey.* Retrieved June 3, 2013 from http://www.americanhockeycenter.com/college_hockey/.

Antshel, K., & Anderman, E. (2000) Social influences on sports participation during adolescence. *Journal of Research and Development in Education, 33,* 85–94.

Beale, A., & Jacobs, J. (2004) Beyond the professional athlete: Introducing middle school students to sports related. *Journal of Career Development, 31,* 111–124.

Dattilio, F. (2007) *Comprehensive Cognitive-Behavior Therapy with Couples and Families: A Schema Based Approach.* Harvard Medical School: Author. PDF document retrieved April 11, 2013 from http://www.dattilio.com/cwo_images/CBSWC_F08b.pdf.

Ferguson, D. (2008) The effects of family stress in sports. *Beyond the Cheers.* Retrieved July 15, 2013 from http://www.beyondthecheers.com/articles/the-affects-of-family-stress-in-sports-by-dave-ferguson/.

Fleischman, B. (1986) Ormsby describes moments before leap. *Philly.com.* Retrieved February 24, 2012 from http://articles.philly.com/1986-12-22/sports/26069929_1_kathy-ormsby-suicide-attempt-penn-relays.

Gee, C. (2010) How does sport psychology actually improve athletic performance? A framework to facilitate athletes' and coaches' understanding. *Behavior Modification,* 34, 386–402.

Halberstam, D. (2002) Just a coach, not a leader. *ESPN Page 2.* Retrieved June 2, 2013 from http://espn.go.com/page2/s/halberstam/021220.html.

Han, Y. J. (2011) Streamlining and licensing versus the first amendment. *Reporters Committee for Freedom of the Press.* Retrieved April 15, 2013 from http://www.rcfp.org/browse-media-law-resources/news-media-law/news-media-and-law-fall-2011/streaming-and-licensing-versu.

Heisler, M. (1986) The Ormsby ordeal: Problem is, Kathy wasn't the first runner to consider jumping. *Los Angeles Times.* Retrieved February 24, 2013 from http://articles.latimes.com/1986-06-29/sports/sp-117_1_pills.

Hensch, L. (2006) Specialization or diversification in youth sport? *Strategies: A Journal for Physical and Sport Educators,* 19, 21–27.

Litsky, F. (1986) Runner quits, leaps from bridge. *New York Times.* Retrieved August 22, 2012 from http://www.nytimes.com/1986/06/06/sports/runner-quits-race-leaps-from-bridge.html.

Lufi, D., & Parish-Plass, J. (2011) Sport-based group therapy program for boys with ADHD or with other behavioral disorders. *Child & Family Behavior Therapy,* 33, 217–230.

Merril, E. (2010) Clay Matthews wanted to be 'that guy.' *ESPN NFL Hot Read.* Retrieved October 26, 2012 from http://sports.espn.go.com/nfl/columns/story?page=hotread04/ClayMatthews&src=mobile.

Patterson, G., & Stouthamer-Loeber, M. (1984) The correlation of family practices and delinquency. *Child Development,* 55, 299–307.

Snow, N. (2010) Violence and aggression in sports: An in-depth look. *Bleacher Report.* Retrieved July 15, 2013 from http://bleacherreport.com/articles/367924-violence-and-aggression-in-sports-an-in-depth-look-part-one.

Sonstroem, E. (2009) Butterflies in your stomach. *Moments in Science.* Retrieved April 21, 2013 from http://indianapublicmedia.org/amomentofscience/butterflies_in_your_stomach/.

Wolverton, B. (2007) Athletics participation prevents many players from choosing majors they want. *Chronicle of Higher Education,* 53, 36.

6 Gender, Sexual Identity, Cultural Issues, and the Student Athlete

Robyn Brammer

Goldberg and Chandler (1995) mentioned some of the strengths of adolescents playing sports (e.g., sense of personal competence, educational aspirations, better achievement identity, and higher graduation rates), but there are also threats to a student's development. One of the most important involves the *stereotype threat*, which occurs when members of a stigmatized group realizes others think negatively about their group identity, which, paradoxically, lowers their achievements (Ståhl, Van Laar, & Ellemers, 2012).

For many minority groups, stereotypes become endemic to the way they are perceived (see Lee, & Opio, 2011; Steinfeldt, Carter, Benton, & Steinfeldt, 2011). For example, if you are tall, you should play basketball. If you are stocky, you should play football. If you are slender, you should be a swimmer or runner. Such stereotypes are not necessarily negative, but they can become negative if you believe you must overcome them to function in society or in a particular discipline.

One of difficulties student athletes face is the perception that their success in academics is only because they are given preferential treatment as sports heroes. This is where stereotype threats become harmful. Granting that we only have a limited ability to process information, if part of your brain is focused on whether someone thinks badly about you, you cannot perform as well as you would without that fear. It is a form of cognitive exhaustion (Logel, Iserman, Davies, Quinn, & Spencer, 2009). Instead of wholly focusing on success, we focus on not looking like the stereotype. The goal becomes one of avoiding mistakes rather than performing well.

Stereotype threats were once thought to only affect the most marginalized groups. We are learning that the problem is much broader. Ethnicity, gender, age, and athletics can all be factors. This is a general psychological process potentially impacting anyone who belongs to a stereotyped group (Stone, 2012).

Bullying, Violence, and the Culture of Winning

Competitive sports necessarily focus on winning. Winning necessarily involves a notion of superiority. If an individual embraces the stereotype of being a superior jock, this perspective may overpower other virtues. Kowalski and Waldron (2010) argued that some coaches place winning above the dignity their athletes. In their study, athletes also endured humiliating and painful activities all in an attempt to build a successful team. The sense of superiority has also been linked with the Greek system, and this trend tends to emphasize in-group/out-group tensions (Hall & Livingston, 2012).

Systems of superiority help make schools simultaneously the safest and most dangerous places for children. As Larkin (2013) notes, young people are least likely to be seriously injured or killed while at school. However, bullying, intimidation, humiliation, and sexual abuse are common within the school system. The more successful a student is in becoming "elite," the more likely the student will earn the support of the adult leaders. If the aggressiveness is viewed as a component of the child's success, coaches and teachers may look the other way. Larkin notes that, if coaches and teachers buy into the notion that another student is "lower" in status or value, they may believe that the disadvantaged youth deserved the treatment they received. Problems are dismissed as "boys being boys," or simply "fooling around" (Larkin, 2013).

The desire to win and the tension to remain superior affect female athletes too. In a phenomenological (interview-based) study with five elite female athletes (ages 18–23 years), Tamminen, Holt, and Neely (2013) found that coach conflicts, eating disorders, sexual abuse, injuries, and bullying were reported. The tension related to these common experiences created a sense of isolation, sadness, anxiety, and the existential angst of self-identity. Similarly, Larkin (2013) found that when females act aggressively toward others, they tend to enhance their own status through psychological methods. Despite being less physical in nature, belittling, minimizing, and rejecting can have powerful consequences.

Although the dangers associated with female superiority systems are significant, schools tend to operate from a position of male power. Male-on-female violence is where the most significant dangers arise. Forbes and colleagues (2006) found that college men who participated in aggressive high school sports were more likely to display greater acceptance of rape myths and greater use of sexual coercion with dating partners compared to other men. Mutz (2012) also found that adolescent males who play sports associated with body building, combat, or hard physical contact approve of violence more often than other students. Such findings tie into Pappas, McKenry, and Catlett's (2004) findings that male athletes may be at risk for using violence both within and beyond their sports involvement, especially when there is alcohol involved and a pervasive objectification of women.

When a culture of objectifying women arises, the community is more likely to accept rape myths. When this happens, a bystander effect may arise. Polanin, Espelage, and Pigott (2012) note in their meta-analysis that observers witness bullying and violence more than 80% of the time, but these witnesses do little to decrease the high rates of childhood violence. For these reasons, it is important to approach rape and violence against women as a school-wide problem. Effective programs will not only be supportive of survivors but it will involve men as allies in preventing future abuses (Moynihan, Banyard, Arnold, Eckstein, & Stapleton, 2010). However, making these programs effective also involves creating new views on masculinity and femininity (Katz, 2010). In order to accomplish this, we must first understand how gender affects the identity of the student athlete.

Cultural Groups

The Male Athlete

For many male student athletes, the stereotype threat they face involves being a *real man* or being cool. Men have long defined their identities as being different from others. As such, a successful student athlete would define himself as being different from non-athletes (Kian, Clavio, Vincent, & Shaw, 2011).

Not only is masculine identity associated with being "different," it is also historically associated with being superior (Griffin, 1993). There are hierarchies associated within male groups and between groups. For example, within a sporting group, there are well established pecking orders. A quarterback, team captain, or other leaders may be viewed as more valuable. They may even win awards such as "Most Valuable Player." Between groups, players of a specific individual sport may argue that their team or their particular sport is more important than someone else's group. Football earns the most money in collegiate sports, so it is often thought of as most important. A lower-powered social group (e.g., women) attempting to change the structure of a hierarchy is likely to be met with resistance (Messner & Solomon, 2007).

One of the dangers associated with the current men's sports movement is the sense that a particular sport (e.g., wrestling or ice hockey) must be preserved simply because it is traditional and masculine. Instead of advocating for a particular sport's advantages, the opposition of wrestling are described as "gay," "pansies," or otherwise effeminate (Abdel-Shehid, 2000). This notion of good versus evil or one-against-another is a potential danger with any social deconstruction (Hägglund, 2004). This is one of the difficulties of a hierarchical identity. It assumes that something associated with those in power (i.e., men) is superior to what is associated with women. However, the relatively recent development of women playing sports such as lacrosse, flag football, or golf does not make them inherently less valuable than better established men's sports. It is difficult to predict if, in several decades, women's sports may be viewed with the same reverence reserved for men's sporting events today.

There are also limits to the hierarchical nature of identity. Sturm, Feltz, and Gilson (2011) explored how identity development differed from student athletes at Division I and Division III schools. They expected to find that Division I men would over-emphasize their athlete identity and under-emphasize their student identity when compared to men of Division III schools. This result was not found. Instead, the researchers found that collegiate athletes' identities differed only by gender. Females held a nearly significant weaker athlete identity and a significantly stronger student identity when compared to males. In other words, being a *student athlete* was important to women, but very important to men. Identifying as a *student* was important to women but less important to men. This helps to explain why other research has found that female student athletes do at least as well as non-athletes academically, but male athletes receive less benefit (Steinfeldt, Carter, Benton, & Steinfeldt, 2011). It appears that male student athletes invest in sports to the point of harming their academic careers, and this may be something school counselors can address.

The way boys conceptualize being student athletes appears to start early in life. Habel, Dittus, De Rosa, Chung, and Kerndt (2010) studied 15,183 middle school students and 19,078 high school students. They found that children participating in sports on a daily basis were more likely to engage in sexual intercourse and oral sex, with boys significantly more likely to follow this trend than girls. The effect of daily sports participation had the biggest impact on middle school children. Middle school male athletes were 70% more likely to have engaged/received oral sex than their non-athlete peers. We do not have enough data to identify traits of at-risk kids for these behaviors, but school counselors can assist by recommending chaperones on bus trips.

Although sexual maladaptive behaviors diminish for collegiate athletes, male athletes at the collegiate level demonstrate higher levels of alcohol abuse and gambling (Weiss, 2010). This led Weiss to conclude that sports may create an institutionalized view of masculinity that includes such stereotypes as alcoholic partying, gambling, and engaging in sex. School counselors can help change this perspective by introducing "real man" programs, for example: The Open Society Foundations curriculum for empowering men of color; the Chicago Public Schools and Chase bank's "real men read" program; or Winston-State's "real men teach" program. What is important in this process is learning how to assess each individual cultural group, train those working with such individuals, build interventions into existing curriculum, create social groups to engage minority students, offer leadership and management, protect the most vulnerable throughout the transition, work with parents and coaches, and offer support. We will discuss these intervention techniques later in the chapter.

When working with males, support and engagement may be most effective by providing positive male role models. Many male-oriented sports conversations focus around their sport, alcohol, and women (Clayton, & Humberstone, 2006). Clayton and Humberstone argue that men may limit academic discussions because they feel inadequate or want to avoid "feminine" conversations. Helping men value academics, scholarship, and learning may help establish a more complete view of masculinity.

The Female Athlete

For female athletes, a different stereotype threat emerges. There is still an assumption that real girls do not play sports. To compensate for this, female athletes may be more susceptible to other feminine stereotypes (Steinfeldt, Carter, Benton, & Steinfeldt, 2011). Blackmer, Searight, and Ratwik (2011) noted the athletes in sports and activities emphasizing leanness may contribute to eating disorders. Sports such as dancing, gymnastics, long-distance running, and wrestling each have weight-related benefits. The authors also noted that athletes coming from warm, nurturing, and supportive families were less likely to have eating disorders, but, regardless of the family upbringing, female athletes were more likely to report body dissatisfaction and weight phobia than non-athletes.

Girls must also contend with the notion that sports are inherently masculine. Steinfeldt, Carter, Benton, and Steinfeldt (2011) explored how female athletes must balance the need for perceived masculine traits with also remaining feminine. They found that female athletes strive to become muscular in order to improve their health, perform better, feel better about themselves, and receive praise from others. Despite craving muscles, the female athletes in the Steinfeldt et al. study also had slightly slower body-mass-index scores than the non-athlete females in their control group. Not only did these women continue to work on being thin, but, 16% of the female student athletes did not want to be muscular. Every male student athlete in this study desired muscularity.

Part of the reason some female student athletes may resist looking muscular could relate to the way their peers treat them. Knifsend and Graham (2012) investigated perceived discrimination for girls in high school. In their ethnically diverse sample from the southwestern United States, they found that girls who participated in sports during 9th grade perceived greater gender discrimination relative to girls who were not involved in sports. Even more importantly, this differential increased over time, with the greatest disparity coming in 12th grade. This discrimination did not come from adults, where there was no perceived difference; it came from other students. The authors hypothesized that girls who start sports early may derive more of their identity from these activities, which may be perceived as anti-feminine. Their study did not differentiate between sports more typically thought of as being feminine in nature (such as dancing or cheerleading), so it is impossible to surmise the reasons for their findings.

Despite the setbacks, girls who participate in sports tend to be more successful than those who do not. This has been the rally cry behind advocating for Title IX. The law states, "No person in the United States shall, on the basis of sex, be excluded from participation in, be denied the benefits of, or be subjected to discrimination under any education program or activity receiving Federal financial assistance…" (Title 20 U.S.C. Sections 1681–1688). However, as more women play sports, their identity continues to differ from that of men. As the Secretary of Education, Arne Duncan (2010) points out, female athletes have higher graduation rates, use fewer drugs, are less likely to become pregnant as teenagers, have lower obesity rates, and may be better at finding employment.

Title IX and Gender

With so many advantages to involving girls in sports, there remain a few setbacks in the social change. The most glaring is the lingering suspicion that Title IX has helped women at the expense of men (Walton & Helstein, 2008). Although the requirement for schools to provide equal access to men and women has changed the way colleges allocate funds, it is important to note that female-based sports are still under represented. Messner and Solomon (2007) note that despite making up the majority of the collegiate student body, women receive a decisive minority of scholarships at United States universities. There is still more to do.

The notion that men have been harmed by Title IX may also relate to the emerging "boy crisis" in academics. There is emerging evidence that participation in stereotypically female-based activities (e.g., household chores, nurturing activities, following directions, visiting museums, attending concerts, taking lessons in music, art, or dance) helps grades, while participation in male-based activities had no direct effect on grades (Orr, 2011). Orr also notes that while both genders are graduating at higher rates than ever, women are excelling at a much faster pace.

Paradoxically, the growing difference between male and female academic success means that Title IX may actually help men in the coming generation. Walton and Helstein (2008) note that the U.S. federal law mandating equal gender opportunities within education is currently focused on male enrollment rather than female sporting activities. The authors continue to explain how the "boy crisis" in education is looking at how cuts in recess time, physical education, and sporting activities have had a disproportionate impact on boys. Although girls are still lacking in some social access, it is becoming likely that women will outpace men in many areas within the coming generation.

Regardless of who is currently benefiting from the law, school counselors and administrators can lessen the polarization by changing the rhetoric associated with gender. Hardin, Simpson, Whiteside, and Garris (2007) recommend those involved with sports find more balanced phrases when discussing the law. Using the term "quota," for example, to explain Title IX is inaccurate and inflammatory. We should also approach gender based questions from the position of a specific individual rather than how a change may impact the status quo. If we start with the question, "How does Title IX affect the NCAA?" we will end with a different result than asking, "How does Title IX affect women?" If we begin around a masculine ideal, we will likely conclude that the law is negative. If we start with assisting equality and women's exercise and identity, the law will be viewed positively.

The Ethnic Athlete

As contentious as Title IX has been, the discussion follows the pattern of other feminist topics. Once a topic focuses on "gender" there is often a tendency to overlook ethnicity and other cultural factors (Henning, 2009). Ethnic minority groups face very different stereotype threats regarding sports. For some minority groups, especially African Americans, they must contend with the stereotype that winning a sporting scholarship may be the only way to attend to college.

African American Student Athletes

Stone, Harrison, and Mottley (2012) identified how African American student athletes are most susceptible to stereotype threats. Within the university setting, there is a perception that African Americans who play sports are only there because they received special treatment (i.e., dumb jocks). In testing this notion, the researchers found that African Americans did worse on difficult classroom-type tests when primed for their identity as athletes. However, when they were primed as "scholar athletes," they not only missed the difficult items, they started missing the easier items. Emphasizing the stereotype threat increases the need for people to waste mental energy to prove the stereotype wrong.

Stereotype threats can also affect how individuals play their sports. Hall and Livingston (2012) wanted to determine if African American football players were more likely to be penalized for actions that looked arrogant. They specially examined "celebrations" in football. The assumption was that high-status groups (i.e., Whites) would be forgiven for celebrating because they are viewed as superior and should celebrate. African Americans who celebrate should be put in their place. They called this a "hubris penalty". In their three experiments, they found that celebration after scoring was generally considered arrogant, but Black players were penalized more severely, even though both groups were considered equally arrogant. Such tensions make it harder for African Americans to succeed. On the one hand, they are told to be aggressive and play hard, but they are also judged more harshly for displaying those behaviors.

Athletics also create a double bind for African American students. On the one hand, they may believe that the only way they can get admitted to college is by becoming an athlete. However, once in college, they are often thought more as a commodity than a student. Beamon (2008) mentioned that many African American males in her study felt like athlete students rather than student athletes. Nineteen of the twenty participants in the study felt they gave more to their university than they received. Several of the students felt forced to change majors because the classes in their majors conflicted with athletic workout times. If the NCAA allows schools to start paying student athletes, universities will have a greater incentive to dictate their athletes' schedules.

Teaching African Americans about the range of discrimination and expectations may help them adapt. Chao, Mallinckrodt, and Wei (2012) examined the records of 1,555 African American clients seen at the counseling centers in predominantly White Midwestern universities. They found that perceived racial discrimination was associated with issues like performance anxiety, adjustment to the university, dating concerns, perfectionism, depression, suicide risk, values confusion, and spiritual/religious concerns. They also noted that men reacted to prejudice through irritability and anger, but women tended to react through procrastination. They concluded that helping students better understand how perceived racism can affect them could help students adapt. Doing this proactively in high school may also help students adjust to college life more readily.

Asian American Athletes

Back in 1999, Ferraro noted common differences between Asian and European American athletes. The author suggests that Asian athletes tend to emphasize perfectionism, family orientation, and hard work. European American athletes emphasize aggressiveness, defeating opponents, and individualism. With aggression and winning key to many sports in the United States, the art of performing the sport perfectly becomes less important. This may be a role for school counselors, to help Asian athletes feel more comfortable with defeating opponents, increasing aggressiveness, and differences between aggression and anger as they relate to guilt.

In addition to discussing how the dominant culture works, it may be useful to discuss how minority athletes feel within their athletic setting. Conversations about ethnicity can help avoid microaggressions. Burdsey (2011) noted that emphasizing a "color-blind ideology" (where race and ethnicity are never discussed) may propagate another form of prejudice. If minority athletes are viewed as being "like everyone else," they may feel pressured to downplay ethnically related "jokes" or "banter." This may create tensions, and there would be no mechanism to address them directly.

Discrimination may be hardest for female Asian athletes. Yu (2009) pointed out that Asia has a long history of a male-dominated society, which has influenced the way the Asian media cover the sports. When examining the summer 2008 Olympics in China, Yu found that sports like diving and the marathon were covered, but more aggressive female sports were not. If sports continue to emphasize gender norms in the dominant culture and ethnic subcultures, Asian American student athletes may face substantial prejudices as they continue through their academic tenure.

Latino Athletes

One similarity between Latino and Asian student athletes is the way they pick role models. In a study of 4,010 multiethnic teens, there was a tendency for African Americans and Whites to pick role models who matched their ethnicity. Latinos and Asians were more likely than their peers to break this trend and have a mentor/hero from another ethnic group. This is important because the type of role model predicted the health of the teen's behaviors. Teens identifying with a teacher had high positive health behaviors. Teens viewing family members or athletes as role models had a smaller but significant association with health-promoting behaviors. But when peers or entertainers/actors were the selected role models, the teens were more likely to engage in health-risk behaviors (Yancey, Grant, Kurosky, Kravitz-Wirtz, & Mistry, 2011). This may mean that having fewer Asian or Latino teachers or sports heroes sets these groups up for health risks. School counselors would be wise to promote scholars and athletes who match the ethnicity of students on their campuses.

The importance of having athletic role models will also tie into shifts regarding college admission. Espenshade, Chung, and Walling (2004) explored which applicant groups were given admission preferences. They found that African Americans received the biggest advantage. Latinos, athletes, and legacies were also given preference. However, the controversies surrounding affirmative action have weakened the preference given to minority students. Even back in 2004, athletes were given greater preference than Latinos and this may increase in the coming decade.

The LGBTQQI Athlete

Although ethnic minorities face unique issues regarding student athletes and role models, lesbian, gay, bisexual, transgender, queer, questioning, and intersexed (LGBTQQI) individuals may face even more challenges. As LGBTQQI students become more conspicuous on school campuses, school counselors must find ways to help such individuals fit into all aspects of campus life. Sports pose a number of difficulties to such an integration, as does the stereotype threat. LGBTQQI individuals might hear that they are "too queer" to fit into athletic life (Hargreaves, 2007). The prototypical athlete in the United States is probably thought of as tough, disciplined, relentless, and male. As LGBTQQI individuals work to show that their sexual/gender identity is not in conflict with their athletic identity, their performance may suffer. For example, if a football player is constantly thinking, "Don't move like a gay guy," the mental effort needed to avoid feminine movements is likely to limit his success at making a great play.

Fontaine (1998) investigated the extent to which school counselors work with adolescents who are questioning their sexual identity or who clearly identify themselves as gay or lesbian. At the middle school (junior high) level, 93% of the counselors surveyed by Fontaine reported working with students who were dealing with sexual identity issues. With this area reaching into nearly all school (even for the past 15 years), school counselors should be well equipped to address their unique concerns. Liu and Chao (2006) explored how well school counselors viewed LGBT issues on their campuses. A strong 60% thought their campuses were LGBT friendly. A sizable minority (34%) had worked with students who faced discrimination for their sexual orientation. But the most striking finding was that only 10% of those surveyed had taken deliberate steps to create a safe and friendly environment for LGBT students. Given that LGBT athletics is an even smaller niche concern, it may be helpful for school counselors to consider how to take proactive steps.

Young people who question or are confused about their gender and sexual orientation are reported to compose 10% of our youth population (Little, 2001). This represents a sizable group facing unique challenges. There are a growing number of students seeking leadership within the LGBT community, but fear keeps many in the closet (Renn & Ozaki, 2010). Transgender students represent an even smaller minority and may face the greatest challenges.

Transgender youth tend to be more victimized, have fewer resources, and they are not often protected by LGB policies (McGuire, Anderson, Toomey, & Russell, 2010). They also face unique problems regarding sports. Even a simple issue like using a locker room could pose significant risks. Imagine a female-to-male student made the varsity basketball team. The team is playing an away game, which is six hours from their home base. After the game, the students may shower in the boys' locker room. Despite being legally male, this student has not had genital reconstruction surgery (which is usually not permitted before the individual turns 18). How should such a situation be handled? The school may have already addressed this issue within their home locker room, but it requires a proactive position to contemplate potential concerns at other schools. Would you have the player shower before or after the rest of the team? Might there be an alternative room for him to use? Would making the request for him to use a separate room marginalize the student? At the collegiate level, the NCAA guidelines recommend allowing athletes to use the locker room or bathroom that matches their perceived gender. They also recommend that school officials consult the athlete and confidentially arrange safe and comfortable facilities at the visiting school (Torre & Epstein, 2012). All of these issues should be explored with the student, coaches, and parents.

No matter how well planned, it is important for the student athlete to realize that society is not fully accepting of LGBTQQI individuals. Coming out is likely to have consequences. They may be rejected by teammates, family members, teachers, peers, and fans.

Homophobia and Transphobia

It is important for school counselors to realize that violence against LGBTQQI individuals can occur unpredictably. There is limited information about LGBTQQI athletes (Lucas-Carr & Krane, 2011). However, there is a growing body of literature about involving academics and gender/sexuality in general.

Even when LGBTQQI individuals can avoid violence in the home, they are likely to face it at school. LGBT youth face substantial risk of being involved in a fight in school (McCabe & Rubinson, 2008). The risk is so great that one study found over 90% of LGB students reporting verbal or physical assaults (compared to 62% of non-LGBT teens) (GLSEN, 2005). This can come in many forms. Gay prejudice has become interwoven into the vernacular of children today. School-aged children use the term "gay" as a euphemism for "stupid," "crazy" or "foolish." The term is used so frequently teachers often fail to reprimand students for using it (McCabe & Rubinson, 2008).

Transphobia may be even more infused into the school system. Sausa (2005) found that teachers often ignored requests for help, minimized punishment when violence occurred against transkids, and would often overlook harassment. When formal complaints were made, teachers would often explain that the child is bringing the harassment on themselves, and attempt to coach the child to act according to the birth-assigned gender (Sausa, 2005).

It is also important to realize that doing nothing with the status quo can perpetuate the sense of inadequacy and pathology. The tendency to assume that all children are heterosexual is often regarded as heterosexism. Chesir-Teran and Hughes (2009) noted that heterosexism and homophobia contribute to the likelihood of school victimization among gays and lesbians. At a time when adolescents are struggling to understand themselves, homosexual students face the added challenges posed by hate crimes, risk of disease, poor self-esteem, isolation, and deciding whether to come out to their friends. In one study, 90% of principals reported having heard antigay slurs in their school, but only 21% initiated changes to their school's policy (GLSEN, 2008). Such antagonism and abuse has also prevented students from participating in sports (Brackenridge, Rivers, Gough, & Llewellyn, 2007). Brackenridge et al. also mention that the emerging anti-bullying campaigns in schools are reaching school-athletic programs very slowly. A more deliberate intervention program for student athletes is necessary.

Definition of Counseling

Even when student athletes desire counseling, they may not have time to seek it (Watson, 2006). Practice sessions, game preparations, and travel can aggravate the time demands of academics. Historically, student athletes have also adopted a rugged individuality. They may focus on the team's needs instead of their own issues (Watson, 2006). For marginalized clients, this may prove even more important. There is some evidence that ethnic minorities are more likely to have high school jobs (Olatunji, 2005). This may limit the amount of time they have available for counseling.

When students create time for counseling, they are likely to gravitate towards counselors who understand their cultural identities. Constantine (2002) studied predictors of ethnic minority clients' satisfaction with their counselors. She found that students who considered their counselors multiculturally competent were more likely to value the counseling experience. What was striking about this study was that ratings for multicultural competence were more significant than ratings for general counseling competence. It is likely that these findings would hold true for student athletes, too. Counselors who can demonstrate an understanding of athletics and ethnic, gender, and sexual orientation will be the ones best able to connect with these students.

In designing an intervention for marginalized athletes, I recommend school counselors follow the ATTEMPTS model: Assess, Train, Teach, Engage, Manage, Protect, Triangulate, and Support.

Assess	No systematic approach can exist before you understand the school's written and unwritten codes. School systems should establish written policies that specifically protect students and staff from discrimination and harassment based on real or perceived sexual orientation. If no policies exist, Boland (n.d.) recommended establishing written policies that specifically protect marginalized students and staff from discrimination. This should exist for harassment based on real or perceived ethnicity, religious beliefs, physical abilities, weight, sexual orientation, or gender identity.
Train	Once policies exist, school systems should provide in-service training opportunities. School counselors can provide insights about the physical, emotional, social, and psychological well-being of at risk student athletes.
Teach	After being trained, school systems should support a curriculum that includes accurate information about marginalized students. School counselors can provide in-class training to discuss these issues. For example, it would be important to discuss the problems with talking about "scalping" your rival football team, saying someone is "too fat to make the swim team," or referring to someone as being "too gay to live." Beyond teaching about safety on the school campus, school counselors can also teach students about preparing for college. They should also realize that being an athlete is only one facet of their identities. They are more complex beings than they may realize.
Engage	Regardless of their minority status, students should have a safe place to meet with like-minded students. Boland (n.d.) recommends supporting the formation of Gay/Straight Alliances or other student activities. Such groups help students understand homophobia and heterosexism within the school setting. McGuire, Anderson, Toomey, and Russell's (2010) study on transgendered youth found that simply creating protective factors did not significantly predict feelings of safety. But creating school protective features did predict connection to adults, which, in turn, predicted feelings of safety. It is the connection that fosters safety, and this only comes when the school structure make students safe enough to risk getting to know their school counselor.
Manage	Effectively engaging marginalized student athletes will include a system of oversight. When I consulted for a local school district, several middle school students told me that oral sex on the bus to sporting events was "expected." This puts cheerleaders and band members particularly at risk. Similarly, younger, "star" athletes are at risk for alcohol and drug abuse because they tend to spend more time with older athletes.
Protect	If an individual is being harassed for participating on a team, the school will need to recreate a safe environment. Although ethnic

minorities, women, and LGB students continue to face harassment, transgender students may be the most at risk (McGuire, Anderson, Toomey, & Russell, 2010). McGuire et al. noted that harassment may lead to switching schools or even dropping out. To combat this, the transgender student needs to know that someone working at the school is an ally. When such connections are formed, they are associated with greater feelings of safety.

Triangulate   Triangulate between athlete, parents, and coach. Parents, coaches, and students may each have different goals and expectations for sports participation. It is also important for coaches, teachers, parents, and students to set up a zero-tolerance program for hazing and bullying (Kowalski & Waldron, 2010). Everyone at the school is part of the team, and all students must be treated with respect for winning to be meaningful.

Support   It is important for school counselors to have students tell their stories. Again, this may be especially true for transgender students who may be at the highest risk of PTSD (Richmond, Burnes, & Carroll, 2012). However, it is unlikely that any marginalized student will finish high school without a story of harassment.

It is also important to realize that the student's goals might ultimately differ from the counselor's. They might start with both of them thinking the college scholarship is the most important thing. But as the session continues, she might come to believe that supporting her parents and staying home takes priority. Until triangulating with the parents and coach, there are more questions than answers.

Given the near infinite range of cultural combinations that may be present, school counselors should be careful about making recommendations or interventions until they let the student teach them about the intricacies involved. A well-intentioned intervention could backfire and create more problems. However, broaching the cultural differences between the counselor and student can help students clarify the situation. They may gain new insights simply by teaching the counselor about their culture and what it means to them.

Summary and Future Recommendations

Little research has been conducted into how sports affect marginalized students in middle school or high school. There is also limited literature about the efficacy of school counselor interventions for these groups. In the future, we are likely to see emerging literature on how various cultural groups benefit or are harmed by sports. We have decades of information about how sports participation affects White males. There is emerging data about how sports benefits girls and young women. But we still need to learn more about how sports affect LGBTQQI students, physically challenged students, obese students, and ethnic minorities.

In reaching this place, it is important for school counselors to create an ATTEMPTS model for their school. Ensuring that the system is safe and ready for students will make it easier to attend to complications when then arise. We have already seen what happens when schools take a more reactive position, especially for LGBTQQI students. A proactive model will ensure that the school best meets the needs for all students. As Richmond, Burnes, and Carroll (2012) point out, we can at least start with the preventative services of labeling discrimination and oppression as trauma (Richmond, Burnes, & Carroll, 2012). Once this occurs, we can all agree to end the trauma with empathy, insight, and creativity.

Questions for Discussion

1. What is a *stereotype threat* and how does this affect various student athlete groups?
2. What are the unique concerns facing male student athletes? How might these concerns change for the next generation of student athletes?
3. Title IX has significantly affected the role of women in athletics. What barriers still exist for female student athletes, and what can be done to promote feminine sporting events in schools?
4. African Americans may face one of the most challenging stereotype threats. How does gender affect these threats? How can the ATTEMPTS model be applied?
5. Asian American student athletes may be harmed by a "color-blind ideology." What does this mean, and how can schools address it? How can the ATTEMPTS model be applied?
6. Latino student athletes are the fastest emerging group. With limited role models, it is important to help these students find people they can follow. Look up a male and female Latino athlete and report on their history, personality, and values.
7. Much of the literature regarding LGB students and athletes has addressed a connection between having an LGB friend or family member and learning to accept others. What can be done to help students better understand LGB issues, and how can social networking assist this process?
8. Transgendered student athletes face the most complex obstacles. How would you intervene if a student were in the process of transitioning but faced harassment from teachers, peers, and parents?

References

Abdel-Shehid, G. (2000) Writing hockey thru race: Rethinking Black hockey in Canada. In R. Walcott (Ed.), *Rude: Contemporary Black Canadian Cultural Criticism* (pp. 69–86). Toronto: Insomniac.

Beamon, K. K. (2008) 'Used goods': Former African American college student athletes' perception of exploitation by Division I universities. *Journal of Negro Education,* 77(4), 352–364.

Blackmer, V., Searight, H., & Ratwik, S. H. (2011) The relationship between eating attitudes, body image and perceived family-of-origin climate among college athletes. *North American Journal of Psychology, 13(3)*, 435–446.

Boland, P. (n.d.) *Vulnerability to Violence Among Gay, Lesbian and Bisexual Youth.* Bethesda, MD: National Association of School Psychologists. Retrieved November 8, 2013 from http://www.nasponline.org/resources/crisis_safety/neat_vulnerability.aspx.

Brackenridge, C., Rivers, I., Gough, B., & Llewellyn, K. (2007) Driving down participation: Homophobic bullying as a deterrent to doing sport. In C. Aitchison (Ed.), *Sport and Gender Identities: Masculinities, Femininities and Sexualities* (pp. 122–139). New York: Routledge/Taylor & Francis Group.

Burdsey, D. (2011) That joke isn't funny anymore: Racial microaggressions, color-blind ideology and the mitigation of racism in English men's first-class cricket. *Sociology of Sport Journal, 28(3)*, 261–283.

Chao, R., Mallinckrodt, B., & Wei, M. (2012) Co-occurring presenting problems in African American college clients reporting racial discrimination distress. *Professional Psychology: Research and Practice, 43(3)*, 199-207. doi:10.1037/a0027861.

Chesir-Teran, D., & Hughes, D. (2009) Heterosexism in high school and victimization among lesbian, gay, bisexual, and questioning students. *Journal of Youth and Adolescence, 38(7)*, 963–975. doi:10.1007/s10964-008-9364-x.

Clayton, B., & Humberstone, B. (2006) Men's talk: A (pro)feminist analysis of male university football players' discourse. *International Review for The Sociology of Sport, 41(3–4)*, 295–316. doi:10.1177/1012690207078380.

Constantine, M. G. (2002) Predictors of satisfaction with counseling: Racial and ethnic minority clients' attitudes toward counseling and ratings of their counselors' general and multicultural counseling competence. *Journal of Counseling Psychology, 49(2)*, 255–263. doi:10.1037/0022-0167.49.2.255.

Duncan, A. (2010) *The Importance of Title IX: Remarks of Secretary of Education Arne Duncan at George Washington University.* U.S. Department of Education. Retrieved August 15, 2013 from http://www.ed.gov/news/speeches/importance-title-ix.

Espenshade, T. J., Chung, C. Y., & Walling, J. L. (2004) Admission preferences for minority students, athletes, and legacies at elite universities. *Social Science Quarterly, 85(5)*, 1422–1446.

Ferraro, T. (1999) Aggression among athletes: An Asian versus American comparison. *Athletic Insight: The Online Journal of Sport Psychology, 1(1)*. Retrieved November 8, 2013 from http://www.athleticinsight.com/Vol1Iss1/Asian_Aggression.htm.

Fontaine, J. H. (1998) Evidencing a need: School counselors' experiences with gay and lesbian students. *Professional School Counseling, 1(3)*, 8–14.

Forbes, G. B., Adams-Curtis, L. E., Pakalka, A. H., & White, K. B. (2006) Dating aggression, sexual coercion, and aggression-supporting attitudes among college men as a function of participation in aggressive high school sports. *Violence Against Women, 12*, 441–454.

GLSEN (2005) *From Teasing to Torment: School Climate in America—A Survey of Students and Teachers.* New York: Harris Interactive, Inc.

GLSEN (2008) *The Principal's Perspective: School Safety, Bullying and Harassment—A Survey of Public School Principals.* New York: Harris Interactive, Inc.

Goldberg, A. D., & Chandler, T. (1995) Sports counseling: Enhancing the development of the high school student athlete. *Journal of Counseling & Development, 74(1)*, 39–44. doi:10.1002/j.1556-6676.1995.tb01820.x.

Griffin, P. (1993) Homophobia in sport: Addressing the needs of lesbian and gay high school athletes. *The High School Journal, 77(1–2)*, 80–87.

Habel, M. A., Dittus, P. J., De Rosa, C. J., Chung, E. Q., & Kerndt, P. R. (2010) Daily participation in sports and students' sexual activity. *Perspectives on Sexual and Reproductive Health, 42(4)*, 244–250. doi:10.1363/4224410.

Hägglund, M. (2004) The necessity of discrimination: Disjoining Derrida and Levinas. *Diacritics, 34(1)*, 40–71.

Hall, E. V., & Livingston, R. W. (2012) The hubris penalty: Biased responses to "celebration" displays of Black football players. *Journal of Experimental Social Psychology, 48(4)*, 899–904.

Hardin, M., Simpson, S., Whiteside, E., & Garris, K. (2007) The gender war in U.S. sport: Winners and losers in news coverage of Title IX. *Mass Communication & Society, 10(2)*, 211–233. doi:10.1080/15205430701265737.

Hargreaves, J. (2007) Men and women and the Gay Games. In A. Tomlinson (Ed.), *The sport studies reader* (pp. 322–363). New York: Routledge/Taylor & Francis Group.

Henning, A. (2009) Review of "Equal play: Title IX and social change". *Gender & Society, 23(3)*, 422–424. doi:10.1177/0891243209336279.

Katz, J. (2010) Reconstructing masculinity in the locker room: The mentors in violence prevention project. In S. R. Harper & F. Harris (Eds.), *College Men and Masculinities: Theory, Research, and Implications for Practice* (pp. 541–552). San Francisco, CA: Jossey-Bass.

Kian, E. M., Clavio, G., Vincent, J., & Shaw, S. D. (2011) Homophobic and sexist yet uncontested: Examining football fan postings on Internet message boards. *Journal of Homosexuality, 58(5)*, 680–699. doi:10.1080/00918369.2011.563672.

Knifsend, C. A., & Graham, S. (2012) Unique challenges facing female athletes in urban high schools. *Sex Roles, 67(3–4)*, 236–246. doi:10.1007/s11199-012-0159-x.

Kowalski, C., & Waldron, J. (2010) Looking the other way: Athletes' perceptions of coaches' responses to hazing. *International Journal of Sports Science & Coaching, 5(1)*, 87–100. doi:10.1260/1747-9541.5.1.87.

Larkin, R. W. (2013) Legitimated adolescent violence: Lessons from Columbine. In N. Böckler, T. Seeger, P. Sitzer, & W. Heitmeyer (Eds.), *School Shootings: International Research, Case Studies, and Concepts for Prevention* (pp. 159–176). New York: Springer Science + Business Media. doi:10.1007/978-1-4614-5526-4_7.

Lee, J., & Opio, T. (2011) Coming to America: Challenges and difficulties faced by African student athletes. *Sport, Education and Society, 16(5)*, 629–644. doi:10.1080/1 3573322.2011.601144.

Little, J. (2001) Embracing gay, lesbian, bisexual, and transgendered youth in school-based settings. *Child & Youth Care Forum, 30(2)*, 99–110.

Liu, A., & Chao, S. (2006) Counseling LGBT youth: A survey research of attitudes towards LGBT and training issues for school counselors. *Chinese Annual Report of Guidance and Counseling, 20*, 201–228.

Logel, C., Iserman, E. C., Davies, P. G., Quinn, D. M., & Spencer, S. J. (2009) The perils of double consciousness: The role of thought suppression in stereotype threat. *Journal of Experimental Social Psychology, 45*, 299–312. doi:10.1016/j.jesp.2008.07.016.

Lucas-Carr, C. B., & Krane, V. (2011) What is the T in LGBT? Supporting transgender athletes through sport psychology. *The Sport Psychologist, 25(4)*, 532–548.

McCabe, P. C., & Rubinson, F. (2008) Committing to social justice: The behavioral intention of school psychology and education trainees to advocate for lesbian, gay, bisexual, and transgendered youth. *School Psychology Review, 37(4)*, 469–486.

McGuire, J. K., Anderson, C. R., Toomey, R. B., & Russell, S. T. (2010) School climate for transgender youth: A mixed method investigation of student experiences and school responses. *Journal of Youth and Adolescence, 39(10)*, 1175–1188.

Messner, M. A., & Solomon, N. M. (2007) Social justice and men's interests: The case of Title IX. *Journal of Sport & Social Issues, 31(2)*, 162–178. doi:10.1177/0193723507301048.

Moynihan, M. M., Banyard, V. L., Arnold, J. S., Eckstein, R. P., & Stapleton, J. G. (2010). Engaging intercollegiate athletes in preventing and intervening in sexual and intimate partner violence. *Journal of American College Health, 59(3)*, 197–204. doi:10.10 80/07448481.2010.502195.

Mutz, M. (2012) Athletic participation and the approval and use of violence: A comparison of adolescent males in different sports disciplines. *EJSS European Journal for Sport and Society, 9(3)*, 177–201.

Olatunji, A. N. (2005) Dropping out of high school among Mexican-origin youths: Is early work experience a factor? *Harvard Educational Review, 75(3)*, 286–305.

Orr, A. J. (2011) Gendered capital: Childhood socialization and the "boy crisis" in education. *Sex Roles, 65(3–4)*, 271–284. doi:10.1007/s11199-011-0016-3.

Pappas, N. T., McKenry, P. C., & Catlett, B. (2004) Athlete aggression on the rink and off the ice: Athlete violence and aggression in hockey and interpersonal relationships. *Men and Masculinities, 6(3)*, 291–312. doi:10.1177/1097184X03257433.

Polanin, J. R., Espelage, D. L., & Pigott, T. D. (2012) A meta-analysis of school-based bulling prevention programs' effects on bystander intervention behavior. *School Psychology Review, 41(1)*, 47–65.

Renn, K. A., & Ozaki, C. (2010) Psychosocial and leadership identities among leaders of identity-based campus organizations. *Journal of Diversity in Higher Education, 3(1)*, 14–26.

Richmond, K. A., Burnes, T., & Carroll, K. (2012) Lost in trans-lation: Interpreting systems of trauma for transgender clients. *Traumatology, 18(1)*, 45–57. doi:10.1177/1534765610396726.

Sausa, L. A. (2005) Translating research into practice: Trans youth recommendations for improving school systems. *Journal of Gay and Lesbian Issues in Education, 3*, 15–28.

Ståhl, T., Van Laar, C., & Ellemers, N. (2012) The role of prevention focus under stereotype threat: Initial cognitive mobilization is followed by depletion. *Journal of Personality and Social Psychology, 102(6)*, 1239–1251. doi:10.1037/a0027678.

Steinfeldt, J. A., Carter, H., Benton, E., & Steinfeldt, M. (2011) Muscularity beliefs of female college student athletes. *Sex Roles, 64(7–8)*, 543–554. doi:10.1007/s11199-011-9935-2.

Stone, J. (2012) A hidden toxicity in the term "student athlete": Stereotype threat for athletes in the college classroom. *Wake Forest Journal of Law & Policy, 2(1)*, 179–197.

Stone, J., Harrison, C. C., & Mottley, J. (2012) "Don't call me a student athlete": The effect of identity priming on stereotype threat for academically engaged African American college athletes. *Basic and Applied Social Psychology, 34(2)*, 99–106. doi:10.1080/01973533.2012.655624.

Sturm, J. E., Feltz, D. L., & Gilson, T. A. (2011) A comparison of athlete and student identity for division I and division III athletes. *Journal of Sport Behavior, 34(3)*, 295–306.

Tamminen, K. A., Holt, N. L., & Neely, K. C. (2013) Exploring adversity and the potential for growth among elite female athletes. *Psychology of Sport and Exercise, 14(1)*, 28–36. doi:10.1016/j.psychsport.2012.07.002.

Torre, P. S., & Epstein, D. (2012) The transgender athlete. *Sports Illustrated*. Retrieved November 8, 2013 from http://sportsillustrated.cnn.com/vault/article/magazine/MAG1198744/index.htm.

Walton, T. A., & Helstein, M. T. (2008) Triumph of backlash: Wrestling community and the "problem" of Title IX. *Sociology of Sport Journal, 25(3)*, 369–386.

Watson, J. C. (2006) Student athletes and counseling: Factors influencing the decision to seek counseling services. *College Student Journal, 40(1)*, 35–42.

Weiss, S. (2010) Cross-addiction on campus: More problems for student athletes. *Substance Use & Misuse, 45(10)*, 1525–1541. doi:10.3109/10826081003682297.

Yancey, A. K., Grant, D., Kurosky, S., Kravitz-Wirtz, N., & Mistry, R. (2011) Role modeling, risk, and resilience in California adolescents. *Journal of Adolescent Health, 48(1)*, 36–43. doi:10.1016/j.jadohealth.2010.05.001.

Yu, C. (2009) A content analysis of news coverage of Asian female Olympic athletes. *International Review for the Sociology of Sport, 44(2–3)*, 283–305. doi:10.1177/1012690209104796.

7 Consultation with Teachers and the Student Athlete

The role of the school counselor as consultant exists for many reasons. There are so many reasons, in fact, that consultation is defined as one of the main roles of the school counselor according to the Ethical Standards of the American School Counselor Association (ASCA, 2010). All individuals and groups served by the consultative process can benefit from it when proper information, interpersonal communication, legal and ethical obligations, and best practices are displayed (Dougherty, 2005; Dinkmeyer & Carlson, 2006). The consultative relationship in and of itself can be a powerful tool for all parties involved because it can involve deep and informative discussions, without the necessarily personal and intrusive nature of psychotherapy and other forms of intervention that can sometimes make others feel that they are being viewed not as collaborative agents, but rather as clients who are being analyzed, evaluated and placed into vulnerable positions that can stir up feelings of defensiveness and conflict which do not serve the students in need.

The Essence of Consultation

It is also important to note that consultation does not always happen in the form of a one-on-one meeting between the school counselor and the school stakeholder in question. Certainly, there are collaborative team meetings that occur on school grounds that enable parents, teachers, administrators, students and other consultative agents to gather and discuss the goals and plans that can best assist the student (Baker, Robichaud, Westforth, Westforth, Wells, & Schreck, 2009; Stone & Dahir, 2006). There are also several general models of consultation (Dinkmeyer & Carlson, 2006; Dougherty, 2005) that have been adapted to the role of the school counselor (Dollarhide & Saginak, 2012; Kampwirth & Powers, 2012). Readers are strongly encouraged to study and adapt these available resources in ways that best reflect the nature of the school(s) in which they work, and the style of consultation that they believe would best serve the needs of all students.

The essential components of the effective consultation process often appear to be aligned with Dougherty's (2005) stages of entry, diagnosis, implementation, and disengagement. In other words, effective consultation requires parties to first *enter*, or engage with, the parties involved and best determine what the needs of the client and consultee are. The next phase is to *diagnose*, or best define, the people, systems, contexts, and goals under which the consultative process will work toward accomplishing its desired outcomes for all parties. The third phase involves *implementation*, or action and selection of intervention to make the progress and outcome possible. Lastly, the *disengagement* phase occurs whereby consultant and consultee gradually scale back their frequency and involvement with one another so as to maintain the outcomes of consultation with follow-ups on an as-needed basis (Dougherty, 2005).

There are ways in which student athletes also have specific needs that are often met by way of the consultation process, and the school counselor must approach these matters in ways that engage parents, coaches, teachers and other related stakeholders. Also, because of the typically goal-structured way in which many student athletes and student-athletic programs are constructed (Fraser-Thomas, Cote, & Deakin, 2005; Lowe & Cook, 2003), it is important to note that some of the entry and diagnostic phases may be largely addressed by simply organizing and facilitating communications between athletic and academic consultees to bring about the needed changes.

The Case of Mike

Referring back to Chapter 1, we were introduced to the case of Mike, who had largely been interested in playing football since the age of 9. This case illustrates some possible scenarios as to how school counselors may wish to proceed when handling a matter relating to a student athlete's struggles within the classroom. Though Mike's situation is not the only type of issue or student athlete that can be encountered, his case is offered as one "template" upon which professionals may wish to apply other principles and guidelines of consultation.

Considering that Mike has been referred for assistance through his football coach(es), he may or may not be fully aware of the work that the school counselor does at his school. Assuming there has been no in-depth meeting in the past with Mike, by which significant rapport or comfort has been established, the school counselor would be strongly advised to gather information about Mike's background and personal characteristics before proceeding. This would likely be a necessary move, since some research suggests that student athletes—especially at the college level—do not traditionally seek counseling and support services (Watson, 2006). These behaviors do not simply appear when an individual goes off to college and, because of demonstrated benefits that counseling and psychological services can have on student athletes' issues of motivation and school performance (Mintz, 2005; Visek, Harris, & Blom, 2009), it is important that the school counselor defines and encourages Mike to understand the role that a school counselor plays when joining with his existing systems to support his development. This transparency is not only comforting, but also sets the stage for establishing appropriate boundaries and ethical guidelines that further enhance the professional nature of the counselor–client relationship and the counselor-as-consultant identity.

Student athletes are involved with several types of networks within the school and community setting. They also collaborate with numerous individuals in order to enhance their motivation and performance goals, including coaches, parents, and peer networks (Keegan, Harwood, Spray, & Lavallee, 2009). This type of action fits quite well with the role of the school counselor in terms of being a resource to further enhance the success of the student athlete; school counselors should bear in mind that, although coaches and peers are often the ones that struggling student athletes turn to for initial support, especially if the issues involve his/her sport performance (Maniar, Curry, Sommers-Flanagan, & Walsh, 2001), they are often involved in the process when it comes to providing resources and additional assistance to the systems that may be unable to assist the student athlete initially. Thus, school counselors should bear in mind they have an ethical responsibility to individually respect the student athlete and also support the systems that (s)he must also engage with to accomplish desired goals, whether or not they are presented as sport-related issues.

Student athletes are often involved with team approaches to accomplishing goals and tasks (Maniar et al., 2001; Stambulova, 2011), and this can complement the school counselor's role as consultant. On some levels, this can serve as an additional comfort to a struggling student athlete, because it may be in line with the typical actions and responses that other people provide him/her when sport-related issues surface. The school counselor should also be prepared for the fact that some of the individuals with whom (s)he may be collaborating are not always familiar with the exact nature of the school counseling profession, and should do his/her best to represent the strengths and limits of what his/her services are. Doing so not only provides the best level of support for the student athlete, but also helps establish meaningful and powerful networks between and among school stakeholders who can further collaborate and consult on future cases.

There are always dual-relationship issues to bear in mind if a school counselor's son or daughter attends school with peers who may seek his/her school counseling services. These individuals may also be teammates on an athletic squad, which could also provide a dual-relationship bias. School counselors are best advised to not take on these cases without first making arrangements with other counselors in the department who do not have such relationships to these clients. There may also be issues to consider with respect to student athletes who are well-known within the school and their surrounding community, because of public identities they have with people who "feel" they know these individuals but are not necessarily involved in a dual relationship. These types of perceptions could lead to biases and other variables that could cloud the nature of the advocacy and consultation needed to address the needs of the student athlete; this is where supervision and personal consultation with other school counseling professionals would also be of significant benefit for the school counselor to use (Stone & Dahir, 2006).

Just as student athletes can have an impact on their community outside of the school system, the same can be said of school counselors. It is important that school counselors align with their school system to provide the necessary resources that student athletes need within the appropriate context of the academic and athletic programs they are enrolled (Stambulova, 2011). There are always questions about where this line gets drawn, but we encourage and remind school counselors that their job title implies that they are representatives of the school and its related systems, not individuals who have private affiliations who happen to be school counselors.

A Note about the Family Educational Rights and Privacy Act (FERPA)

One other matter for school counselors to bear in mind is the Family Educational Rights and Privacy Act (1974). This is a legal matter not only for the role of consultation, but for any school-related service that applies to students, their families, and related systems. As is directly stated by the U.S. Department of Education:

> The Family Educational Rights and Privacy Act (FERPA) (20 U.S.C. §
> 1232g; 34 CFR Part 99) is a Federal law that protects the privacy of student education records. The law applies to all schools that receive funds under an applicable program of the U.S. Department of Education. FERPA gives parents certain rights with respect to their children's education records. These rights transfer to the student when he or she reaches the age of 18 or attends a school beyond the high school level. Students to whom the rights have transferred are "eligible students."
> (U.S. Department of Education, 1974)

Thus a school counselor may be best served to have permission and consent forms available to the student athlete and his/her parent and/or guardian, in order to best ensure effective communication between all consultative parties. It is likely that the school has documentation in place to cover such matters for the school counselor, but it would be unwise to assume this. Transparency about this sharing of information helps to build trust into the counselor–student relationship and helps the school counselor communicate with consultees effectively. Considering the amount of data that teachers often have on their students, abiding by FERPA also helps establish trust between school counselors and teachers.

Teachers as Consultees

Stone and Dahir (2006) have an effective classification system of teacher-as-consultee types that are important to consider when working in the consultant role. Although their is not the only or perfect way to classify teachers-as-consultees, as far as working with student athletes, each type provides an effective foundation upon which a counseling professional can provide consultation services. It is also important to remember that there are coaches who are also teachers, so the classification of teachers for the purpose of this chapter is meant to mainly apply to working with individuals who mainly provide academic instruction and not athletic guidance. The dynamic of working with the student athlete relationship, however, can cause these types to manifest in slightly different ways to the manner(s) in which Stone and Dahir state in their experience with typical classroom and school climate issues. For the purposes of this chapter, the types will be addressed in both fashions.

Stone and Dahir (2006) suggested that these types of teacher characteristics may unfold during the consultation process: *confident, questioning, dependent, absentee,* and *dominating.*

Confident Teacher as Consultee

The *confident* teacher is typically defined as one who is accustomed to successful outcomes when working with students. The relationship (s)he has with students and school professionals usually brings them to the consultation relationship with the idea of getting information and resources from the school counselor, such as agencies, materials, and other stakeholders, who can assist with the issues related to the students' needs. Within consultation sessions, they tend to be appreciative and supportive of what the school counselor can provide, even if nothing more than validation and agreement (Stone & Dahir, 2006).

When it comes to working with student athletes, confident teachers are often found to be the ones who utilize these students in various roles within the classroom. They do not necessarily shine a spotlight on the academic or athletic accomplishments of such students, at least not for the sake of simply doing so. They also tend to be familiar with the schedules and practices associated with the student athlete's season and team responsibilities, and freely consult with coaches, athletic directors, and the school counselor as ways of assisting with the progress of a struggling student athlete.

In the case of Mike, the school counselor is recommended to know what resources have already been provided to him and incorporated into the confident teacher's classroom. For example, has Mike's Math teacher employed a folder system for keeping track of work? Is there a policy or procedure in place that has taken visiting games and practice schedules into account? Sometimes, the confident teacher may have the resources available, but the scheduled athletic events and activities have been modified in some fashion from previous years and/or semesters, and the student athlete may not be able to adjust properly to this timing aspect. The use of evaluation within the consultative relationship can be an effective way by which this issue can be addressed, and can effectively balance the insight of the consultant with the expertise of the consultee (Visek et al., 2009). The evaluation methods should be agreed to in terms of who provides them, how developmentally appropriate they are for the student(s) involved, the appropriate factors that are being assessed, when these evaluation periods are to happen, and the manner by which these evaluations will occur (Anderson, Miles, Mahoney, & Robinson, 2002; Visek et al., 2009). Regardless, the use of objective data can provide the problem-solving angle that a confident teacher may be able to benefit from when figuring out what otherwise successful techniques and resources may be stymieing the progress of a student athlete like Mike. After reaching an agreed outcome level of work productivity and quality, consultant and consultee would be able to effectively disengage and monitor progress on an as-needed basis.

Questioning Teacher as Consultee

The *questioning* teacher is typically defined as one who has not achieved a successful outcome with students. The relationship (s)he has with students and school professionals usually brings them to the consultation relationship with the idea of getting "unstuck" from their unsuccessful state of affairs. This teacher is largely seeking a novel approach and new voice from the consultant, and within consultation sessions, appears to be easy to work with because of a desire to share responsibility for success and a willingness to cooperate with the school counselor throughout the process (Stone & Dahir, 2006).

When it comes to working with student athletes, the questioning teacher may not know how to approach such a situation due to a parallel process of being "stuck" in the same slump that the student athlete may also be involved with, due to a recent experience or series of frustrations that has not been properly worked through. The questioning teacher may also have a bit of a reputation for not being understanding of the student athlete's schedule or programmatic demands, which can sometimes make the working alliance between teacher and student athlete more challenging. Since both teacher and student are usually competent and performing at decent levels, it can be initially difficult for either party to acknowledge and recognize that there has been a recent change. The need to acknowledge the struggle and recognize that it is possible to work through this matter can be important for both the teacher and the student athlete.

In the case of Mike, the questioning teacher may use the same option of a folder system and/or scheduling approach to assist with Mike's struggling productivity in the classroom. However, because of the desire for novelty and fresh perspective that is often associated with this consultee style, other approaches to assist the teacher's perspective may also aid the consultation process. Facilitating connections between the teacher and coaching staff (with, of course, appropriate consent from all consultative parties) may also provide a way of assisting the development of Mike and similar cases, by shedding some light on how progress is made athletically and academically, and looking for some synergistic ties that can be applied to both systems. Also, considering research and literature that supports the idea that coaches who adopt reinforcement approaches (Smoll, Smith, Barnett, & Everett, 1993) and child-involved democratic coaching styles (Fraser-Thomas, Cote, & Deakin, 2005) are often well-received by student athletes, encouraging this type of connection between such a coach and a questioning teacher may provide reinforcement for all parties. The disengagement phase may also be assisted through this coach–teacher connection because continued discussion between these parties will reduce the need for action on the part of the school counselor.

Dependent Teacher as Consultee

The *dependent* teacher is typically defined as one who is largely overwhelmed by student and classroom behaviors. The relationship (s)he has with students and school professionals usually brings them to the consultation relationship in the hopes that situations and behaviors can be immediately corrected mostly by the efforts of the consultant. This teacher often presents with a "fix the child" mentality and can often seek out the school counselor in multiple instances that all come across as crisis-oriented approaches within consultation sessions, even if they do not warrant crisis responses (Stone & Dahir, 2006).

When it comes to working with student athletes, the dependent teacher may lack a fundamental understanding of what the strengths of the student are. Since some student athletes are involved with leadership positions within their athletic roles, dependent teachers may have a difficult time sharing a classroom space with another leadership type. This teacher may be perceived by student athletes as "out of touch" with student-athletic culture. It can also be difficult for the dependent teacher to understand the athletic roles and responsibilities of the student athlete, because of a tendency to anchor his/her perceptions of the student around the classroom environment alone.

Similar to the approach of the questioning teacher, some encouragement from the school counselor as consultant to communicate with the coaching staff may prove useful in assisting with the work (s)he can accomplish with the case of Mike. Also, if parent–teacher consultations have not been previously undertaken, it may be possible for this type of engagement to help get Mike more on track in the classroom. However, it is important to establish important ground rules and guidelines for the nature of these communications at the start of consultation, so as to ensure a norm of collaboration can occur (Visek et al., 2009; Dougherty, 2005) and minimize the chances of creating conflict and confirmation bias that "fixing" the child is the main issue. The theme of viewing the student athlete as a person (Stambulova, 2011) needs to be present, and the school counselor may have to model and encourage this behavior when making these moves within the consultation relationship, so that the dependent teacher can follow this theme accordingly. Communicating with the parents and coaches, just as in the case of the questioning teacher, could also enable an effective disengagement from the school counselor-as-consultant relationship, as former parties are able to report on Mike's progress on assignments and on the football field as a result.

Absentee Teacher as Consultee

The *absentee* teacher is typically defined as one who never seeks the assistance of the school counselor as a consultant. It is difficult to determine the success or non-success rate of this teacher type when it comes to student–teacher relationships and relationships with other professionals, mainly due to the fact that these individuals keep to themselves and do not call upon others for assistance. Developing a consultative relationship may be a gradual process with this type of teacher because of the tendency not to admit that problems exist (Stone & Dahir, 2006).

When working with student athletes, the absentee teacher often appears uninterested or disconnected from the students and related situations at hand. This can perhaps manifest itself in the form of disengaged or lack of school spirit, or inability to recognize accomplishments of student athletes beyond the scope of in-the-moment classroom-based tasks. For example, students who remain on-task within a classroom setting may not be praised or punished by such a teacher because they are getting the task done, but the absentee teacher may not be able to further relate to these students because (s)he is not looking to engage with their learning and development beyond the scope of the task at hand. The teacher is missing some of the teachable moments that parallel the student athlete's learning and development on the field, in other parts of the school, and within the community. It is believed that exposure to school functions and sporting events can bridge some of this gap. However, the absentee teacher may also require some collaboration from the school counselor and athletic stakeholders in order to operate in more of a team-oriented fashion, so that accountability and engagement become more likely throughout the consultation process.

In the case of Mike, the school counselor may wish to encourage a teaching-team approach, whereby some classroom guidance, consultation with coaches, and parent input could be applied. There are program curricula and various materials that are available to schools for such a purpose, one of the more notable being the Play It Smart program (Petitpas, Van Raalte, Cornelius, & Presbrey, 2004). This program is mainly facilitated through the work of academic coaches who provide contact with the student athletes on and off the field, but with the accountability of reporting to school personnel, parents, and athletic coaches. Even if the entire program cannot be implemented at the school in question, the notion of a team building and team-focused approach to information gathering about what works can more readily engage an absentee teacher in the process of aligning with Mike's classroom goals and academic progress. The disengagement phase could be brought about by encouraging the teacher to provide feedback to the school counselor about the classroom guidance activities and/or curriculum adjustments that have been improving the student outcomes. In other words, the shift of power, from being the observer of intervention and change to the active evaluator of change and progress, allows the absentee teacher to invest more in the student/classroom and less in the structured schedule of the counselor–teacher consultation process. This shifting of engagement level from the counselor-as-consultant to the classroom and student is what allows the disengagement from consultation to occur in both a gradual and non-intrusive manner, which will hopefully guard against future "absenteeism."

Dominating Teacher as Consultee

The *dominating* teacher is typically defined as one who monopolizes the time of the consultant. Their relationship to students and other professionals suggests that one must approach the consultative relationship with clearly defined boundaries, schedules and appointment times. Though they are able to collaborate with the school counselor as a consultant, this type of teacher as consultee can spend a significant amount of time dictating the flow and direction of the consultation session. It is important, therefore, to develop a balance of listening skills and instruction when it comes to working with this type of teacher as consultee (Stone & Dahir, 2006).

When it comes to working with student athletes, the dominant teacher may overuse information or over-identify with issues that the student athlete is experiencing, because of perceived expertise about how to bring about changes. This is not to say that this teacher's knowledge is unwarranted or inauthentic, but the information (s)he may have can be overused when addressing the needs of the student athlete and the interventions that are needed to bring about change. It is a difficult balance that needs to be present, so that the consultee does not feel discredited or on the losing end of the relationship.

In the case of Mike, working with a dominant teacher would likely involve the same methods and actions used for an absentee teacher, with the possible exception that instead of encouraging communication between stakeholders and the teacher, the school counselor may wish to incorporate the use of observation and assessment in order to anchor communications between all parties around the idea of objective progress as opposed to subjective data. For example, reporting to coaches and parents the progress Mike has made through homework completion records can enable communication to occur between stakeholders without creating too much space for over-interpretation of behavior and/or experience. The school counselor can still speak about and reflect upon subjective material with the teacher on a one-on-one basis, and this may balance the need for elaboration and validation of expertise. Also, when reflecting on the progress and positives of the student more than the obstacles and issues, better rapport and relationships can be developed over time (Petitpas et al., 2004; Dougherty, 2005). Noting Mike's improvements can also reinforce some of his leadership and prosocial skills within the classroom, which can also enable a dominating teacher to focus less on off-task behaviors that can still occasionally occur (Albert, 1996), but are not necessarily indicative of a crisis or regression. In other words, student and teacher can mutually benefit from the patience and progress that each is likely to make as the relationship develops. As would also be expected, the shift away from prolonged face-to-face encounters with the school counselor as consultant, as well as the shift toward focusing on the student's improvements, would enable effective disengagement from the consultation relationship.

Important Consultation Skills

Regardless of the type of issue or teacher-as-consultee involved with the consultation process, there are recommended skills that school counselors are advised to use when working with student athlete cases. I and other school stakeholders believe these skills can be applied to other types of students and consultative issues, but have found them particularly helpful when addressing many of the student athlete cases we have encountered. They are also shared by several consultation models and approaches to interpersonal communication involved with school stakeholders (Dougherty, 2005; Dinkmeyer & Carlson, 2006): the *one-down* approach, *data gathering with reframing, positive asset search*, and *planning and follow-up* (Zagelbaum, 2011).

One-Down Approach

The limited time teachers have to formally sit down and consult with the school counselor necessitates significant appreciation and regard for the teacher-as-consultee. When initially engaging with a teacher during the consultation process, it is advisable to approach him/her from the perspective that (s)he has valuable information to provide and that it is not something that needs to be forced out of him/her by way of the consultation process. In other words, though the school counselor has some perceived or established expertise when called upon as a consultant (Dougherty, 2005; Dinkmeyer & Carlson, 2006), approaching the teacher-as-consultee from the perspective of being an equal-footed colleague assists with rapport and allows for freer communication regarding the student athlete's issues in the classroom (Zagelbaum, 2011). It is similar to motivational interviewing and counseling skills, in that an intentional counselor tries to first humanistically engage with the client, so that any reservations and/or apprehensions (s)he may have about counseling can be comfortably discussed before embarking on the process of change (Ivey, Ivey, & Zalaquett, 2010). It also enables consultees to know that the consultant appreciates the variety of skills and duties they perform, and is not merely attempting to reduce their presence in the consultative relationship solely to the description of problem behaviors.

Data Gathering with Reframing Approach

When first diagnosing or analyzing the problem(s) involved with the student athlete, some observations or details provided by the teacher-as-consultee can be viewed with a negative bent (Czech, Whalen, Burdette, Metzler, & Zwald, 2006). Being able to reframe these data as neutral matters or possible strengths can help the consultation session stay on course in terms of diagnosis and decision-making, because it reduces the subjective nature of the discussion (Dougherty, 2005), which can lead to more searching for problems which may or may not be related to the core of the student athlete's concerns (Zagelbaum, 2011). It is similar to the way in which interpersonal processing can lead some clients to get lost in their experience(s) of a problem and not allow for levels of resistance to drop so that actions toward change can be taken (Teyber, 1992). The school counselor is advised to be a good listener to the teacher-as-consultee, but to also help objectify data about the student athlete, so that goals and objectives can be established more effectively. It also enables consultees to know that problem solving is possible for the student athlete they are currently experiencing difficulties with, and that resources are possible to find.

Positive Asset Search

This may go without saying, but it is important to engage teachers-as-consultees in discussions about what strengths and positive skills the student athlete has, just as much as the problem issues that served as antecedents to the consultation session. Focus on the behaviors and steps that are needed for change can be such that the teacher-as-consultee can lose sight of the potential a student athlete has for developing these behaviors (Albert, 1996). Focusing on solutions is not always the same as focusing on the person who is performing the solutions (Hoigaard & Johansen, 2004; Albert, 1996), and school counselors need to reinforce the personal strengths of the student athlete as much as possible, so that this focus can remain balanced between both the goals of supervision and the individual(s) who can benefit from making the change(s). It is a form of advocacy, in the sense that school counselors are trying to focus the teacher-as-consultant on the student's potential for success (Stone & Dahir, 2006), and also a form of modeling that can assist a teacher with reframing negative perceptions into possible avenues for change. This can not only change the consultee's view of the student athlete, but it can also change the way (s)he views other systemic matters that may be involved in the consultation process (Zagelbaum, 2011). Positive asset search is one of the cornerstones of building an effective therapeutic relationship (Ivey et al., 2010), and it seems that it greatly assists with consultative relationships in a similar manner by enabling an internal, efficacious dialogue about a student and the consultee to exist.

Planning and Follow-Up

Similar to the disengagement stage of consultation, the making of plans and follow-up meetings can provide a sense of closure and balance to working with a teacher-as-consultee (Dougherty, 2005). Some consultees may have a hard time following through on plans and goals if there is no set schedule or process established early and often. Some consultees may rely too heavily on the school counselor as a resource throughout the consultation process that the full implementation of a plan or intervention does not occur efficiently. Planning and follow-up are not only essential elements of consultation that allow a collaborative dynamic to be established between consultant and consultee (Dougherty, 2005; Dinkmeyer & Carlson, 2006), but they can also demonstrate a commitment on the part of counselor and consultee to see their responsibilities through (Zagelbaum, 2011).

Summary

The process of consultation can make some specific demands of the school counselor when working with a student athlete. This chapter mainly emphasizes the essential components of consulting with teachers and recognizes that coaches can also be teachers of student athletes within K-12 settings, though they are not always the exclusive instructors of all students. Regardless, teachers are often one of the most significant and initially critical stakeholders for a school counselor-as-consultant to collaborate with when it comes to addressing the needs of student athletes, and recognizing what type of teacher-as-consultee is in the room can be extremely helpful when it comes to planning, approaching, and maintaining consultative interventions and approaches. There are also specific ethical guidelines and laws such as FERPA that should be used to provide structure to the consultative relationship, and school counselors should abide by appropriate boundaries and privacies in order to ensure the greatest care and the least harm when speaking to all interested parties who are overseeing the progress of a student athlete. Though some of these matters can be addressed through documentation, others are more complex and may require the school counselor to seek consultation of another colleague and/or supervisor to ensure the best care as well as the most productive and efficient use of time for all parties who are attempting to service all students.

Questions for Discussion

1. How would your approach to teacher consultation change if you were consulting with a teacher/coach?
2. How would your approach to teacher consultation change if you were encountering a case like Mike in a middle/junior high school?

References

Albert, L. (1996) *Cooperative Discipline*. Circle Pines, MN: AGS Publishing.

Anderson, A. G., Miles, A., Mahoney, C., & Robinson, P. (2002) Evaluating the effectiveness of applied sport psychology practice: Making the case of a case study approach. *The Sport Psychologist, 16*, 432–453.

ASCA (American School Counseling Association) (2010) *Ethical Code for School Counselors*. Alexandria, VA: Author.

Baker, S. B., Robichaud, T. A., Westforth, V. C., Westforth, D., Wells, S. C., & Schreck, R. E. (2009) School counsellor consultation: A pathway to advocacy, collaboration, and leadership. *Professional School Counseling, 12(3)*, 200–206.

Czech, D. R., Whalen, S. J., Burdette, G. P., Metzler, J. N., & Zwald, D. (2006) Optimism and pessimism in sport and in the classroom: Applied tips for teacher-coaches. *Georgia Association for Health, Physical Education, Recreation and Dance Journal, 39(3)*, 15–17.

Dinkmeyer, D. C., & Carlson, J. (2006) *Consultation: Creating School-based Interventions* (3rd ed.). New York: Routledge.

Dollarhide, C. T., & Saginak, K. A. (2012) *Comprehensive School Counseling Programs: K-12 Delivery Systems in Action* (2nd ed.). Upper Saddle River, NJ: Pearson.

Dougherty, A. M. (2005) *Psychological Consultation and Collaboration in School and Community Settings* (5th ed.). Belmont, CA: Brooks/Cole.

Fraser-Thomas, J. L., Cote, J., & Deakin, J. (2005) Youth sport programs: An avenue to foster positive youth development. *Physical Education and Sport Psychology, 10(1)*, 19–40.

Hoigaard, R. & Johansen, B. (2004) The solution-focused approach in sport psychology. *The Sport Psychologist, 18*, 218–228.

Ivey, A. E., Ivey, M. B., & Zalaquett, C. P. (2010) *Intentional Interviewing and Counseling: Facilitating Client Development in a Multicultural Society* (7th ed.). Belmont, CA: Brooks/Cole.

Kampwirth, T. J., & Powers, K. M. (2012) *Collaborative Consultation in the Schools: Effective Practices for Students with Learning and Behavior Problems* (4th ed.). Upper Saddle River, NJ: Pearson.

Keegan, R. J., Harwood, C. G., Spray, C. M., & Lavallee, D. E. (2009) A qualitative investigation exploring the motivational climate in early career sports participants: Coach, parent and peer influences on sport motivation. *Psychology of Sport and Science, 10*, 361–372.

Lowe, H. & Cook, A. (2003) Mind the gap: Are students prepared for higher education? *Journal of Further and Higher Education, 27(1)*, 53–76.

Maniar, S. D., Curry, L. A., Sommers-Flanagan, J., & Walsh, J. A. (2001) Student athlete preferences in seeking help when confronted with sport performance problems. *The Sport Psychologist, 15*, 205–223.

Mintz, M. L. (2005) The school psychologist and sport: A natural interface to promote optimal functioning between student athlete, family and school personnel. *Journal of Applied School Psychology, 21(2)*, 25–40.

Petitpas, A. J., Van Raalte, J. L., Cornelius, A. E., & Presbrey, J. (2004) A life skills development program for high school student athletes. *The Journal of Primary Prevention, 24(3)*, 325–334.

Smoll, F. L., Smith, R. E., Barnett, N. P., & Everett, J. J. (1993) Enhancement of children's self-esteem through social support training for youth sport coaches. *Journal of Applied Sport Psychology,78*, 602–610.

Stambulova, N. (2011) The Mobilization Model of counseling athletes in crisis-transitions: An educational intervention tool. *Journal of Sport Psychology in Action, 2*, 156–170.

Stone, C. B., & Dahir, C. A. (2006) *The Transformed School Counselor*. Boston: Lahaska Press.

Teyber, E. (1992) *Interpersonal Process in Psychotherapy: A Guide for Clinical Training* (2nd ed.). Belmont, CA: Wadsworth.

U.S. Department of Education (1974) The Family Educational Rights and Privacy Act (FERPA): General. Washington, DC: Author.

Visek, A. J., Harris, B. S., & Blom, L. C. (2009) Doing sport psychology: A youth sport consulting model for practitioners. *The Sport Psychologist, 23*, 271–291.

Watson, J. C. (2006) Student athletes and counseling: Factors influencing the decision to seek counseling services. *College Student Journal, 40(1)*, 35–42.

Zagelbaum, A. (2011) *Counseling the Student athlete*. Alexandria, VA: Alexander Street Press.

8 Consultation with Coaches and the Student Athlete

In the previous chapter, we examined the role of school counselors as consultants to teachers working with student athletes. Specifically, we looked at the American School Counselor Association's (ASCA's) Code of Ethics and Standards of Practice in order to guide this examination of content and process of consultation. For this chapter, we also take into consideration the Code of Ethics for coaches, as defined by respective coaches' associations identified by the National Collegiate Athletic Association (NCAA), National Association of Intercollegiate Athletics (NAIA) and National Junior College Athletic Association (NJCAA); likewise we take into account the Code of Ethics for athletic trainers as defined by the National Athletic Trainers' Association (NATA; 2005).

One of the more detailed ethical codes associated with the NCAA is that of the U.S. Track & Field and Cross Country Coaches Association (USTFCCCA; 2009). Issues of confidentiality and record dissemination, to personal well-being and conduct, are explicitly detailed. There are many other sports and coaches represented by the NCAA, but the core principles regarding the work related to student athlete relationships appear largely in line with this one.

Elements of NAIA's Code of Ethics (NAIA, n.d.) shows similar principles, in that coaches are to work with admissions offices of educational institutions in a way that does not permit records or transcripts of prospective student athletes to pass through their offices, and that coaches' personal conduct does not conflict with the educational aims of the institution.

Also, NJCAA's Region XIX provides a general overview of coaching responsibilities within its Code of Ethics in the following way:

> Individuals employed by (or associated with) a member institution to administer, conduct or coach intercollegiate athletics shall conduct themselves with honesty and sportsmanship at all times so that their institutions and they, as individuals, shall represent the honor and dignity of fair play and the generally recognized high standards associated with wholesome competitive sports.
>
> (NJCAA, 2003)

Thus, it also follows that emphasizing points of athletic and non-athletic relationships are integral components to both understanding and approaching coaches when engaged in the consultation process. It also appears to follow the codes for athletic trainers.

Though it should be clear that coaches are not always teachers and athletic trainers, taking NATA's Code of Ethics into account can assist the school counselor as consultant when aligning with a coach as consultee. There are certain common elements regarding confidentiality and boundary issues that can assist coach and counselor by recognizing the ways in which the goals of consultation can strive for mutual beneficial outcomes along with respect for the expertise that each professional brings to the consultative relationship. The Principles of the NATA Code reads as follows:

Principle 1   Members shall respect the rights, welfare and dignity of all.
Principle 2   Members shall comply with the laws and regulations governing the practice of athletic training.
Principle 3   Members shall maintain and promote high standards in their provision of services.
Principle 4   Members shall not engage in conduct that could be construed as a conflict of interest or that reflects negatively on the profession.

It appears that ASCA, NCAA, NAIA, NJCAA and NATA hold professionals to significant levels of accountability and expectations of placing the need of the student athlete first. Though athletic trainers are more likely to be involved with on-the-field issues affecting the performance and personal issues of the student athlete, the way in which their conduct is guided off-the-field by NATA standards helps school counselors recognize how to collaborate with them fully during the consultation process. It also helps the school counselor remember the additional expectations and responsibilities that coaches have when working with student athletes by saliently displaying principles that define the sport and non-sport-related issues involved with student athletics.

Sports Counseling and Consultation

The application of Sports Counseling also provides important guidelines and approaches for school counselors to consider when working with coaches and student athletes. As a specialty, this field has a very recent history for Counselor Educators (Petitpas, Buntrock, Van Raalte, & Brewer, 1995) and school counselors (Goldberg & Chandler, 1995). The American Counseling Association (ACA) has a Sports Counseling Interest Network (SCIN) which has been an effective collection of professionals who support the practices of this type of counseling and continue to advance it towards becoming a specialty (Rollins, 2007). Additionally, the growing body of research and prominence of sport culture within schools has presented counseling professionals with several important strategies and approaches to take with athletic stakeholders when it comes to addressing developmental issues of student athletes.

The developmental issues defined by Goldberg and Chandler (1995) that seem to impact most student athletes at the K-12 level are: *identity, personal competence, interpersonal behavior,* and *future planning. Identity* issues stem from the roles and values that student athletes experience along with their expectations of success (Yopyk & Prentice, 2005). Athletes often turn to their coaches first when identity issues impact sport performance (Maniar, Curry, Sommers-Flanagan, & Walsh, 2001), but also rely on other professionals when facing similar issues that relate to pressures they face from community and school-related venues (Magen, 1998; Watson, 2006). *Personal competence* refers to the ability of a student athlete to develop into an individual who can perform tasks in the world largely driven through intrinsic reward and with a sense of independence that does not significantly require connections to other adults (Goldberg & Chandler, 1995). Athletes can struggle with this issue because of the largely dependent nature that coach–athlete connections often have (Ting, 2009; Lubker, Visek, Geer, Watson II, 2008). As a result, student athletes can develop limited interpersonal skills and have difficulty generalizing perceptions and behaviors into other settings and relationships that they may eventually encounter (Goldberg & Chandler, 1995). *Interpersonal behavior* issues refer simply to how adolescent athletes relate to others. Because of the context in which sports can be played, some student athletes develop a team-oriented focus that can make certain social situations difficult to handle because team-mates are not always around (Goldberg & Chandler, 1995). There is also a difficulty for some athletes to perceive or display vulnerability in social situations because of the notion that being "tough" is often associated with winning and success (Frey, 1991; Watson, 2006; Steinfeldt, Rutkowski, Vaughan, & Steinfeldt, 2011). Thus, being able to consciously recognize and alter behaviors away from the athletic context is an important matter for school counselors and coaches to collaboratively address. *Future planning,* as the label would imply, refers to a student athlete's ability to develop strategies that enable effective transitions to be made, whether continuing with or moving away from a sports career (Goldberg & Chandler, 1995). This concept will be more fully addressed in Chapter 13, but in terms of the consultative nature of this developmental issue, it is important for counselor and coach to recognize how effective and appropriate the student athlete's decision-making abilities are, and how aware (s)he is of the risks and benefits associated with the outcomes of certain decisions. Goldberg and Chandler (1995) strongly advocate for the use of psycho-educational approaches to address all developmental issues, mainly because they tend to integrate interpersonal skill development and social learning theory—two approaches that are often used in coaching and school-based counseling services (Baker, 1992). The ability to concretely describe what skills look like, as well as demonstrate and practice them, enable clients to believe they are possible to learn (Goldstein & McGinnis, 1997), and for consultees and consultants to define goals in a jointly shared and mutually identifiable fashion (Kampwirth & Powers, 2012). It is this collaborative effort that enables sports counseling, school counseling, and work with coaching staff/stakeholders to truly produce an effective approach to consultation. Each of these developmental issues can be uncovered during the entry and/or diagnostic stages of consultation (Dougherty, 2005), but it is important for a school counselor to bear in mind that the issues themselves may not be in line with the expectations that coaches and student athletes have for the consultation process. Recognizing the distinction between sport issues and student issues is an important way for a consultant to appropriately join with the athletic system.

Consulting Expectations of Sport Issues

When working with athletes, teams, and coaches, sports psychologists often address issues related to sport performance and enhancement. The Association of Applied Sport Psychology (AASP) has specific guidelines and certification standards that all sports consultants are required to meet, and it is important for school-based counseling professionals to recognize that their work is not specifically designed to venture into this area of expertise and specialization. However, research by Lubker and colleagues (2008), reveals some interesting characteristics that student athletes perceive as being important for effective sport consultants to have. Student athletes placed significant value on sports consultants' *professional status* (how well-trained they are to deal with sport and athletic-based issues), *athletic background* (how personally and professionally knowledgeable they are to understand what it means to be an athlete who plays sports), *sport culture* (how knowledgeable they are when speaking the language and understanding the mentality and attitude of sport), and *physical characteristics* (how well-matched to the physicality of the athlete and coaching staff, as well as how physically healthy the consultant appears to be) (Lubker et al., 2008). However, there was one factor that was valued by student athletes as more valuable and significant than all of these: interpersonal skills.

Student athletes appear to value *positive interpersonal skills* as the most significant characteristic for a consultant to have when addressing sport-related issues (Lubker et al., 2008). More specifically, they value notions of being friendly, approachable, trustworthy, and the ability to maintain confidentiality. Even though there can be perceptions that sport-related issues are not always indicative of deep-rooted psychological matters (Cox, 2002), student athletes greatly prefer that a sport psychology consultant (SPC) possesses qualities that align with many factors associated with therapeutic rapport within the psychological counseling relationship (Carkhuff, 2010; Ivey, Ivey, & Zalaquett, 2010; Cormier & Cormier, 1995). This information may indicate that school counselors who may not feel they have expertise regarding sports and athletics do not have to be greatly concerned that most student athletes will not view their role as helpful, because it seems that the person-centered connection(s) between client and consultant are cornerstones to the overall process of consultation. Parents have also reported that quality of communication with school and sport staff is one of the most significant and enduring stressors that they experience while their children are involved in student athletics (Harwood, Drew, & Knight, 2010). Thus, it can also be said that school counselors and coaches can be effective consultants and consultees to one another when using these person-centered characteristics to engage the consultative process.

The Case of Mike

Again, we return to the case of Mike, presented at the beginning of Chapter 1, to illustrate possible approaches to take as a school-counselor-as-consultant working with coaches. It may help to re-read the case at this point.

In terms of consultation, it is likely that a teacher who has been noticing Mike's struggles would also refer Mike to the school counselor, if communication between coach and parents can not be done effectively or is logistically difficult to arrange. There are different models and approaches that can exist from school to school, and all school counselors are strongly advised to know the protocol that is largely in place for addressing such a case at the school they serve (Dollarhide & Saginak, 2012; Kampwirth & Powers, 2012). However, knowing the type of coach-as-consultee can assist the school counselor address him/her at all stages of the consultation process.

Types of Coaches-as-Consultees

When defining types of coaches, Keegan, Harwood, Spray and Lavallee (2009) present an effective qualitatively defined system that appears to significantly apply to consultation roles. All coaches have particular leadership styles, emotional and affective responses, and instructional/pedagogic approaches that are important to consider when engaged in the consultative process. As is always the case, though, readers are reminded that there can be exceptions to these suggested types of coaches. Previous chapters have noted that there have been examples in the media of coaches who have adopted a "win-at-all-costs" mentality that can be at odds with ethical and legal guidelines meant to protect individuals from mistreatment and harm. Coaches who take a distant or blind approach to dealing with players who violate conduct policies on and off the field, for example, can present significant challenges not only to players and their families, but also to school stakeholders and the surrounding community because they can be inadvertently condoning misbehavior and/or criminal acts that perpetuate harm. Coaches who violate rules and policy in order to have athletes play on their team and preserve winning records can send mixed and misunderstood messages to student athletes and school stakeholders about what moral and ethical guidelines should be established. Also, coaches who push their players to play through injury and capacities that can be of risk to the student athlete's personal health can present significant issues to student athletes who may suffer long-term consequences because of such demands and short-sighted decisions. These types of coaches can exist, and it is important for school-based counseling professionals to engage with administration and athletic staff so that appropriate actions and ethical guidelines can be followed and disciplinary actions enforced when required. However, readers are reminded that these types of cases are usually few in number and frequency, and, given that the goal involving the case of Mike involves maintaining a balance between academic and athletic focus, we will describe the types of coaches in relation to this scenario.

Leadership Continuum

There are two main points along the leadership style continuum that Keegan et al. (2009) define for coaches: *controlling/autocratic* style and *autonomy supportive/democratic* style.

The *controlling/autocratic* style is characterized by sport-related decision-making that involves little to no input on the part of the student athlete. For example, if a player is needed to fill a particular position on a team, a controlling/autocratic coach will assign the student athlete to that position without gathering significant input about the student athlete's opinion or perception regarding the assignment.

The *autonomy supportive/democratic* style is characterized by sport-related decision-making that involves more input from the student athlete in order to inform the coach's choice. Thus, instead of simply assigning the player to a particular team position, the democratic coach will ask the student athlete where (s)he feels comfortable and or wants to play before making the specific assignment. This is not to say that positions can only be filled if a player chooses to do so, but the use of the student athlete's thoughts, feelings and comfort-level are used to inform the coach's decision.

The styles that help define what point along this continuum a coach may fit appear to boil down to the use of collaboration and/or the use of control. At the entry stage of consultation (Dougherty, 2005), the school counselor may get a sense of what style the coach uses by simply asking him/her to define the concerns about Mike's academic and athletic performance issues. A controlling coach when asked for input about Mike's underperformance may simply state "I believe in him, but until he shows the improvement, we can only do so much." This can often be taken by the student athlete as additional stress and criticisms that can impact psychosocial development (Ommundsen, Roberts, Lemyre, & Miller, 2006). The school-counselor-as-consultant may wish to ask this type of coach for strategies and suggestions that (s)he may have about what has worked for Mike in the past; also, if Mike has ever gone through a slump in sport-performance, perhaps asking the coach about what tactics were employed to turn this trend around could provide important insights into how other strategies can be adopted for this current situation. The collaborative coach, on the other hand, when asked for input about Mike's underperformance may state various variables and matters that could present several opportunities for the consultation process to progress. There may be specific characteristics about Mike that the coach is able to readily identify as important to assisting with his progress (e.g., "Mike shows up to practices on time but sometimes has difficulty focusing on his assignments"), and there may also be team-related characteristics that the coach may provide as well [e.g., "Mike is viewed by his teammates as a leader when they take the field."). However, it should be noted that collaboration is not always synonymous with leadership, and some aspects of limit-setting and decision-making can be beneficial for student athletes and coaches alike. The school-counselor-as-consultant may wish to gather information about which skills and goals are given priority attention, and perhaps collaborate with the coach to create plans and strategies that align with these primary observations.

Instructional and Pedagogic Approaches

There are also instructional and pedagogic approaches that Keegan et al. (2009) identify as unique to coaches. Though they primarily refer to sport-related responsibilities regarding game plans and team construction, they do relate to aspects of consultation where strategies and interventions can be implemented. One of these approaches, *equal treatment and perceived fairness*, refers to how coaches apply discipline and structure to the team. For example, if a coach rewards players for good behavior but occasionally spares punishments for the sake of team-building, some players may perceive this as a block to momentum and motivation to perform. Mike may be struggling academically and athletically because he may be acting out or resisting some of the requests made of him because he feels unfairly treated and is not sure how to resolve this issue. A school counselor may be able to explore this with Mike in a brief session independently from coaches and teachers. Though the school counselor should be aware not to take on a clinical role with Mike (ASCA, 2012; Watson, 2006), and must be aware of power dynamics that exist between coach and student athlete (Ward, Sandstedt, Cox, & Beck, 2005; Visek, Harris, & Blom, 2009), uncovering this insight may be able to help the consultee and client establish better communication and agreements about how to adjust performance and expectations in the future.

Another pedagogic approach, *one-to-one coaching*, refers to the amount of specialized attention that coaches devote to student athletes on an individual basis (Keegan et al., 2009). Coaches that are able to provide this type of attention—whether it be to deliver feedback, instruction, or evaluation of performance—are often perceived by student athletes to have a positive effect on motivation. This could also be helpful for a school-counselor-as-consultant who may wish to join coach and student together for some part of the consultation process in order to facilitate greater levels of compliance and follow-up agreement (Dougherty, 2005; Zagelbaum, 2011).

Task design is an approach that coaches normally use to establish competition and focus during practices and scrimmage games (Keegan et al., 2009).

Coaches who have used this strategy toward the latter part of practice sessions have been generally viewed as more favorable than those who engage in this process at the start of practices (Keegan et al., 2009). Thus, if Mike is experiencing a drop in performance or motivation because of perceived or actual inability to effectively compete with others, it may be possible to see if adjustment to the task design, on or off the field, may assist with getting him back on track. If this sense of competition is affecting his classroom performance, assisting coaches and teachers with this conceptualization of task design could also be of benefit.

One possible way to vary task design relates to another approach: *variety and fun*. Essentially, student athletes tend to derive greater levels of motivation from coaches who vary the types of tasks and skills that are to be developed, as opposed to only emphasizing one skill at a time until a certain level of mastery occurs (Keegan et al., 2009). It may be possible that Mike is devoting so much time to one particular aspect of his student athlete responsibilities that he is tuning out and/or disregarding other ones. Facilitating a dialogue between coach and student as well as teacher and student may enable Mike to reconnect with some of these "lost" responsibilities, at least because of the conscious attention that can be given (Maniar, Curry, Sommers-Flannagan, & Walsh, 2001; Ommundsen et al., 2006; Visek, Harris, & Blom, 2009).

One other approach, *evaluation criteria*, is what coaches focus on in order to make sport-related decisions regarding teams and individuals; it is not the same as providing feedback about performance, because it does not necessarily involve communication of the performance process as much as it involves discussion about the outcome (Keegan et al., 2009). Coaches were either perceived by student athletes as being *fault-finders* (emphasizing mostly the deficits and indicators of poor performance) or as being *effort and improvement focused* (emphasizing the ways in which student athletes have made progress since their last evaluation). The former approach appears to correlate strongly with fear-of-failure perceptions which often discourage some student athletes from approaching future tasks with a sense of hopefulness (Harwood et al., 2010; Keegan et al., 2009; Magen, 1998; Maniar et al., 2001; Seligman, 2006). Being able to connect coach and client with a discussion of skills and strengths can likely assist with the consultation process and help to establish an understanding that a lack of progress toward goals does not mean that Mike has already failed. However, it must be understood that progress must be defined and displayed in order to achieve a desired result (Dougherty, 2005; Keegan et al., 2009).

Gaining Credibility

Given that we have examined the types of coaches and approaches they often use to athletically challenge and develop student athletes, we should also emphasize ways in which a school counselor can gain credibility and effective entry into the coach–student collaboration process. Consultation with coaches and athletic staff is not likely to be effective if a school counselor joins with this system without a sense of sport culture and the demands that coaches have when it comes to working with student athletes (Harwood et al., 2010; Mintz, 2005; Ward et al., 2005).

In order to encourage credible rapport and working alliances, Janssen and Dale (2002) have identified specific factors that apply specifically to coaches working with student athletes and developing professional athletes. Essentially, credible coaches are found by players to:

1. have a broader definition of success that goes beyond the results of winning or losing a competition;
2. expect the striving toward success with honest effort from players;
3. rebound from losses in a quick but effective manner that serves as a good behavioral example for players;
4. encourage self-determination from players and self-regulation from teams and players alike; and
5. focus on intrinsic motivation, commitment and confidence when it comes to performance.

These qualities have a strong correlation to the working alliance in counseling and consultative relationships as well. Again, it must be noted that school counselors are not involved in the consultation process to alter the personality of coaches and/or student athletes. The awareness of these credible factors should not encourage school counselors to point out what a coach is doing wrong in order to solve performance problems. However, by using these factors as guidelines when discussing problems with coaches and athletic staff, a school counselor-as-consultant has the ability to model these skills and reinforce a dialogue that allows for the coach-as-consultee to reframe expectations of a struggling student athlete in a way that bridges a gap between sport-specific difficulties and issues outside of the athletic system. It also helps consultant and consultee draw parallels between their levels of expertise and what unique strengths they bring to the consultative relationship, so that collaboration is more likely (Dinkmeyer & Carlson, 2006; Dougherty, 2005). In other words, a dispositional flow can be created by using coaching principles to guide the collaborative efforts between consultant and consultee, which can impact the efforts of the student athlete (Moreno, Cervello, & Gonzalez-Cutre, 2010).

The simple use of reflective listening can help this process along. When defining the problem, reflective statements such as "I'm hearing that Mike has a strong ability to..." can help normalize concerns and encourage a problem-solving discussion to take place, instead of dwelling too long on the shortcomings and inabilities which may obscure solutions (Dinkmeyer & Carlson, 2006; Teyber, 1992). This is not to say that coaches are not able to use these skills without prompting, but even the most collaborative and understanding of coaches can inadvertently lose sight of these observations when the pressures of competition mount (Fletcher, Benshoff, & Richburg, 2003). Reflecting these strengths and skills of the student athlete enables the coach to have a sense of agreement and validation from the school counselor-as-consultant about how to approach the consultative relationship, without feeling a sense of one-upmanship or defensiveness about what information (s)he has not been able to previously use. It also enables the school counselor to introduce other sources of data and observations from other stakeholders regarding the student athlete in question, so that the coach can be made aware of consistencies that exist on and off the field. Such information, when presented with the same strengths-based focus as the communication between consultant and consultee, creates a sense of commonality and collaboration among stakeholders and helps more clearly define what the goals and outcomes for consultation should be (Dougherty, 2005; Lubker et al., 2008). The school counselor does not need to be the one in control of the consultative process, but should do his/her best to encourage the collaborative elements of consultation to form and crystallize among all parties.

Further Tips

Though we have mainly addressed the relationship and communication variables that can impact the consultative efforts between school counselor and coach, there are also other tips to bear in mind when engaging in this process. First and foremost, the school counselor should be aware of the schedules of coaches and coaching staff. Even though all school staff and stakeholders have busy lives and multiple responsibilities, the coaches and athletic staff also have duties which involve team travel outside of the school campus, practice schedules, teaching responsibilities, and various other organized team activities which do not allow them to keep as regular a schedule as a dedicated classroom teacher. This does not mean that they are more privileged or unique than other school staff members, but recognizing the demands of their job and joining with coaches in a way that expresses appreciation for their accessibility and availability can go a long way towards establishing an effective consultative relationship (Dinkmeyer & Carlson, 2006; Zagelbaum, 2011) and establishing a parallel link of support among athletic and academic systems (Wieskhamp, 2008). This one-down approach reduces the potential for power struggles between consultant and consultee, and serves as an effective modeling technique for the ways in which subsequent communications are likely to occur (Dougherty, 2005).

Given that academic and athletic struggles can relate to on- and off-the-field issues, school counselors are encouraged to meet with teachers and other school staff involved with the student athlete prior to consultation with the coach if such communications have not yet occurred. It is important to adhere to Family Educational Rights and Privacy Act rules (Baker, 1992), but having these communications among parents, students, staff, and related stakeholders can enable these details to be handled appropriately. It also displays an attitude and style of transparency on the part of the school counselor which, in terms of consultative actions, can go a long way toward compliance and collaboration (Dougherty, 2005; Zagelbaum, 2011). These initial meetings can be brief in nature and can allow stakeholders to express interest in meeting with each other, not just through the facilitative efforts of the school counselor. Since the school system can be very intricate in some areas, coaches, teachers, counselors, and other related stakeholders may not always cross paths. The school counselor-as-consultant has an opportunity to facilitate these collaborative relationships between systems just as much as (s)he can in a one-to-one meeting with each stakeholder separately (Mintz, 2005).

It is also important for the school counselor to recognize that a lack of athletic background and/or understanding of sport culture are not automatic barriers to consultation with coaches. There are certainly advantages for professionals who have a significant sports background to work with individuals who are currently involved with sports (Lubker et al., 2008), but being sincere and genuine about gaining an understanding of the sport and the demands placed upon coaches and student athletes helps to establish rapport and bonds that make the focus of consultation about life skills which can apply to both academic and athletic goals (Petitpas, Van Raalte, Cornelius, & Presbrey, 2004). Some individuals may appreciate how sports can serve as a metaphor for life, while some may be bothered by the fact that someone not directly affiliated with sports is attempting to make such connections. There is not necessarily a right or wrong way to engage in this discussion, if it is to be included at all. As is the case within counseling and therapeutic relationships, it is advisable to allow consultees to bring up these metaphors first, so that there is a greater likelihood of a joining with the consultee over this issue, as opposed to forcing a connection to be seen that may not be of significant shared value (Cormier & Cormier, 1995; Zagelbaum, 2011). It is helpful for a consultant to know the role that a coach has in the life of a student athlete, but the consultee is not meant to be the focus of the consultation (Dougherty, 2005), and school counselors should not attempt to bond with coaches simply because of their athletic and/or sporting backgrounds.

Summary

When addressing issues of student athletes, consultation with coaches is one of the more powerful actions that a school counselor can take toward assisting with change. Though coaches and athletic staff have similar duties and responsibilities within schools that are shared by teachers and administrators, it is important to consider the unique demands and responsibilities they have in terms of schedule, external agency connections, and athletic organizations. The likelihood of student athletes turning to coaches in times of struggle is often stronger than other school staff members (Maniar et al., 2001; Watson, 2006). However, when issues appear to be interfering with issues beyond the athletic relationship, the school counselor can be of valuable service toward gaining further insights and approaches toward getting the student athlete back on track. There are types of coaches that can be autocratic or democratic in terms of their leadership style, which may provide some valuable insight as to how they may approach the consultative relationship. Recognizing the types of strategies used by each type of coach can enable the consultant to address the consultee in ways that speak to his/her strengths as a leader, so that resistance and defensiveness can be reduced and collaboration has a better chance of occurring. It is also likely that a joint meeting between coach and student, student and teacher, and/or all three could assist with the collaborative process, but it is not always easy to accomplish solely through the consultative efforts of the school counselor. However, the use of parallel processes and observations of strengths that all stakeholders share, may enable interests and proactive efforts to increase among these individuals, which can in turn create a feedback loop and progress-reporting dynamic that can assist the student athlete accomplish his/her academic and athletic goals. There are interpersonal dynamics and conflicts that can also surface when a student athlete is struggling, but these can usually be addressed through counseling work, and explorations of these matters are discussed in greater detail within subsequent chapters. In the end, however, the school counselor-as-consultant can build an effective team approach toward assisting the student athlete in much the same way that a collaborative coach can gain credibility from his/her players: by looking at the totality of the efforts, attitudes, and ethics of the individuals (s)he works with, and encouraging full potential to be applied to required tasks.

Questions for Discussion

1. How would your approach to consultation change if you were consulting with coaches at levels other than high school?
2. How would you address issues of conflict between coach and student athlete?

References

ASCA (American School Counselor Association) (2012) *The ASCA National Model: A Framework for School Counseling Programs* (3rd ed.). Alexandria, VA: Author.

Baker, S. (1992) *School Counseling for the 21st Century*. New York: Merrill.

Carkhuff, R. R. (2010) *The Art of Helping in the 21st Century*. Amherst, MA: Human Resource Development Press, Inc.

Cormier, W. H., & Cormier, L. S. (1995) *Interviewing Strategies for Helpers* (2nd ed.). Pacific Grove, CA: Brooks/Cole.

Cox, R. H. (2002) *Sport Psychology: Concepts and Applications* (5th ed.). Boston: McGraw-Hill.

Dinkmeyer, D. C., & Carlson, J. (2006) *Consultation: Creating School-Based Interventions* (3rd ed.). New York: Routledge.

Dollarhide, C. T., & Saginak, K. A. (2012) *Comprehensive School Counseling Programs: K-12 Delivery Systems in Action*. Upper Saddle River, NJ: Pearson.

Dougherty, A. M. (2005) *Psychological Consultation and Collaboration in School and Community Settings* (5th ed.). Belmont, CA: Brooks/Cole.

Fletcher, T. B., Benshoff, J. M., & Richburg, M. J. (2003) A systems approach to understanding and counseling college student athletes. *Journal of College Counseling, 6,* 35–45.

Frey, J. (1991) Social risk and the meaning of sport. *Sociology of Sport Journal, 8,* 136–145.

Goldberg, A. D., & Chandler, T. (1995) Sports counseling: Enhancing the development of the high school student athlete. *Journal of Counseling and Development, 74,* 39–44.

Goldstein, A., & McGinnis, E. (1997) *Skillstreaming the Adolescent: New Strategies and Perspectives for Teaching Prosocial Skills.* Champaign, IL: Research Press.

Harwood, C., Drew, A., & Knight, C. J. (2010) Parental stressors in professional youth football academies: A qualitative investigation of specializing stage parents. *Qualitative Research in Sport and Exercise, 2(1),* 39–55.

Ivey, A. E., Ivey, M. B., & Zalaquett, C. P. (2010) *Intentional Interviewing and Counseling: Facilitating Client Development in a Multicultural Society* (7th ed.). Belmont, CA: Brooks/Cole.

Janssen, J., & Dale, G. A. (2002) *The Seven Secrets of Successful Coaches.* Tuscon, AZ: Winning the Mental Game.

Kampwirth, T. J., & Powers, K. M. (2012) *Collaborative Consultation in the Schools: Effective Practices for Students with Learning and Behavior Problems* (4th ed.). Upper Saddle River, NJ: Pearson.

Keegan, R. J., Harwood, C. G., Spray, C. M., & Lavallee, D. (2009) A qualitative investigation exploring the motivational climate in early career sports participants: Coach, parent and peer influences on sport motivation. *Psychology of Sport and Exercise, 10,* 361–372.

Lubker, J. R., Visek, A. J., Geer, J. R., & Watson II, J. C. (2008) Characteristics of an effective sport psychology consultant: Perspectives from athletes and consultants. *Journal of Sport Behavior, 31(2),* 147–165.

Magen, Z. (1998) *Exploring Adolescent Happiness: Commitment, Purpose, and Fulfillment.* Thousand Oaks, CA: Sage.

Maniar, S. D., Curry, L. A., Sommers-Flannagan, J., & Walsh, J. A. (2001) Student-athlete preferences in seeking help when confronted with sport performance problems. *The Sport Psychologist, 15,* 205–223.

Mintz, M. L. (2005) The school psychologist and sport: A natural interface to promote optimal functioning between student-athlete, family and school personnel. *Journal of Applied School Psychology, 21(2),* 25–40.

Moreno, J. A., Cerevello, E., & Gonzalez-Cutre, D. (2010) The achievement goal and self-determination theories as predictors of dispositional flow in young athletes. *Anales de Psicologia, 26(2),* 390–399.

NAIA (National Association of Intercollegiate Athletics) (n.d.). *NAIA Champions of Character: Code of Ethics.* Kansas City, MO: Author. Retrieved June 8, 2012 from http://www.championsofcharacter.org/fls/27910/1NAIA/doc/NAIAChampionsofCharacter_CodeofEthics.pdf?DB_OEM_ID=27900.

NATA (National Athletic Trainers' Association) (2005) *Code of Ethics.* Retrieved June 2, 2012 from http://www.nata.org/codeofethics.

NJCAA (National Junior College Athletics Association: Region XIX) (2003) *Code of Ethics.* Retrieved 6/8/12 from http://www.region19.org/f/Code_of_Ethics.php.

Ommundsen, Y., Roberts, G. C., Lemyre, P., & Miller, B. W. (2006) Parental and coach support or pressure on psychosocial outcomes of pediatric athletes in soccer. *Clinical Journal of Sport Medicine, 16(6),* 522–526.

Petitpas, A. J., Buntrock, C. L., Van Raalte, J. L., & Brewer, B. W. (1995) Counseling athletes: A new specialty in counselor education. *Counselor Education & Supervision, 34*, 212–219.

Petitpas, A. J., Van Raalte, J. L., Cornelius, A. E., & Presbrey, J. (2004) A life skills development program for high school student athletes. *The Journal of Primary Prevention, 24(3)*, 325–334.

Rollins, J. (2007) Giving counseling a sporting chance. *Counseling Today Online.* Retrieved June 2, 2012 from http://www.calu.edu/academics/online-programs/sports-counseling/_files/Counseling_Today_Online_Giving_Counseling_Today_a_Sporting_Chance.pdf.

Seligman, M. E. P. (2006) *Learned Optimism: How to Change Your Mind and Life.* New York: Vintage.

Steinfeldt, J. A., Rutkowski, L. A., Vaughan, E. L., & Steinfeldt, M. C. (2011) Masculinity, moral atmosphere, and moral functioning of high school football players. *Journal of Sport & Exercise Psychology, 33*, 215–234.

Teyber, E. (1992) *Interpersonal Process in Psychotherapy: A Guide for Clinical Training* (2nd ed.). Pacific Grove, CA: Brooks/Cole.

Ting, S. R. (2009) Impact of noncognitive factors on first-year academic performance and persistence of NCAA Division I student athletes. *Journal of Humanistic Counseling, Education, and Development, 48*, 215–228.

USTFCCCA (United States Track & Field and Cross Country Coaches Association) (2009) *Code of Ethics.* New Orleans, LA: Author.

Visek, A. J., Harris, B. S., & Blom, L. C. (2009) Doing sport psychology: A youth sport consulting model for practitioners. *The Sport Psychologist, 23*, 271–291.

Ward, D. G., Sandstedt, S. D., Cox, R. H., & Beck, N. C. (2005) Athlete-counseling competencies for U.S. Psychologists working with athletes. *The Sport Psychologist, 19*, 318–334.

Watson, J. C. (2006) Student athletes and counseling: Factors influencing the decision to seek counseling services. *College Student Journal, 40(1)*, 35–42.

Wieskamp, K. (2008) No athlete left behind: An athletic academic support program. *Interscholastic Athletic Administration, 34(4)*, 22–23.

Yopyk, D. J., & Prentice, D. A. (2005) Am I an athlete or student? Identity salience and stereotype threat in student-athletes. *Basic and Applied Social Psychology, 27(4)*, 329–336.

Zagelbaum, A. (2011) *Counseling the Student athlete.* Alexandria, VA: Alexander Street Press.

9 Consultation with Parents and the Student Athlete

The greatest influence on student athletes other than coaches tends to involve family members, most notably parents. Certainly, coaches, teachers, peers, and school staff are important, but significant research and literature has long focused on parental influence when it comes to examining virtually all forms of success in school. There are significant opportunities for parents to involve themselves with the athletic development of their children, from volunteering to assist with team events, to attending sport competitions, to coaching, and at various other points in between.

It is also understood that parents have particular rights, and that very specific protocol must be followed in cases where students are identified as having (or are suspected to have) special needs and accommodations that must be made in order to enable appropriate interventions to occur. The use of Student Study/ Support Teams (SSTs), Individualized Education Program (IEP) Teams, Transition Planning Teams (TPT), 504 Plans, and various other resources have particular guidelines and protocols that effective consultants must adhere to and know how to implement within particular school districts and systems (Dinkmeyer & Carlson, 2006; Dougherty, 2005; Kampwirth & Powers, 2012). The Individuals with Disabilities Education Act (IDEA), otherwise known as P.L. 108–446 (December 3, 2004), makes very clear provisions for what types of communication, use of data, and services/resources must be provided to all parties involved with consultative efforts to assist with such cases. Parents also have specific rights under the Family Educational Rights and Privacy Act (FERPA), which school counselors are also specifically advised to follow and align with the practices of the school campus and district within which they serve. There are several examples of how support and resources can be provided for student athletes who struggle with hearing impairments (Stewart & Ellis, 2005), physical impairments requiring the use of wheelchairs (Swanson, Colwell, & Zhao, 2008), emotional disorders (Kamm, 2008), and "invisible" disabilities that are defined within the mild range of assessment (Byer, Flores, & Vargas-Tonsing, 2009; Weiss, 2011). This chapter does not attempt to minimize these points, but rather emphasizes that, in order to serve all students, thorough examination and application of these laws must be applied. However, in order to best address specific aspects of consultation with parents and student athletes, another important foundation to consider are the guidelines established by the Parent Teacher Association (PTA).

In order to best serve parents, guardians, and families, the National Parent Teacher Association (1996) has six National Standards for Parent/Family Involvement Programs that clearly apply to both school counseling and school athletic programs. These standards are primarily designed to: promote and encourage meaningful and significant parent/family participation among all educational programs associated with the development of children; help raise awareness about characteristics of effective programs; and establish guidelines for schools attempting to evaluate, develop, and improve such programs. An effective consultant should bear these specific standards in mind. They include:

1. *Communicating*: Communication between home and school is regular, two-way, and meaningful.
2. *Parenting*: Parenting skills are promoted and supported.
3. *Student Learning*: Parents play an integral role in assisting student learning.
4. *Volunteering*: Parents are welcome in the school, and their support and assistance are sought.
5. *School Decision-Making and Advocacy*: Parents are full partners in the decisions that affect children and families.
6. *Collaborating with Community*: Community resources are used to strengthen schools, families and student learning.

Though athletic development is not explicitly stated within these National Standards, it is clear that athletic development and academic development can be important influences on children and families (Fraser-Thomas, Cote, & Deakin, 2005; Petrie & Stover, 1997; Sagar & Lavallee, 2010) and provide foundations upon which student athletes further develop their academic, personal/social, and career potentials beyond their K-12 years (Fraser-Thomas, Cote, & Deakin, 2005; Lubker & Etzel, 2007; Steinfeldt, Rutkowski, Vaughan, & Steinfeldt, 2011).

There are also particular ethical codes that the American School Counselor Association (ASCA, 2010) specifically applies to the work school counselors perform with parents and guardians. Most notably, when forming relationships with parents and guardians, professional school counselors:

B.1.a. Respect the rights and responsibilities of parents/guardians for their children and endeavor to establish, as appropriate, a collaborative relationship with parents/guardians to facilitate students' maximum development.

b. Adhere to laws, local guidelines and ethical standards of practice when assisting parents/guardians experiencing family difficulties interfering with the student's effectiveness and welfare.

c. Are sensitive to diversity among families and recognize that all parents/ guardians, custodial and noncustodial, are vested with certain rights and responsibilities for their children's welfare by virtue of their role and according to law.

(ASCA, 2010)

Clearly, the opportunity to work with parents can take various forms, but the effective school counselor applies all of these principles to consultative efforts regardless of other services and needs that parents have when student athletes are struggling. If parents are in need of assistance with scholarship and athletic program application, the school counselor must be familiar with eligibility guidelines associated with the college or university being applied to, as well as the National Collegiate Athletic Association, National Junior College Athletic Association, and/or the National Association of Intercollegiate Athletics, so that appropriate information can be disseminated and deadlines can be met. In cases where struggles are more associated with classroom and field-performance behaviors, however, the range of services can be more complex and intricate than information-giving. The former matter will be addressed in another chapter, but for the purposes of understanding consultation with parents and student athletes, this chapter will examine approaches to the latter.

The Case of Mike

We will once again use the case of Mike to illustrate the concepts and approaches to possible consultative efforts that school counselors may wish to take. It is recognized that Mike is a very particular case that does not represent every student athlete, and that Mike's parents do not represent every type of parent with whom school counselors can interact with. The full vignette is presented at the start of Chapter 1.

In the early phases of consultation, it is recommended to get a sense of what interaction(s), if any, have occurred between parents and coaches, parents and teachers, and any other possible stakeholders. Though these interactions are not predictors of all behaviors and characteristics of every interaction a parent provides to others, it may prepare the school counselor-as-consultant for how best to join with him/her during the initial phases of consultation.

It is important to note that parents have varying levels of influence on their children at several levels of development, regardless of sports or other areas of life, such academics and socialization (Fredricks & Eccles, 2004). However, the pressures that most children face during the middle periods of school as well as their sports careers tend to bring out some of the more negative behaviors in both parents and children alike (Harwood, Drew, & Knight, 2010; Lauer, Gould, Roman, & Pierce, 2010; Ommundsen, Roberts, Lemyre, & Miller, 2006). This is a time period where peers, coaches, teachers, and other influences beyond the scope of the family are consciously becoming a more active part of a child's identity, and physical changes are also shifting the child's identity into a different state of mind as well as a different level of appearance. The potential for conflicts and confusion about how parents deal with their children's sport and non-sport related behaviors and goals is high (Harwood et al., 2010; Hellstedt, 2005), and the school counselor must carefully navigate the family and athletic systems of the child in order to best develop working alliances during the consultation process. Considering that Mike Sr. was a football player himself, there could be potential for some conflicts because of expectations he may have for his son that are biased to a particular level or degree that may not be completely appropriate for Mike Jr's ability. Mike's mother, Linda, may also have potential for conflicts because of her concern for Mike's health and safety, which may be creating stress for Mike to feel a certain way about his athletic career. It is also possible that Mike and Mike Sr. are heavily bonded because of their sport background, and this may be overshadowing other responsibilities that Mike has regarding academics and classroom behavior. Also, considering Linda's support for both Mike Sr. and Mike Jr., such a sense of bonding may also be present. The point of these hypotheses is to make clear the fact that the school counselor should be mindful of his/her role as consultant when engaging with parents (Dollarhide & Saginak, 2012; Stone & Dahir, 2006), and be careful not to become too intensely involved with the therapeutic elements of family counseling and therapy in order to engage with the family and athletic systems of the student athlete (Kampwirth & Powers, 2012; Mintz, 2005). The objective and observable data regarding parent engagement and behavior tends to be more valuable for the school counselor-as-consultant for working with various types of parents during the consultation process.

Types of Parents

There are three main styles of parenting that Holt, Tamminen, Black, Mandigo, and Fox (2009) identify as significant to the development of children in youth sports: *autonomy-supportive, controlling,* and *mixed.* Each of these styles can be defined through the level of involvement that the parent has with his/her child, the structure by which expectations, rules, and guidance are given to a child within the family system, and the environment that allows the child to feel like (s)he has a stake in behavioral approaches to tasks and decision-making. It is likely that these styles are not indicators of how parents behave or respond to their children in every scenario, but rather they represent a continuum that parent control exists within, with controlling parents exhibiting the greatest amount, followed by mixed parenting, then autonomy-supportive. A synopsis of each style may elucidate further.

Controlling parents are highly involved with the lives of their children, to the point at which little to no decision-making exists on the part of the child (Holt et al., 2009). These are the types of parents who are able to label themselves as strict, demanding, and regimented in terms of approaching tasks, duties, and responsibilities. Sometimes confrontation plays a part in how feedback and guidance are provided to the child(ren). This appears to be partially related to the fact that these parents have difficulty reading the mood of their child(ren) and largely focus on the deficits of performance so as to motivate improvement. In Mike's case, his father was particularly demanding about keeping a home practice schedule, and was known for being tough on his son because of his ability to "make it" at the next level. Mike Sr.'s status in the community, because of his athletic past, helped to emphasize this point of power because of perceived expertise and ability that seemed to put just as much pressure on him to succeed in motivating his son as his son had to perform athletically and academically. It was clear that Mike respected his father's methods and the authority figure role he had within the household, but they would not have a lot of discussion regarding academic struggles. His mother appeared to be protective of him in many ways, because of concern for injury and health, but this did not permit a significant amount of open communication about struggles Mike was having within some of his subjects of study. Linda seemed to be focused on providing Mike encouraging words in order to inspire his success, but did not often comment on the reality of his struggles or how frustrating these struggles could be. The school counselor might be able to assist these parents because, as a consultant, the use of strategies and problem-solving approaches could provide an opportunity for the parents to focus on collaborative efforts that can take Mike's strengths and weaknesses into account (Dinkmeyer & Carlson, 2006; Dougherty, 2005). Thus, instead of analyzing the personality of each parent, the consultation process helps to educate the parents-as-consultants about methods and strategies that often help to improve the struggles of students like Mike. This is by no means a simple process, but the emphasis of planning and strategy is more likely to join with the expectations of Mike and Linda during the initial stages of consultation, and result in a better working alliance. This working alliance can enable consultant and consultee(s) to develop a balance of power, and perhaps encourage autonomy-supportive approaches that Holt and colleagues (2009) have found more indicative of helping student athletes deal with difficult situations.

Autonomy-supportive parents are not only highly involved with the lives of their children, but they also tend to encourage behaviors more from their children, rather than trying to pressure them to engage in such behaviors (Holt et al., 2009). In other words, decision-making appears to be the energy that drives this vehicle of behavior as opposed to a show of dominance. For example, if Mike has weekend homework to complete, Linda may approach him before the week is over in order to ask him when he plans on setting aside the time to complete it. His ability to decide when to do it, with the understanding that it must be done before the weekend is over permits greater autonomy on Mike's behalf without neglecting his full plate of responsibilities.

It should also follow from this example that autonomy-supportive parents tend to provide an appropriate structure and expectations for their children (Holt et al., 2009). This still means that the parents exert power in order to create the structure, but the child has some degree of flexibility to operate within this structure. Just as previously noted, Mike's mother keeps a schedule for him to finish his homework, but allows Mike to appropriately anchor the time(s) under which he is to complete the tasks that still allows him to have a say in how the schedule is to be kept. Mike understands the schedule, but can adapt to it instead of rebelling from it when it conflicts with other tasks.

Also, autonomy-supportive parents were found to mostly be able to read their children's mood, and use open communication skills when conveying ideas about sport and related behaviors (Holt et al., 2009). For example, if Mike Sr. were to attend one of Mike's practices and notice a sense of frustration on his son's behalf after it was over, he would approach him about it in a one-on-one venue, and comment on what things he observed that Mike performed well in addition to what areas of development appeared. In other words, Mike Sr. is aware of the fact that Mike has room for improvement and that Mike is upset about how much needs to be improved, but is not publicly calling out his son in order to merely focus on the faults. The balance between commenting on strengths and weaknesses is also likely to encourage Mike to ask questions of his dad in order to come up with strategies for improvement, as opposed to feeling uncomfortable and embarrassed about the fact that improvements are needed. This two-way communication is helpful not only for family dynamics (Hellstedt, 2005), but also for athletic development (Lauer et al., 2010) and academic development (Sagar & Lavallee, 2010).

Mixed parenting styles, as the name would imply, involve elements of both autonomy-support and control (Holt et al., 2009). The mixed style mostly exists within a family system that has inconsistency between parents in terms of their overall styles, and/or inconsistency across the situations in which parenting styles are practiced. For example, Mike's mother, in comparison to Mike's father, may take a less critical approach about her son's performance because of her concern for his overall health and safety. This communication of support may be a little more autonomy-supportive than Mike Sr.'s otherwise controlling style to rigorously having Mike practice and demonstrating improvement in his athletic areas of weakness. It is difficult to determine with certainty how mixed a parent or parental unit can be, but in terms of situational data, consultation with coaches can provide some insight into how controlling a parent can be in certain sport-related situations.

Parent Types when Interacting with Coaches

Smoll, Smith, Barnett, and Everett (1993) provided an interesting classification system regarding parental interactions with coaches of youth sports. Each of their five categories are derived from how involved a parent is when it comes to relationships with family and athletic influences linked to his/her child(ren). Though not all coaches may be aware of all communication patterns and interactions that every parent possesses at all times, recognizing differences between parents who are *disinterested, overcritical, screaming behind the bench,* [acting as] *sideline coaches*, and *overprotective* can provide counseling professionals with valuable insights if further work is needed with such individuals in the future (Harwood et al., 2010; Mintz, 2005; Ommundsen et al., 2006).

The *disinterested* parent is largely absent from team events and activities, to the point where the student athlete becomes emotionally affected by this non-presence (Smoll et al., 1993). Such a parent seems similar to the laissez-faire type who does not hold a child accountable for his/her actions and tends to let matters be within the household (Cline & Fay, 2006). Some of this behavior may be due to a lack of motivation on the parent's behalf, or perhaps a desire to have the child figure out things for him/herself. Regardless, knowledge of this communication style can be addressed by encouraging more connections to other parent volunteers on the athletic staff, or facilitating more communication between coach and parent at various times during the season (Smoll et al., 1993). Collaborations like this are essential when coaches are not teachers within the school in addition to their coaching duties, and can help parent and coach develop a fuller picture of the needs and demands of the student athlete as a result (Petitpas, Van Raalte, Cornelius, & Presbrey, 2004). Mintz (2005) also suggests more preseason communication with psychological and counseling professionals as a way of better linking such a parent to the related systems of the student athlete.

The *overcritical* parent tends to use scolding and down-putting terminology in order to address performance issues of the student athlete (Smoll et al., 1993). Some of this behavior may be due to a perceived over-identification with the student athlete or link to the competition that becomes personal in nature. Horn (2011) recommends that such parents be reminded that coaches, related stakeholders, and players have a commitment to all members, and that over-stressing the role of one member can be detrimental to the overall goal of the sport in question. This reminder may help to educate such a parent that concern for his/her child's performance, though respectable in terms of intent, should be channeled in the proper direction, so that appropriate context and team mindedness are not lost on the child or the athletic stakeholders who are trying to support him/her.

The parent who *screams behind the bench* is often verbally abusive to players, officials, coaches, and various other individuals during competitions in addition to his/her own child(ren) (Smoll et al., 1993). This style appears somewhat like the drill-sergeant type who expects compliance and perfection and has a strong sense of control, whether perceived or actual (Cline & Fay, 2006). Sometimes, disciplinary action brought by league administrators and athletic directors may intervene in such cases. This type of parent may not be best engaged in the consultation process at first but, perhaps with appropriate space to vent frustration, the school counselor may be in a position to educate such an individual about effective ways to channel this passion in order to better meet the developmental needs of his/her child (Thompson, 2002).

Parents who are figurative *sideline coaches* tend to take on the coaching role and can create disruption and interference with the team as a result (Smoll et al.,

1993). Coaches are often recommended to establish clear ground rules and protocol for such individuals during parent-coach meetings, usually held at the beginning of the season (Jenkins, 2011). It may also be possible to engage this type of parent in some type of assistant role to the team, but careful attention must be given to ensure dual-relationships are minimized (Lubker, Visek, Geer, & Watson II, 2008).

Overprotective parents are those who are concerned about their child(ren) to the point they threaten to remove him/her/them from sports altogether (Smoll et al., 1993). These threats may be active or passive in nature, and are not isolated instances. This style appears similar to the "helicopter" and "turbo-attack helicopter" parent, in that they both involve blaming other factors for a child's struggles and go to significant lengths to protect a child from consequences, even if they are natural consequences of an average event (Cline & Fay, 2006). It is important to provide concrete and objective information when working with such a parent in order to balance the anxiety and emotionally charged perspective that can often be taken during the initial stages of consultation and collaboration (Dougherty, 2005). However, a humanistic approach that allows empathic listening and positive regard of the parent's love and care for his/her child(ren) can also assist in gaining trust and improving social connections within the athletic and academic systems of the child (Mintz, 2005; Thompson, 2002).

Regardless of a parent's style, specific communication skills are recommended when approaching parents of student athletes for consultative purposes. These skills are found to be effective when parents address student athletes in terms of motivation and performance-related goals, and appear to be applicable for consultants (Keegan, Harwood, Spray, & Lavallee, 2009). Specifically, parents who were found to be supportive and facilitative of their child(ren)'s development tend to engage in behaviors that communicated material and emotional support, and were present as spectators during athletic competitions. This largely meant that parents would be able to make sacrifices of their own time and energy in order to transport and/or supply their child(ren) with accessibility to practices and competitions when possible. Also, when present at events, they were appreciative of their child(ren)'s efforts and did not provide conditional messages of support and encouragement based on outcome. In other words, the actions of interest and support were louder than the actions of showing up, and are necessary complements for one another to communicate effective autonomy to the student athlete. Other studies have also shown that game attendance and material support from parents have significant impact on lifetime sport involvement, especially for female student athletes (Dixon, Warner, & Bruening, 2008). Even parents within families of privilege can struggle with conveying the non-material messages of support to their children (Harwood, et al., 2010; Levine, 2006), and the school counselor-as-consultant can be one of the first school stakeholders to tap into this concept with parents by engaging in a supportive dialogue. This effect may also occur in families that are struggling to provide material support, but have a strong desire to express nonmaterial support for their children through encouragement and positive expectations about their participation in sport. Also, because of the educational opportunity available during the consultation process, school counselors-as-consultants can assist parents with identifying messages of support versus messages of pressure, which can also relate to a student athlete's struggles both on and off the field (Ommundsen et al., 2006).

Parents also serve as teachers to their child(ren) in terms of student-athletic development, and can influence their child(ren)'s development and competence within this communicative role as well (Harwood et al., 2010; Keegan et al., 2009). When playing with and teaching their children, parents were found to be more effective and supportive by student athletes when they encouraged practice, observed the skills of the child, and gave immediate praise of capabilities. In other words, they were involved with the efforts that their child(ren) placed in their sporting activities outside of school and team activities. Interaction with the child need not be on a constant basis, but without this type of engagement between parent and child, student athletes can experience more pressure and confusion about their capabilities (Ommundsen et al., 2006). It can also create an environment in which student athletes are uncertain about their suitability for sport and school (Dixon et al., 2008). The school counselor's ability as consultant to establish a norm of positive expectations and a "catch-them-being-good" attitude during the initial phases of consultation can help model these effective engagement patterns for parents who struggle with these skills (Czech, Whalen, Burdette, Metzler, & Zwald, 2006; Dinkmeyer & Carlson, 2006).

In order to facilitate these types of norms, school counselors are recommended to focus on positive assets and when gathering data from parents regarding perceived issues, and to reframe these items as strengths whenever possible (Ivey, Ivey, & Zalaquett, 2010; Zagelbaum, 2011). For example, a parent who acts as a sideline coach can be given some recognition for his/her understanding of the game and passion for results. This mild level of acknowledgement can serve as a form of validation that may not otherwise be recognized by a coach, athletic stakeholder, or student athlete, and can create an outlet by which (s)he can channel other feelings of frustrations in ways that do not manifest on the playing field and/or disrupt a sport team. Over time, the school counselor may also advocate that a parent like this volunteer for other possible connections to the athletic department, such as assisting the team parent or team sponsor. Though conflicts between coach and parent may still be possible, interactions with the school counselor can serve as effective modeling points upon which better communication and direction for such a parent can be identified and coordinated with the athletic system of his/her child(ren) (Lubker et al., 2008). Sometimes, gathering information through discussion of sport-specific problems can provide this insight for parents, coaches, and counseling professionals. Donohue, Miller, Crammer, Cross and Covassin (2007) have a standardized measure by which student athletes can identify the supportive and non-supportive relationships surrounding their sport-specific issues. Their research specifically identifies overall happiness within family relationships and the contributions of family members to be of greatest influence on student athletes' sport performance issues, which further encourages the need for school counselors when consulting with parents to reframe and encourage positive expectations of these individuals whenever possible. Further examination of the Student Athlete Relationship Instrument (SARI) may also assist school counselors consult with coaches and teachers (Donohue et al., 2007), but the school counselor must be careful not to create a power dynamic between said stakeholders, especially since (s)he may not have the athletic expertise to intervene ethically in such a manner.

Recognizing the ethical boundaries and limits that consultation can provide can further assist this process, as long as the school counselor-as-consultant remains clear and consistent about what interactions with coaches, athletic coordinators, and team assistants are beyond his/her limits (Moore, 2003). However, considering the competencies and guidelines that coaches and other school stakeholders often have when working with the psychological needs of student athletes, these boundaries do not need to be covert or silent elements within the consultation process (Ward, Sandstedt, Cox, & Beck, 2005). The school counselor-as-consultant can be of significant assistance to parents by being a facilitative resource and listening agent that helps encourage strength-based dialogue between themselves and students, coaches, and teachers, and the use of a collaborative approach as opposed to a top-down approach where (s)he is perceived to be an expert tends to enable this to happen (Dougherty, 2005; Stone & Dahir, 2006).

Summary

Consultation with parents can be a rewarding—though complex—process by which school counselors can assist student athletes. It can be mostly information-driven, such as when parents need to be informed about academic eligibility issues and application procedures when their child applies to college and/or university level; it can be advocacy-driven, such as when special needs necessitate resources from academic and athletic stakeholders; and it can be social-emotional, such as when conflicts and barriers to progress are perceived by student and parent, parent and coach, student and teacher, and any other combination of individuals impacting the school climate of the child in question. Often, communication between parents and coaches can occur at the beginning of the season, and behavioral and communicative guidelines and expectations can be firmly established as a result. However, when communication becomes more challenging and student-athletic performance falls short of expectations, a referral to the school counselor-as-consultant can be a valuable tool to help defuse conflict-driven communications and increase strength-based methods to inspire appropriate change within the student athlete's systems as well as within his/her own belief system. However, the importance of being transparent with all parties involved cannot be overstated, because of the need for collaboration that drives this process. Since teams are what the student athlete is used to dealing with in terms of sport, team approaches are most familiar to them when consultation is needed to assist with struggles on and off the field.

Questions for Discussion

1. What potential for conflicts can be foreseen for each type of parent listed in this chapter? How would you as a school counseling consultant be able to deal with such conflicts?
2. How do you view the role of observation and assessment in the consultation process?
3. How do you engage a parent in a dialogue about how off-the-field behaviors can impact on-the-field behaviors?

References

ASCA (American School Counseling Association) (2010) *Ethical Code for School Counselors*. Alexandria, VA: Author.

Byer, R., Flores, M. M., & Vargas-Tonsing, T. M. (2009) Strategies and methods for coaching athletes with invisible disabilities in youth sport activities. *The Journal of Youth Sports, 4(2)*, 10–15.

Cline, F., & Fay, F. (2006) *Parenting with Love and Logic* (2nd ed.). Colorado Springs: CO: Pinon Press.

Czech, D. R., Whalen, S. J., Burdette, G. P., Metzler, J. N., & Zwald, D. (2006) Optimism and pessimism in sport and in the classroom: Applied tips for teacher-coaches. *Georgia Association for Health, Physical Education, Recreation and Dance Journal, 39(3)*, 15–17.

Dinkmeyer, D. C., & Carlson, J. (2006) *Consultation: Creating School-based Interventions* (3rd ed.). New York: Routledge.

Dixon, M. A., Warner, S. M., & Bruening, J. E. (2008) More than just letting them play: Parental influence on women's lifetime sport involvement. *Sociology of Sport Journal, 25*, 538–559.

Dollarhide, C. T., & Saginak, K. A. (2012) *Comprehensive School Counseling Programs: K-12 Delivery Systems in Action* (2nd ed.). Upper Saddle River, NJ: Pearson.

Donohue, B., Miller, A., Crammer, L., Cross, C., & Covassin, T. (2007) A standardized method of assessing sport specific problems in the relationships of athletes with their coaches, teammates, family and peers. *Journal of Sport Behavior, 30(4)*, 375–397.

Dougherty, A. M. (2005) *Psychological Consultation and Collaboration in School and Community Settings* (5th ed.). Belmont, CA: Brooks/Cole.

Fraser-Thomas, J. L., Cote, J., & Deakin, J. (2005) Youth sport programs: An avenue to foster positive youth development. *Physical Education and Sport Pedagogy, 10(1)*, 19–40.

Fredricks, J. A., & Eccles, J. S. (2004) Parental influences on youth involvement in sport. In M. R. Weiss (Ed.), *Developmental Sport and Exercise Psychology: A Lifespan Perspective* (pp. 145–164). Morgantown, WV: Fitness Information Technology.

Harwood, C., Drew, A., & Knight, C. J. (2010) Parental stressors in professional youth football academies: A qualitative investigation of specializing stage parents. *Qualitative Research in Sport and Exercise, 2(1)*, 39–55.

Hellstedt, J. (2005) Invisible players: A family systems model. *Clinics in Sports Medicine, 24,* 899–928.

Holt, N. L., Tamminen, K. A., Black, D. E., Mandingo, J. L., & Fox, K. R. (2009) Youth sport parenting and practices. *Journal of Sport and Exercise Psychology, 31,* 37–59.

Horn, T. S. (2011) Enhancing coach–parent relationships in youth sports: Increasing harmony and minimizing hassle. *International Journal of Sports Science & Coaching, 6(1),* 27–31.

Ivey, A. E., Ivey, M. B., & Zalaquett, C. P. (2010) *Intentional Interviewing and Counseling: Facilitating Client Development in a Multicultural Society* (7th ed.). Belmont, CA: Brooks/Cole.

Jenkins, S. (2011) Coaching philosophy and storytelling. *International Journal of Sports Science & Coaching, 6(1),* iii–ix.

Kamm, R. L. (2008) Diagnosing emotional disorders in athletes: A sport psychiatrist's perspective. *Journal of Clinical Sport Psychology, 2,* 178–201.

Kampwirth, T. J., & Powers, K. M. (2012) *Collaborative Consultation in the Schools: Effective Practices for Students with Learning and Behavior Problems* (4th ed.). Upper Saddle River, NJ: Pearson.

Keegan, R. J., Harwood, C. G., Spray, C. M., & Lavallee, D. E. (2009) A qualitative investigation exploring the motivational climate in early-career sports participants: Coach, parent and peer influences on sport motivation. *Psychology of Sport & Exercise, 10,* 361–372.

Lauer, L., Gould, D., Roman, N., & Pierce, M. (2010) Parental behaviors that affect junior tennis player development. *Psychology of Sport and Exercise, 11,* 487–496.

Levine, M. (2006) *The Price of Privilege: How Parental Pressure and Material Advantage are Creating a Generation of Disconnected and Unhappy Kids.* New York: Harper & Row.

Lubker, J. R., & Etzel, E. F. (2007) College adjustment experiences of first-year students: Disengaged athletes, nonathletes, and current varsity athletes. *National Association of Student Personnel Administrators Journal, 44(3),* 457–480.

Lubker, J. R., Visek, A. J., Geer, J. R., & Watson II, J. C. (2008) Characteristics of an effective sport psychology consultant: Perspectives from athletes and consultants. *Journal of Sport Behavior, 31(2),* 147–165.

Mintz, M. L. (2005) The school psychologist and sport: A natural interface to promote optimal functioning between student-athlete, family and school personnel. *Journal of Applied School Psychology, 21(2),* 25–40.

Moore, Z. E. (2003) Ethical dilemmas in sport psychology: Discussion and recommendations for practice. *Professional Psychology: Research and Practice, 34,* 601–610.

National Parent Teacher Association (1996) *National Standards for Parent/Family Involvement Programs.* Chicago: Author.

Ommundsen, Y., Roberts, G. C., Lemyre, P., & Miller, B. W. (2006) Parental and coach support or pressure on psychosocial outcomes of pediatric athletes in soccer. *Clinical Journal of Sport Medicine, 16(6),* 522–526.

Petitpas, A. J., Van Raalte, J. L., Cornelius, A. E., & Presbrey, J. (2004) A life skills development program for high school student athletes. *The Journal of Primary Prevention, 24(3),* 325–334.

Petrie, T. A., & Stover, S. (1997) Academic and nonacademic predictors of female student athletes' academic performances. *Journal of College Student Development, 38(6),* 599–608.

Sagar, S. S., & Lavallee, D. (2010) The developmental origins of fear of failure in adolescent athletes: Examining parental practices. *Psychology of Sport and Exercise, 11,* 177–187.

Smoll, F. L., Smith, R. E., Barnett, N. P., & Everett, J. J. (1993) Enhancement of children's self-esteem through social support training for youth sport coaches. *Journal of Applied Psychology, 78,* 602–610.

Steinfeldt, J. A., Rutkowski, L. A., Vaughan, E. L., & Steinfeldt, M. C. (2011) Masculinity, moral atmosphere, and moral functioning of high school football players. *Journal of Sport & Exercise Psychology, 33,* 215–234.

Stewart, D. A., & Ellis, M. K. (2005) Sports and the deaf child. *American Annals of the Deaf, 150(1),* 59–66.

Stone, C. B., & Dahir, C. A. (2006) *The Transformed School Counselor.* Boston: Lahaska Press.

Swanson, S. R., Colwell, T., & Zhao, Y. (2008) Motives for participation and importance of social support for athletes with physical disabilities. *Journal of Clinical Sports Psychology, 2,* 317–336.

Thompson, R. A. (2002) *School counseling: Best practices for working in the schools* (2nd ed.). Hove, UK: Brunner-Routledge.

Ward, D. G., Sandstedt, S. D., Cox, R. H., & Beck, N. C. (2005) Athlete-counseling competencies for U.S. psychologists working with athletes. *The Sport Psychologist, 19,* 318–334.

Weiss, M. P. (2011) *Journal of Postsecondary Education and Disability, 24(2),* 161–163.

Zagelbaum, A. (2011) *Counseling the Student athlete.* Alexandria, VA: Alexander Street Press.

10 Academic Issues for the Student Athlete

The athletic landscape has continually changed when it comes to the role academics play in the lives of student athletes. Mixed messages about the importance of academics and athletics appear to occur quite frequently, either through perceptions or observations. In the 1980s, for example, five men's football teams within the Pacific 10 Conference were declared ineligible for the Conference Championship and barred from making bowl game appearances because of alleged improper academic issues; these played out through the media via coaches and athletic directors making several statements that suggested more frustration about the punishments than the actions which led to the irregularities (Miles, 1980). Arguably, this remains one of the largest-scale academic controversies associated with college athletics. Benford (2007) also recounts numerous academic scandals which took place at major colleges and university athletic programs throughout the 1990s and into the early 2000s, which strongly suggests these controversies are a long-standing problem. Lapchick (1987) reported that "all the problems of college sport exist at the high school level" (p. 104). This was primarily in response to what, at the time, was a push for year-round sports within middle/junior high and high schools; a demand for athletic practice and competition that seemed to reduce study time and academic preparation of student athletes, and the ability for some student athletes to be able to play sports with grade point averages at the D+ level, or even with no statewide academic requirements. The creation of Proposition 48 initiated some steps toward change by requiring higher academic standards by colleges and universities, and emphasized stronger levels of preparation for high school student athletes that also focused on standardized test scores. There were concerns about how such requirements would impact culturally different student athletes, because of concerns over test biases, but measures were passed (Lapchick, 1987). Now, academic eligibility standards are being revised again, and the emphasis on core courses, higher GPAs and scaled test score performances require the school counselor be completely up-to-date with respect to such particulars. There also remains concern about balanced students who play sports can be when it comes to academics (Lapchick, 1989), especially since it is not always clear how time devoted to these two endeavors can be balanced within some school districts and systems (Ward Jr., 2008). Even gifted and talented student athletes have difficulty striking this balance and this is prompting various school stakeholders to reconsider how to best prepare student athletes for effective transitions toward or away from sports at the next level (Tranckle & Cushion, 2006). However, with recent public statements that have been made by National Collegiate Athletics Association President Mark Emmert, with respect to student athletes and coaches needing to make educational opportunities a priority, along with abiding by rules (Associated Press Sports Writer, 2012), academic development of the student athlete is a critical matter for numerous stakeholders to address. This chapter is designed to sort out necessary terminology and contemporary issues that affect the academic development of student athletes, and suggests a framework for school counselors to use in their roles within K-12 settings to address these matters positively.

When addressing academic issues for student athletes who are college-bound, it is essential to first understand the three levels of qualification. Each level is based on academic outcome and, though they mainly apply to Division I schools, there are parallel levels of qualification within other divisions and associations. The National Collegiate Athletics Association (NCAA, 2012) lists the level of qualification as follows:

Full Qualifier	A college-bound student athlete may receive athletics aid (scholarship), practice and compete in the first year of enrollment at the Division I college or university.
Academic Redshirt	A college-bound student athlete may receive athletics aid (scholarship) in the first year of enrollment and may practice in the first regular academic term (semester or quarter) but may not compete in the first year of enrollment. After the first term is complete, the college-bound student athlete must be academically successful at his/her college or university to continue to practice for the rest of the year.
Non-qualifier	A college-bound student athlete cannot receive athletics aid (scholarship), cannot practice, and cannot compete in the first year of enrollment.

The most recent eligibility requirements for the National Collegiate Athletic Association (NCAA, 2012) are as follows:

College bound student athletes before August 1, 2016 who are to enroll full-time at an NCAA Division I college or university as full qualifiers must:

1. Complete 16 core courses, ten of which must be completed before the seventh semester (senior year) of high school. Of these core courses, 7 out of 10 must be in English, math or science.

2. Have a minimum core-course grade point average (GPA) of 2.300, with the understanding that grades earned in the 10 required courses required before the senior year are "locked in" for the purposes of GPA calculation; though repeating a course is possible, improving a GPA can only be done if a repeated course is taken prior to the beginning of the seventh semester.

3. Meet the competition sliding scale requirement of GPA and American College Test (ACT)/Scholastic Aptitude Test (SAT) score. The ACT score is defined through the Summary Score of all sections and the SAT score is compiled through critical reading and math sections only; and

4. Graduate from high school.

Students who are to be academic redshirts must:

1. Complete the 16 core courses [the same as full qualifiers]

2. Have a minimum GPA of 2.000

3. Meet academic redshirt sliding scale requirement of GPA and ACT/SAT score [determined through the same test sections for full qualifiers]; and

4. Graduate from high school.

Non-qualifiers are not able to meet the standards listed above for qualifiers and redshirts.

The National Junior College Athletic Association (NJCAA, 2012–13) follows similar requirements to the NCAA, with some details that are specific to international student athletes. Specific requirements for entering and continuing student athletes are defined as follows:

A. A student athlete must be a graduate of a high school with an academic diploma of a General Education diploma.

B. An international student athlete (non-U.S. citizen/non-permanent resident) reaching his/her 21st birthday prior to August 1st each year will be charged with one (1) season of NJCAA eligibility regardless of participation provided (s)he has NJCAA eligibility remaining. An international student athlete (non-U.S. citizen/non-permanent resident) reaching his/her 22nd birthday prior to each year will be charged with two (2) seasons of NJCAA eligibility regardless of participation.

There are also specific eligibility requirements for student athletes to follow once they are within junior college, depending on whether they are on a semester or quarter system. Essentially, these NJCAA requirements boil down to two fundamental rules:

1. On or before the 15th calendar day from the beginning date of the term for the second full-time quarter/semester, as published in the college catalog, a student athlete must have passed 12 quarter hours with a 1.75 GPA or higher; and

2. On or before the 15th calendar day from the beginning date of the term for the third full-time quarter/semester, and all subsequent quarters/ semesters thereafter, as published in the college catalog, a student athlete must satisfy one of four requirements.

The four additional requirements primarily involve obtaining and maintaining a 2.000 GPA or higher, along with passing the appropriate number of semester/ quarter hours based on years in school and season within which the sport is played. There are also rules for certified disabled student athletes that enable appropriate adjustments to eligibility requirements to be made, which require specific documentation and review. The NJCAA (2012–13) has various forms and guidelines to assist the student athlete, coaching staff, and admissions and counseling professionals with this process.

The National Association of Intercollegiate Athletics (NAIA, 2011–12) has the following guidelines in place for student eligibility:

1. An entering freshman student must be a graduate of an accredited high school or be accepted as a regular student in good standing as defined by the enrolling institution.

2. An entering freshman student must meet two of the three entry-level requirements:

   a. A minimum score of 18 on the ACT or 860 on the SAT (for tests taken on or after April 1, 1995).

   b. An overall high school grade point average of 2.000 or higher on a 4.000 scale;

   c. Graduate in the upper half of the student's high school graduating class. The class rank must appear on the student's transcript, leaving certificate or other academic document. If the student's class rank does not appear on the above mentioned documents, a letter from the student's principal or head-master, written on the school's letterhead and with the school's official seal, stating that the student meets the class rank requirement can be accepted.

Thus it is clear that there are parallels of GPA, standardized test scores, and graduation from high school that apply to NAIA institutions as well. Though some high schools may delegate many of these academic monitoring responsibilities to athletic departments, it is clear that the school counselor's role of maintaining case records and files for all students makes him/her a necessary part of the student athlete's academic development.

These guidelines are particularly important to make clear to students, especially because of the intricacies involved in applying to colleges and universities in the first place. Considering that athletic scholarships and admissions are also linked to some student athletes' goals, the school counselor must be particularly organized and clear to these individuals about what actions are required. The 2001 case of *Sain v. Cedar Rapids Community School District* has become an important reminder of this notion. A high school guidance counselor was accused of negligence when he informed a male basketball student athlete that an English class he was choosing would be in line with NCAA core course eligibility requirements for incoming freshmen student athletes. This did not turn out to be the case, and the student ended up losing a scholarship and initial playing eligibility at Northern Illinois University, a Division I program, as a result (Bennett, 2002). This case appears to be a sobering and significant illustration of the need for consistent and clear communication about all academic requirements for prospective student athletes that coaches, teachers, administrators, and school counselors must be able to emphasize to students, their families, and all related stakeholders. A school counselor serving the academic needs of student athletes must know the organizational system in place for handling such processes, and find the collaborative agents to best assist this process whenever possible. Though it is clear that these educational and organizational roles are necessary and beneficial to student athletes and their families, there are also psychosocial factors that appear to link to academic issues for which school counselors may be one of the only resources available to address.

When it comes to addressing academic issues for the student athlete, significant attention has been given to adolescents' perceptions of self within their scholastic and athletic roles. Chandler and Goldberg (1990) discovered that academic grades were valued by a significant portion of high school students, but males perceived high grades and athletic success as the most important factors with respect to defining "success" in terms of social status and personal history. Female high school students perceived getting high grades and leadership status as more important factors, and athletics were not significantly linked to these factors. Males also projected the identity of a scholar athlete to be more status-enhancing than females, who expressed a preference for the role of scholar for this purpose than that of athlete or scholar athlete. Both boys and girls also agreed that athletic skills of boys were more likely to garner popularity with girls, while athletic ability did not carry this weight for girls' popularity with boys (Chandler & Goldberg, 1990). To add further depth to this understanding of academic issue, there is also perception data associated with the idea of being a "jock" versus an "athlete".

Miller, Melnick, Barnes, Farrell, and Sabo (2005) surveyed a significant sample of high school students who identified themselves as either athletes or jocks; the former indicating a self-perception of an individual who favors their athletic performance and ability as well as their academic performance, while the latter represented a self-perception of an individual who favors their athletic performance and ability regardless of academic performance. Of the 600 students within this study's sample, almost 65% stated that they were actively participating in school sports, and over 35% of this portion identified themselves as jocks. Though athletic involvement was reported at higher levels for boys than for girls, it was nearly the same for Black and White students. White students, however, were more likely to self-identify as jocks than Black students (Miller et al., 2005).

When comparing athletes to non-athletes, Miller et al. (2005) noticed some interesting differences for grade performance averages (GPA). Over a two-year period, starting from middle school and following into high school for the majority of sampled students, female athletes reported having a higher GPA as opposed to non-athletes, while male athletes reported having slightly lower grades than male non-athletes. Female jocks initially reported higher GPAs than female non-jocks, but did not maintain such results after two years. Female jocks also stated that they had lower overall grades than female non-jocks, while male jocks and non-jocks were not reported to be different during any point in time. Female athletes also reported greater instances of school misconduct after two years' time than female non-athletes; these specific behaviors included skipping classes, skipping school, requiring calls to be placed to parent(s)/guardian(s), and being referred to the principal's office. Male athletes, however, engaged in less misconduct than male non-athletes after two years. Though having a jock identity had no significant effect on the grades for White students, Black jocks stated that they had lower overall grades than Black non-jocks. This information provides a different emphasis on the strength and power of sports when it comes to academic motivation and performance than some past studies (Eccles & Barber, 1999; Pintrich & Shunk, 2001). In their study involving 132 schools throughout the United States at both the middle and high school level, Rees and Sabia (2010) also found that participation in sports can increase the academic performance of student athletes, but not at a significantly high outcome/causal level. However, they do emphasize and argue that the social capital and adaptability involved with students who play sports may assist with effective transitions and learning experiences that these students can make as they head to college and/or beyond.

Also, it appears that, at the college level, the salient self-identity of the student role appears to greatly assist student athletes when it comes to completing academic tasks, such as taking tests (Yopyk & Prentice, 2005) and carving out effective studying time (Woodruff & Schallert, 2008). Though these studies do not differentiate between "jock" identity and athlete identity, it is clear that the student identity within the context of college and university settings is a powerful mechanism by which student athletes matriculate and succeed. These findings also appear to be relevant for athletes who perform beyond college and university level because of the ability to make achievement a central theme in their lives (Comeaux & Harrison, 2011), regardless of sport performance or other forms of achievement (Mallett & Hanrahan,

2004; Stone, 2002). Thus the school counselor provides an important link to life-skills and approaches to academic tasks that student athletes may not always receive through contact with coaches and trainers.

Pearson, Crissey, and Riegle-Crumb (2009) explored the impact that athletic participation appeared to have with students' advanced course taking during high school years. Their sample was derived from the same initial source that Rees and Sabia (2010) used to explore athletic identity and academic performance. Though overall results revealed that both male and female student athletes were more likely to take foreign language and Physics courses than same sex non-athlete peers, female athletes demonstrated the strongest effect for enrolling in Physics classes among all students sampled in their study. Even after controlling for academic performance, interpersonal and intrapersonal resources, personal background data, and level of school integration, these students were 71% more likely to take Physics courses as compared to their non-athlete peers. It seems that the attachments formed with teachers and educational stakeholders, along with a sense of competitive drive toward success and belongingness to the school, helped to encourage these students to enroll and achieve within a course that traditionally has been perceived by many to be a masculine-dominated subject area (Riegle-Crumb, Farkas, & Muller, 2006; Pearson et al., 2009). However, not all students experienced the same outcomes with respect to racial differences.

Pearson et al. (2009) noted that White female students expressed more positive associations about Physics courses and sport participation than was the case among African American and Asian female students, which could also suggest that there are climate and perception issues that may account for certain academic issues regarding some students. Also, when comparing White and Asian male student athletes, data indicated male Asian students who played sports had a significantly greater likelihood of taking advanced foreign language courses, even after taking overall academic achievement into account. Latina girls who participated in sports were actually found to be less likely to complete foreign language classes at the advanced level, but some effects of integration into mainstream classrooms may account for this particular finding (Pearson et al., 2009). Castillo, Duda, Balaguer, and Tomas (2009) conducted a separate study on Spanish adolescents with respect to sport and academic performance and perceived levels of success and satisfaction. Students were classified as those who attributed their successes to hard work and effort on tasks (*task orientation*) or those who attributed their successes to personal ability and the use of deceptive tactics (*ego orientation*). The use of standardized assessment measures across sport contexts and classroom contexts indicated that both orientations carried over to both contexts. However, those who adopted a task theory expressed greater satisfaction regarding their performances within sport and classroom contexts than those who adopted an ego theory, who actually expressed higher levels of boredom and lower levels of interest within both contexts. Specific to classroom context, students with a task theory orientation also expressed higher levels of personal competence than students with an ego theory orientation, which also suggested that non-voluntary activities such as academic tasks can also have an effect on how students achieve. In other words, students who perceive their personal efforts as the main reason for success, but are working within contexts where they are required to be present, such as an academic core classroom, may have a harder time connecting to tasks and understanding point and purpose. Certain sport and student cultures, where participation is voluntary, can allow ego-oriented individuals to drop out or withdraw when they perceive inadequacies that they may not be able to improve right away, thus not allowing for as great a disconnect or level of dissatisfaction to occur (Castillo et al., 2009). Thus, positive expectations associated with sport-related participation goals may not translate consistently into all academic-related opportunities that all students are believed to have.

It is also important to bear in mind the types of impact a positive stereotype can have on a student athlete. Within middle school years, coaches and educators are encouraged to help students develop positive senses of self within academic and athletic domains, because data suggest that this support helps students transition into secondary school (Marsh, Gerlach, Trautwein, Ludtke, & Brettschneider, 2007). However, many student groups are often more engaged in athletics and/or academics than others, and sometimes calling attention to these differences—even with positive encouragement in mind— can impact their perception and performance of tasks and goals. Harrison and colleagues (2009) demonstrated that, when male college athletes were primed about their athletic ability before taking an academic verbal ability test, they tended to perform better than when they were primed only about their academic identity, especially on test items deemed to be more academically challenging. Female college student athletes performed worse on the academic test when primed about both their academic and athletic identities. None of the students in this study withdrew or completed fewer items on the test, and displayed what appeared to be consistent effort throughout all phases of the study. Thus, even though the title of "student athlete" or "scholar athlete" is encouraged as a moniker to designate a balance of athletic and academic ability, it can sometimes create pressures or additional expectations for some students to avoid confirming negative perceptions that can sometimes be associated with one who is able play sports while attending school (Harrison et al., 2009). Ting (2009) also managed to confirm this finding for first-year student athletes attending NCAA Division I schools, and found that emphasizing non-cognitive abilities (such as positive self-concept, preference for long-term goals, demonstrated community service, and acquired knowledge in a field of study) were factors that tended to successfully predict academic success. The nonspecific emphasis of athletic identity and/or academic identity appeared to be helpful for academic and psychosocial adjustment of student athletes in this study (Ting, 2009). Also, in a study examining the effects of positive stereotypes on peer perceptions related to schoolwork, Czopp (2010) found that, when giving career and academic support to one another, White male students who largely endorsed positive racial stereotypes encouraged Black male students to focus more on athletic skills than academic skills while encouraging White males students to focus more on academic skills than sports. Female students did not provide significantly different encouragement for White or Black students, but generally advised students to focus more on academics than athletics. Though these were undergraduate students, the results indicate that perceptions of peers related to the identity of a student athlete can influence motivation and development even after K-12 matriculation has occurred. It also provides further evidence of previous research suggesting that students involved with high school sports that have relative senses of autonomy with respect to their academic and athletic development, a positive social identification that associates with sports and sports culture within their school and community, and a task orientation tend to demonstrate greater scholastic competence regardless of gender and type of sport they play (Ryska, 2003). Noting these significant factors provides ample evidence for why school counselors can further assist student athletes with academic issues beyond the scope of gaining eligibility and obtaining scholarships.

The American School Counselor Association (ASCA, 2012) specifically states in its Student Standards that school counselors are to explicitly assist all students so that academic issues can be effectively addressed. The Student Standards seem to nicely parallel how many counseling, psychological and athletic professionals are trained and prepared to assist student athletes. For example, the Council of Accreditation for Counseling and Related Educational Programs (CACREP, 2009) explicitly define standards for its professionals regarding knowledge and application of human growth and development concepts. At minimum, its counselors are expected to possess "a general framework for addressing exceptional abilities and strategies for differentiated interventions...[and use] theories for facilitating optimum development and wellness over the lifespan" (CACREP, 2009, p. 11). Academic issues certainly can involve exceptional needs and impact a student athlete's future, and the school counselor is an important link to these factors.

The American Psychology Association's Division 47 in Exercise and Sports Psychology (APA, 2012) effectively links to the school counselor's role through their mission statement, which encourages "training in the development and use of psychological skills for optimal performance of athletes, in the well-being of athletes, in the systemic issues associated with sports settings and organizations and in developmental and social aspects of sports participation." This also appears to link to the Association of Applied Sport Psychology (AASP, 2007–2012) which states in its code of ethics that "members respect the central importance of freedom of inquiry and expression in research, teaching, and consulting." Though academics is not an explicit part of AASP's roles with student athlete development, teaching and decision-making regarding the learning potential of individuals helps to inform the ways in which student athletes develop their overall potential and are taken into account by AASP members. Academic issues of student athletes are also not an explicit detail addressed by the National Athletic Trainers' Association (NATA, 2005), but are composed of a group of members who, in part, are educators and researchers and have a stake in assisting student athletes' learning and cognitive development. Thus, regardless of how academic issues are defined, one of the most effective approaches that is often taken with respect to assisting the student athlete is a systemic one. The school counselor may not be the main person involved with all facets of a student athlete's academic issues, but (s)he can be one of the most important links within the school system to assist the struggling student athlete.

For example, an unfortunate issue that has been fairly or unfairly associated with some student athletes is the issue of academic dishonesty. Cheating—either by way of plagiarism, improper protocol on examinations, or the completion of academic tasks by someone other than the student receiving the evaluation—have long been concerns for educational professionals at the middle school level and beyond (Alutu & Aluede, 2006; Finn & Frone, 2004; Honz, Kiewra, & Yang, 2010; Schmelkin, Gilbert, & Sliva, 2010; McQuillan & Zito, 2011). Some of these behaviors appear to increase during transitional periods from middle school to high school (Anderman & Midgley, 2004; Strom & Strom, 2007). Some of these behaviors are viewed by the students who engage in them as responses to limited time demands and competitive tactics that can be used in order to accomplish assigned tasks (Sisti, 2007). One study among undergraduates indicated that student athletes reported more instances of academic dishonesty than nonathletes, citing specific reasons related to lack of available time to devote to classes because of athletic schedules, needing to maintain eligibility requirements, and/or a belief that it is acceptable to do so unless one is caught (Storch, Storch, & Clark, 2002). However, it is not often the job of the school counselor to provide discipline for or the policing of such practices among the student body. Collaborating with other school and athletic stakeholders, though, provides an important opportunity to address these issues.

Coaches have been found to be important sources of student athletes' moral development, primarily because they set the tone and example for teams and their moral climate (Steinfeldt, Rutkowski, Vaughan, & Steinfeldt, 2011; Valentine & Taub, 1999). School counselors may not be able to explicitly address academic honesty issues with an entire sports team, but providing a classroom guidance lesson and/or character education presentation in conjoint effort with coaches, athletic directors, and/or parents/family of student athletes can serve as a preventative measure by which moral reasoning and decision-making on and off the field can become a more salient practice (Parmer, 1994; Stein, Richin, Banyon, Banyon, & Stein, 2001). Interactions like these not only serve as prosocial modeling strategies that increase peer support and goal motivation for student athletes (Fletcher, Benshoff, & Richburg, 2003; Mouratidis, Vansteenkiste, Lens, & Sideridis, 2008; Weiss & Smith, 2002), but they also allow school counselors to join with the athletic system in a way that does not place a disciplinary label onto his/her role (Valentine & Taub, 1999).

Also, considering that school counselors are often responsible for very large caseloads and coaching staff may not always consist of members who are directly connected to the educational staff of a school, such opportunities to work collaboratively can potentially benefit all parties including the student athletes.

Examples of Programs that Work

Clearly, when addressing academic issues of student athletes, the most significant approaches that athletic and academic stakeholders use involves a combination of collaboration and goal planning (Wang, Yang, & Sabatelle, 2011). One of the most popular and successful programs to assist student athlete development is the *Play It Smart* program (Petitpas, Van Raalte, Cornelius, & Presbrey, 2004). This systemic approach, originally used for underserved students within inner city neighborhoods, uses the resources of community members as well as athletic coaches, teachers, and school counseling professionals to serve in both an educational and mentoring role when assisting its participants. Community mentors are available for social skill development outside of normal school hours; coaches are available during practice and competition times to assist with athletic development and further life skill encouragement; educators are able to assist with classroom and related academic experiences; and school counselors are able to assist with transitions and adjustments that student athletes are expected to make as they matriculate through their grade levels and into post-secondary options (Petitpas et al., 2004).

Another program, *Athletes for Better Education* (AFBE), uses very similar resources to Play It Smart in a year-round fashion that also involves summer residential camp programming, follow-up sessions, and college placement (Miles, 1980). Another aspect of AFBE also involves alternative planning strategies for student athletes to consider if they are not able to continue with sports at the next level for reasons varying from injury to ineligibility. Regardless, this aspect of reality and decision-making strategies overseen by school counselors, educators, and coaches also helps student athletes recognize the need to be mindful of—but not discouraged about—the effort and ability needed to plan for life developments, for which both academics and athletics can be helpful skill-building tools.

One other program that is used at the pre-collegiate and college level is the *Scholar-Baller* (SB) curriculum, which also uses a team of educators, counseling professionals, researchers, professional athletes, and popular media figures to assist student athletes address issues with their development and progress in culturally and socially relevant manners (Comeaux & Harrison, 2011). Though the resources for this type of program can vary, individual lesson plans that address self-identity and expectations parallel many of the same approaches that have been used to assist student athletes with understanding the importance of recognizing academic and athletic skills, which can be effectively addressed through interpersonal counseling dialogues with students as early as middle school (Parmer, 1994). The use of popular media also helps young student athletes feel connected to the material in a way that connects to social aspects of their lives, which helps to saliently identify how academic development and personal identity extend beyond the scope of the classroom and playing field. Thus, regardless of what program or lesson a school counselor wishes to use, it is clear that team-based approaches that use positive feedback and a moderate sense of reality about what it means to be eligible or ineligible to play sports appear to be the elements upon which effective work with student athletes dealing with academic issues can evolve.

Summary

While it is clear that not all student athletes struggle with academics, the expectations that are placed on them to perform and excel inside and outside the classroom can still make for stressful academic experiences. Resources that are sometimes provided for athletic programs can be disproportionate to academic programs, which can also send mixed messages to students and communities about what type of balance is needed between academic and athletic expectations. The school counselor must also be highly aware of what academic requirements are needed for the student athlete to meet and should be in constant contact with colleges and universities along with appropriate athletic organizations in order to best assist all student athletes and their families; the consequences of misinformation can be quite detrimental. However, research and program evaluation data has shown that one of the more powerful tools for assisting student athletes address academic issues is the understanding of self and planning strategies, which fortunately aligns well with ASCA Student Standards and places the school counselor in a position by which student athletes can seek help without a sense of discipline or control being used to guide the process. It also allows opportunities for collaborative efforts to exist between school counselors and athletic staff who greatly influence the sport and team culture present at their school. It seems the more coordinated efforts that are made, the greater the chances for reducing conflicts and struggles associated with maintaining an athletic and academic schedule.

Questions for Discussion

1. What role(s) should the school counselor have when a student athlete is underperforming academically? How would you work with resistance on the part of the student athlete regarding academic performance issues?
2. What role(s) should the school counselor have when academic dishonesty issues surface?
3. What techniques or strategies would you use to help student athletes identify where they reside on the scholar athlete continuum?

References

AASP (Association for Applied Sport Psychology) (2007–2012) *Ethics code*. Indianapolis, IN: Author.

Alutu, N. G., & Aluede, O. (2006) Secondary schools student's perception of examination malpractices and examination ethics. *Journal of Human Ecology, 20(4)*, 295–300.

Anderman, E. M., & Midgley, C. (2004) Changes in self-reported academic cheating across the transition from middle school to high school. *Contemporary Educational Psychology, 29*, 499–517.

APA (American Psychological Association – Division 47: Exercise and Sports Psychology) (2012) *Proficiency in Sports Psychology*. Washington, DC: Author. Retrieved June 17, 2012 from http://www.apadivisions.org/division-47/index.aspx.

ASCA (American School Counselor Association) (2012) *The ASCA National Model: A Framework for School Counseling Programs* (3rd ed.). Alexandria, VA: Author.

Associated Press Sports Writer (2012) NCAA President pushes to clean up college sports. *Associated Press*. Retrieved November 8, 2013 from http://www.columbian.com/news/2012/jan/12/ncaa-president-pushes-to-clean-up-college-sports/.

Benford, R. D. (2007) The college sports reform movement: Reframing the "edutainment" industry. *The Sociological Quarterly, 48*, 1–28.

Bennett, T. C. (2002) Negligent misrepresentation – High school guidance counselors can be held liable when their erroneous advice prevents a student athlete from obtaining an athletic scholarship: *Sain v. Cedar Rapids Community School District, 626 N.W.2d 115 (Iowa 2001)*. *Seaton Hall Journal of Sport Law, 12*, 311–331.

CACREP (Council of Accreditation for Counseling and Related Educational Programs) (2009) *Council of Accreditation for Counseling and Related Educational Programs: 2009 Standards*. Alexandria, VA: Author.

Castillo, I., Duda, J. L., Balaguer, I., & Tomas, I. (2009) Cross-domain generality of achievement motivation across sport and the classroom: The case of Spanish adolescents. *Adolescence, 44(175)*, 569–580.

Chandler, T. J. L., & Goldberg, A. D. (1990) The Academic All-American as vaunted adolescent role-identity. *Sociology of Sport Journal, 7*, 287–293.

Commeaux, E., & Harrison, C. K. (2011) A conceptual model of academic success for student athletes. *Educational Researcher, 40(5)*, 235–245.

Czopp, A. M. (2010) Studying is lame when he got game: Racial stereotypes and the discouragement of Black student athletes from schoolwork. *Social Psychology of Education, 13*, 485–498.

Eccles, J. S., & Barber, B. L. (1999) Student council, volunteering, basketball, or marching band: What kind of extracurricular involvement matters? *Journal of Adolescent Research, 14(1)*, 10–43.

Finn, K. V., & Frone, M. R. (2004) Academic performance and cheating: Moderating role of school identification and self-efficacy. *The Journal of Educational Research, 97(3)*, 115–122.

Fletcher, T. B., Benshoff, J. M., & Richburg, M. J. (2003) A systems approach to understanding and counseling college student athletes. *Journal of College Counseling, 6*, 35–45.

Harrison, C. K., Stone, J., Shapiro, J., Yee, S., Boyd, J. A., & Rullan, V. (2009) The role of gender identities and stereotype salience with the academic performance of male and female college athletes. *Journal of Sport and Social Issues, 33(1)*, 78–96.

Honz, K., Kiewra, K. A., & Yang, Y. (2010) Cheating perceptions and prevalence across academic settings. *Mid-Western Educational Researcher, 23(2)*, 10–17.

Lapchick, R. E. (1987) The high school athlete as the future college student athlete. *Journal of Sport and Social Issues, 11*, 104–124.

Lapchick, R. E. (1989) *Pass to play: Student athletes and academics.* Washington, DC: National Education Association.

McQuillan, P. J., & Zito, N. (2011) It's not my fault: Using neutralization theory to understand cheating by middle school students. *Current Issues in Education, 13(3)*, 1–23.

Mallett, C. J., & Hanrahan, S. J. (2004) Elite athletes: Why does the fire burn so brightly? *Psychology of Sport and Exercise, 5*, 183–200.

Marsh, H. W., Gerlach, E., Trautwein, U., Ludtke, O., & Brettschneider, W. D. (2007) Longitudinal study of preadolescent sport self-concept and performance: Reciprocal effects and causal ordering. *Child Development, 78(6)*, 1640–1656.

Miles, B. (1980) Letting student athletes know the score. *National ACAC Journal, 25(2)*, 3–9.

Miller, K. E., Melnick, M. J., Barnes, G. M., Farrell, M. P., & Sabo, D. (2005) Untangling the links among athletic involvement, gender, race, and adolescent academic outcomes. *Sociology of Sport Journal, 22*, 178–193.

Mouratidis, A., Vansteenkiste, M., Lens, W., & Sideridis, G. (2008) The motivating role of positive feedback in sport and physical education: Evidence for a motivational model. *Journal of Sport & Exercise Psychology, 30*, 240–268.

NAIA (National Association of Intercollegiate Athletics) (2011–12) *NAIA Handbook 2011.* Kansas City, MO: Author.

NATA (National Athletic Trainers' Association) (2005) *NATA Code of Ethics.* Dallas, TX: Author.

NCAA (National Collegiate Athletics Association) (2012) *New NCAA Division I Initial-Eligibility Standards.* Indianapolis, IN: Author.

NJCAA (National Junior College Athletic Association) (2012–13) *Eligibility Rules of the National Junior College Athletic Association.* Colorado Springs, CO: Author.

Parmer, T. (1994) The athletic dream and the Black male student: Primary prevention implications for counselors. *Professional School Counselor, 41(5)*, 333–338.

Pearson, J., Crissey, S. R., & Riegle-Crumb, C. (2009) Gendered fields: Sports and advanced course taking in high school. *Sex Roles, 61*, 519–535.

Petitpas, A. J., Van Raalte, J. L., Cornelius, A. E., & Presbrey, J. (2004) A life skills development program for high school student athletes. *The Journal of Primary Prevention, 24(3)*, 325–334.

Pintrich, P. R., & Schunk, D. H. (2001) *Motivation in Education: Theory, Research, and Applications* (2nd ed.). New York: Prentice Hall.

Rees, D. I., & Sabia, J. J. (2010) Sports participation and academic performance: Evidence from the National Longitudinal Study of Adolescent Health. *Economics of Education Review, 29*, 751–759.

Riegle-Crumb, C., Farkas, G., & Muller, C. (2006) The role of gender and friendship in advanced course taking. *Sociology of Education, 79*, 206–228.

Ryska, T. A. (2003) Sport involvement and perceived scholastic competence in student-athletes: A multivariate analysis. *International Sports Journal, 7(1)*, 155–171.

Schmelkin, L. P., Gilbert, K. A., & Silva, R. (2010) Multidimensional scaling of high school students' perceptions of academic dishonesty. *High School Journal, 93*, 156–165.

Sisti, D. A. (2007) How do high school students justify internet plagiarism? *Ethics & Behavior, 17(3)*, 215–231.

140 Academic Issues

Stein, R., Richin, R., Banyon, R., Banyon, F., & Stein, M. (2001) *Connecting Character to Conduct: Helping Students Do the Right Things*. Alexandria, VA: Association of Supervision and Curriculum Development.

Steinfeldt, J. A., Rutkowski, L. A., Vaughan, E. L., & Steinfeldt, M. C. (2011) Masculinity, moral atmosphere, and moral functioning of high school football players. *Journal of Sport & Exercise Psychology, 33,* 215–234.

Stone, J. (2002) Battling doubt by avoiding practice: The effects of stereotype threat on self-handicapping in White athletes. *Personality and Social Psychology Bulletin, 28,* 1667–1678.

Storch, J. B., Storch, E. A., & Clark, P. (2002) Academic dishonesty and neutralization theory: A comparison of intercollegiate athletes and nonathletes. *Journal of College Student Development, 43(6),* 921–930.

Strom, P. S., & Strom, R. D. (2007) Cheating in middle and high school. *The Educational Forum, 71,* 104–116.

Ting, S. (2009) Impact of noncognitive factors on first-year academic performance and persistence of NCAA Division I student athletes. *Journal of Humanistic Counseling, Education, and Development, 48,* 215–228.

Tranckle, P., & Cushion, C. J. (2006) Rethinking giftedness and talent and sport. *National Association for Kinesiology and Physical Education in Higher Education, 58,* 265–282.

Valentine, J. J., & Taub, D. J. (1999) Responding to the developmental needs of student athletes. *Journal of College Counseling, 2,* 164–179.

Wang, J., Yang, G., & Sabatelle, M. (2011) Coaching psychology: Every high school coach should know. *Youth First: The Journal of Youth Sports, 6(1),* 18–23.

Ward Jr., R. E. (2008) Athletic expenditures and the academic mission of American schools: A group-level analysis. *Sociology of Sport Journal, 25,* 560–578.

Weiss, M. R., & Smith, A. L. (2002) Friendship quality in youth sport: Relationship to age, gender, and motivational variables. *Journal of Sport & Exercise Psychology, 24,* 420–437.

Woodruff, A. L., & Schallert, D. L. (2008) Studying to play, playing to study: Nine college student athletes' motivational sense of self. *Contemporary Educational Psychology, 33,* 34–57.

Yopyk, D. J. A., & Prentice, D. A. (2005) Am I an athlete or a student? Identity salience and stereotype threat in student athletes. *Basic and Applied Social Psychology, 27(4),* 329–336.

11 Career and College Issues for the Student Athlete

Gregg Kuehl

Student athletes have a number of issues to consider when they transition from high school to college and to career. In recent years, the influence of sports in society has grown significantly. Sports have become big business with talented athletes highly sought after and, in many instances, highly rewarded. It is not unreasonable to assume, therefore, that sports participation generates career goals among adolescents (Lee, 1983). While many high school students view professional athletics as an attractive career option, reality indicates that it is likely not a practical one.

According to Figler and Figler (1984), only about 1% of all student athletes will advance to any level of professional sport. High school student athletes and their parents need to have realistic expectations about their futures. They need to be realistic about receiving an athletic scholarship to play sports in college. High school student athletes must also have pragmatic expectations about having a professional career in sports. Because of the small percentage of student athletes who advance to play college or even professional sports, it is important for student athletes to prepare for other careers. In order to prepare for other careers, student athletes need to be prepared for the full college experience beyond the athletic arena.

The transition from high school to college for the student athlete can be especially demanding (Goldberg, 1991). Socialized to be tough, athletes' natural feelings of homesickness that often accompany the transition to college may be viewed as socially unacceptable and weak. In many institutions athletes are set apart from the larger student culture which limits their social network to just their teammates and fellow athletes; this then limits their ability and desire to relate to others (Golden, 1984). Student athletes in college face greater demands on their time than their peers because of their involvement in sport. Student athletes also face public scrutiny that their non-athlete peers don't face. As a result, many of the transitional issues faced by their peers can be intensified under the time constraints of being an athlete and a student.

While considerable attention has been placed on counseling as a means of enhancing individual athletic performance, a principle contribution a counselor can make is in helping the student athlete adjust to the college environment.

Counselors can help student athletes prepare for their careers and other challenges. For students who do choose to continue their athletic careers at the collegiate level, counselors can be invaluable in helping the students and their parents navigate the difficult decisions that they will face in finding the right school.

Student athletes tend to focus on one dimension of their search and application process: which college will give them the most playing time (College Board, 2009). The counselor's task is to encourage students to look at the broader picture in terms of finding the right school and helping the student athlete on a path of success. A number of factors play into choosing the right school, such as location, size of the school, major the student might choose, and other considerations. Counselors must help the student athlete look at life beyond sport.

Counselors should help remind students that sport is only one issue to consider when applying for college. Counselors should help students look beyond their sport to other factors that will help them be successful students, should their involvement in sports come to an end. Counselors can also help students and their parents better understand the admissions requirements established by athletic associations in order to play intercollegiate athletics. Counselors can help students cope, should their dream of playing sport in college not come true, or if they have to take an alternate path to the one they had hoped for. For example, some students might have to begin their college career at a junior college to improve their academic standing before going on to an NCAA-endorsed university.

Counselors working with student athletes must be knowledgeable about the different associations within college athletics. Colleges fielding intercollegiate athletics are organized into various associations (College Board, 2009), such as the National Association of Intercollegiate Athletics (NAIA), the National Junior College Athletic Association (NJCAA) and the National Collegiate Athletic Association (NCAA). Counselors should also note that NCAA members include large colleges and universities, and that Division I schools allocate significantly more money to athletics than do Division II and III schools.

Counselors should know the academic requirements and eligibility rules for college athletics as determined by the college athletic associations (College Board, 2009). Counselors working with student athletes should also be aware of the culture and climate differences at the different collegiate levels of competition. In addition those previously mentioned, there are a few other such groups, including the National Christian College Athletic Association and the Association of Christian College Athletics. Each of these organizations has its own website that keeps current information posted.

Intercollegiate Athletic Organizations

The NCAA, the largest athletic association, offers or oversees the most athletic scholarship money (College Board, 2009). The intercollegiate athletic program is regulated by one of three divisions (four for football), and colleges sometimes have sports in different divisions. Division I colleges are the most competitive athletically. Division I institutions can offer full scholarships and partial scholarships to their athletes. Students must meet academic eligibility guidelines to play. The eight Ivy League schools (Harvard, Yale, Princeton, Cornell, Columbia, University of Pennsylvania, Dartmouth and Brown) field Division I teams but do not provide NCAA scholarships. The NCAA allows Division I sports to have more practice time and longer seasons than the other divisions.

Less competitive athletically than Division I, colleges in Division II have different academic eligibility guidelines as well (College Board, 2009). Colleges in Division II are in general somewhat smaller than Division I schools. Furthermore, athletic aid is available in lesser amounts for Division II than for Division I sports. There are maximum financial aid awards for each sport that a Division II school must not exceed. Division II teams usually feature a number of local or in-state student athletes. Often Division II student athletes fund their schooling through a combination of scholarship money, grants, student loans and employment earnings.

Division III schools are less competitive than Division II schools. These colleges have no academic eligibility requirements (College Board, 2009). No NCAA financial aid is provided at the Division III level, but these colleges may offer athletic scholarships of their own. Division III athletics encourages participation by maximizing the number and variety of athletics opportunities available to students, placing primary emphasis on regional in-season and conference competition.

There are nearly 300 colleges affiliated with the National Association of Intercollegiate Athletics (NAIA), offering 13 sports (College Board, 2009). Most are small colleges with members in every region of the United States. Student athletes competing in the NAIA must meet eligibility requirements to remain in college and to continue to play just as those in the NCAA. However, the regulations are simpler and fewer than those of the NCAA. NAIA colleges do have athletic scholarships. Each individual college determines how much scholarship money each coach will be allowed to offer to student athletes.

There are also 510 junior and community colleges that are members of the National Junior College Athletic Association (NJCAA) where student athletes can participate in sports (College Board, 2009). Junior colleges can compete at three different levels, the Division I, II or III level. Like the NCAA, NJCAA Division I colleges may offer full athletic scholarships. Division II colleges are limited to awarding tuition, fees, and books. NJCAA Division III schools may provide no athletically related financial assistance.

Student athletes' experiences can differ based on NCAA Division level (Watt & Moore III, 2001). Division I student athletes might have fewer opportunities to be a part of the traditional college experience because of the demands of athletic participation at that level. Depending on the sport, the student athlete may face media attention and scrutiny at the Division I level. The focus at many Division II and III schools is different. Most Division II and III institutions try to integrate the student athlete into the college environment. It is generally thought that athletes who compete at the Division II and III level do so for the love of the sport rather than for external rewards often associated with Division I athletics. Given these differences, it is important for counselors to assess the impact the particular institution's division classification has on student athletes' experiences. A general listing of academic requirements for all Athletic Associations can be found in Chapter 10, which also provides important background information about college issues that many student athletes can face.

College Issues

Students choosing to participate in intercollegiate athletics face a unique set of challenges and conditions as they transition from high school to college (Jordan & Denson, 1990). One might assume that the differences between those who are students and those who are student athletes are minimal. Both groups attend college with all the developmental issues related with that experience. The main dissimilarity seemingly is that one group competes in intercollegiate athletics and the other group does not. Playing an intercollegiate sport, however, adds a complex layer to student life (Watt & Moore III, 2001).

Student athletes must deal with such things as living away from home for the first time, developing new social groups, and assuming responsibility of self-discipline just as other college students must (Jordan & Denson, 1990). However, student athletes must also learn to balance their athletic and academic life. In addition to the normal daily routine that other college students engage in, student athletes have their sports related activities also. These activities include going to practice every day and traveling to away games. In terms of their academic performance, student athletes have an added obligation to the coach, the team, and the rules and regulations of the NCAA (Watt & Moore III, 2001). Student athletes face different identity issues than other college students. They might also face stigma for being an athlete in college.

Time Constraints

Student athletes face difficulties related to academic success just as other college students do, however student athletes must face those issues under different time constraints. Student athletes' schedules may be very demanding. Student athletes must deal with the challenge of being away from faculty and devoting time to athletic training and competition (Simiyu, 2010). Student athletes may not have as much control over their schedules as traditional students. They have to schedule their classes and academic activities around their athletic schedule. The major demands for time that student athletes face include: practice, games, traveling, film sessions, weight training, injury/recovery treatment, media responsibilities, and alumni/community related duties (Thomas, 2008). Additional time is needed for travel to these actives, packing for trips, and other unforeseen issues that can eat into the athletes' time. Student athletes may spend 30 to 40 or more hours a week devoted to their sport (Simon, Bosworth, Fujita, & Jenson, 2007).

The time demands placed on student athletes could be potentially overwhelming. In fact Humphrey, Yow, and Bowden (2000) found that 95% of male athletes and 86% of female athletes were stressed by factors such as: tests and examinations, preparing papers for class, missing classes because of travel, and making up assignments. Many athletes may find that they are unprepared for academic life in college. Additionally, athletes may falsely believe that they will be treated differently in the classroom because they are athletes (Papanikolaou, Nikolaidis, Patsiaouras, & Alexopoulos, 2003).

Student athletes who devote a disproportionately high percentage of their time to athletic pursuits at the expense of academic priorities fair poorly in terms of their class attendance and, in so doing, compromise their progression toward graduation (Simiyu, 2010). Class attendance and participation suffers when the student athlete invests time and energy into their sport which represents a reduction in the time and energy that the student has to devote to class attendance and related assignments. Student athletes should therefore be guided to balance their athletic and academic commitments.

Counselors can help prepare student athletes for the time demands that they will face in their college careers. Counselors can help by educating student athletes on what to expect when they get to college and the resources that they might utilize. Counselors can help prepare student athletes for the academic expectations college professors will have and the fact that their status as student athlete will not afford them special privilege. Counselors can assist with time management skills. Counselors can help with the development of life skills intended to assist the student athletes with issues they will confront during their college years and beyond. Counselors can develop programs that can be presented to student athletes as a group or they can work individually with student athletes.

Identity Issues

Student athletes receive both positive and negative reinforcement from their surroundings (Watt & Moore III, 2001). These reinforcements can facilitate development of an identity as student and athlete or can encourage the student athlete to focus on one aspect of that identity to the detriment of the other. The immediate, short-term rewards received from athletic participation invite over-identification with the athletic role. Therefore, for many student athletes, the identity as student takes a backseat to the identity as athlete. This can cause the athlete to neglect their academic responsibilities.

By neglecting their academic responsibilities the student athlete continues to require rewards that are contingent on athletic prowess (Goldberg, 1991). This need for rewards based on superior athletic performance does little to establish feelings of self-worth and an internal locus of control. As a result, student athletes are prone to chronic feelings of poor self-esteem and dependence on sources outside themselves for approval and confirmation.

College student athletes who make a strong commitment to the athletic identity may lag behind their peers in terms of career maturity. Murphy, Petitpas, and Brewer (1996) found an inverse relationship between athletic identity and career maturity. That is, identifying strongly and exclusively with the athlete role may reduce examination of non-sport career possibilities. The researchers found that male student athletes in revenue-producing sports may be especially at risk for impaired attainment of career decision-making skills.

Strum, Feltz, and Gilson (2011) found that gender was a key distinguishing variable in relation to identity. They found that females reported higher levels of student identity and help lower perceptions of athlete identity, compared to males. Their findings also suggest that student athletes at Division I schools have similar athlete and student identity levels as student athletes at Division III schools. These findings are limited due to the modest number of universities sampled; however, the implication is that, despite the different missions of Division I and Division III schools, there may be a more balanced perspective when it comes to academic and athletic emphasis.

In many cases, the sports identity, the status enjoyed by student athletes, and preferential treatment that student athletes often experience can create a sense of entitlement, permissiveness, and dependence (Wooten Jr., 1994). According to Wooten Jr., many student athletes hold the irrational belief that they are special and, because of their status, things will be handled for them. This irrational belief can create a number of difficulties for the student athlete.

This irrational belief is often created by the institution and exacerbated by the adulation that the student athlete receives from fan support. Often the student athletes' school supplies are free to them. Student athletes often get free athletic gear to wear and free backpacks to use. Student athletes are also privy to tutoring services that the rest of the standard, non-athletic-scholarship students have to go out of their way for or otherwise not have. The privileges enjoyed by student athletes further sets them apart from the rest of the student body and adds to the belief that they are to be treated specially.

It is not new to intercollegiate athletics to have academic fraud, pay-for-play scandals, overzealous booster involvement, and athletes enrolled in school with little desire or motivation to focus on academic and social development (Ridpath, 2002). Critics contend that participation in sports is more likely to create characters than character (Goldberg, 1991).

Individual athletes might expect preferential treatment for class deadlines or they may expect better grades than they deserve. This belief system can have detrimental effects on the student athlete, with the realization that he or she is not as special as was once thought. Faculty members may react negatively toward student athletes' absences from class and their attitudes toward academic work. Some faculty members genuinely run out of patience and understanding or empathy for the special needs and requirements of student athletes (Simiyu, 2010).

A life-skills development approach will again work well for counselors working with these student athlete issues. Helping the student athlete with personal accountability and understanding of personal responsibility can help them prepare for dealing with demands from two different worlds. Counselors can help student athletes with issues related to their identity conflict. They can assist student athletes examine disruptive beliefs that might interfere with their success outside of the athletic arena. Pinkerton, Hinz, and Barrow (1989) suggested that solution-focused therapy and cognitive behavioral therapy are the most important intervention techniques for use with student athletes.

One proposal to help reduce the separation of student athletes with other college students at the institutional level has been proposed by the Drake Group (Ridpath, 2008). The Drake Group affirms that athletes are an integral part of the student body and that there is no more need to call them "student athletes" than there is to call members of the marching band student-band members. This is one step that can be taken right away to help reduce special status.

Athletic Stigma

Athletes in college are expected to be both successful in the athletic and academic domains. They must meet the same academic demands as other students while also devoting energy to their sport. Student athletes must satisfy demanding coaches whose livelihood depends upon their athletic performance and maintain self-esteem by performing up to their own, coaches', and family and friends' expectations (Simon et al., 2007). A less recognized burden faced by student athletes is the negative perceptions and expectations by faculty and other students about their academic capacity and motivation.

Student athletes may be stigmatized as being a "dumb jock" while at the same time they may be idolized for their athletic skill. In a study of 538 collegiate athletes, it was revealed that 33% reported being perceived negatively by professors and 59.1% by students (Simon et al., 2007). These numbers suggest that student athletes may not be as positively received or as popular as they believed they would be when they went to college.

Counselors must be aware of and sensitive to the stigma athletes might face in different areas of their life. They need to be aware of how this stigma might cause student athletes to overcompensate in one area or the other. As a result of being perceived negatively by professors, a student athlete might gravitate more toward their athletic pursuits for self-esteem. On the other hand, they might try to overcompensate for the stigma by working harder in the classroom, which might affect their athletic performance detrimentally. Counselors can help student athletes develop a balanced view of their college experience.

Student Athlete Transitions Beyond College

Transitions occur throughout life and can be a source of stress. Students must prepare for a future that does not involve participation in sports. Separation from sports participation can be a difficult time for the student athlete. Counselors working with student athletes should be aware of the difficulties that student athletes' career ends can present, and also how they can intervene to assist in this transitional time.

Student athletes who face retirement from their sport face a number of adjustment issues, some of which are explored at the K-12 level in Chapter 13. One of the only inevitabilities of sport participation is that eventually every competitor will have to end his or her sporting career (Lavallee, 2005). There are a number of factors that could lead the student athlete to end his or her participation in sports. The retirement from sport could be sudden and unexpected or it could be a gradual process. The retirement could be one of choice or could be forced upon the athlete. The four factors most responsible for athletes transitioning out of sport are: age, deselection, injury, and free will or choice (Fisher & Wrisberg, 2007). Clearly, not making the team can be a heartbreaking experience. The consequences of not making the team may affect the self-esteem of those who are cut (Pearson & Petitpas, 1990). Being cut may also impact interpersonal relationships. The student athlete may no longer have as much access to former teammates and must develop different social relationships at college. The individual who does not make the team is also faced with a sense of loss. The athlete must now explore other life options.

One option for some is to participate in athletics at the junior college level and then to try to transfer to a NCAA institution in the future. Students taking this route may have to work extra hard in the classroom to become academically eligible for the NCAA or may have to work harder on their sport if they weren't skilled enough. An athlete may spend some time allowing their physical attributes to develop and improve their skill level and then attempt to transfer to another school. This presents another transitional situation and another possible rejection. Once the player has transferred to the NCAA institution, there may be new issues of overcompensation due to being rejected the first time. The transfer student could also have similar developmental issues to an incoming freshman as they are experiencing university life for the first time.

Many athletes have had their careers ended by serious injury. The end of an athletic career may be the result of acute or chronic injury. Like the athlete who was deselected, the injured athlete is faced with a grief reaction (Danish, 1986). Danish outlined some of the other effects, such as impairment of the self-concept, disconfirmation of deeply held values, disruption of social and occupational functioning, and loss of emotional equilibrium. The full impact of athletic injuries varies depending on a number of variables. The variables that add to the impact of an injury include the nature and severity of the injury, the availability of social support following the injury, and the level to which the individual identified with sport (Pearson & Petitpas, 1990).

Whatever brings about the end of the collegiate athletic career, the student athlete will have to deal with a life transition (Pearson & Petitpas, 1990). Grove, Lavallee, Gordon, and Harvey (1998) found, in a review of the research that has examined and documented adjustment difficulties associated with retirement from sport, that 20% of the athletes required considerable psychological adjustment upon their career termination. Athletes separating from sport may experience a number of physical and psychological effects. These effects include loss of appetite, weight fluctuation, skipped menstrual cycles, insomnia, mood changes, a sense of being out of control, sadness about the loss of teammates, decline in motivation, and loss of trust in others (Blinde & Stratta, 1993).

The effects of not being selected, of being cut from the team, or of having one's athletic career ended prematurely due to injury can be devastating for the student athlete. Counselors can help with the psychological adjustment to life without sport. They can once again help the student athlete see the bigger picture and help broaden their perspective. They can help with the grieving process brought on by the role transition.

Summary

Counselors working with student athletes need to be attentive to the many issues facing this special population. In addition to academic eligibility counselors need to focus on enhancing the academic, personal, and athletic development of the student athlete (Broughton & Neyer, 2001). Counselors need to be aware of the many issues that student athletes face and to be able to provide appropriate counseling for the student athlete whether they are for developmental or clinical issues.

Counseling interventions for college student athletes must focus on developing coping skills in response to or in anticipation of transition from sport (Wooten, Jr., 1994). Counselors can help with the transition into and out of sport during the college years. Counselors can help with disputing the irrational beliefs that student athletes may hold about special privileges that they will be granted once they reach the college campus. Counselors can then help the student athlete set more realistic beliefs about what they can expect in and out of the classroom. They can also help the student athlete focus on their academic demands and to help with career decisions that the student athlete may have ignored.

Questions for Discussion

1. How might counseling approaches vary according to the NCAA Division that the student athlete belongs to? NAIA? NJCAA?
2. How might a counselor overcome the stigma that student athletes face about seeking psychological services?
3. How might a counselor work with a student athlete who is transferring from a junior college to a larger more athletically competitive university?
4. How might parents affect a student athlete and what can a counselor do to help facilitate a positive relationship?
5. How might a counselor help with the grief reaction of a student athlete who was cut from the team?

References

Blinde, E. M., & Stratta, T. M. (1993) The "Sport Career Death" of college athletes: Involuntary and unanticipated sport exits. *The Journal of Sport Behavior, 15*, 3–20.

Broughton, E., & Neyer, M. (2001) Advising and counseling student athletes. *New Directions for Student Services, 93*, 47–53.

College Board (2009) *College Counseling Sourcebook: Advice and Strategies from Experienced School Counselors.* New York: Author.

Danish, S. J. (1986) Psychological aspects in the care and treatment of athletic injuries. In P. E. Vinger & E. F. Horner (Eds.), *Sports Injuries: The Unthwarted Epidemic* (2nd ed., pp. 345–353). Boston: John Wright.

Figler, S., & Figler, H. (1984) *Athlete's Game Plan for College and Career.* Princeton, NJ: Peterson's Guides.

Fisher, L. A., & Wrisberg, C. A. (2007) How to handle athletes transitioning out of sport. *Athletic Therapy Today, 12(2),* 49–50.

Goldberg, A. D. (1991) Counseling the high school student athlete. *School Counselor, 38(5),* 332–341.

Golden, D. (1984) Supervising college athletics: The role of the chief student services officer. *New Directions for Student Services, 28,* 59–70.

Grove, J. R., Lavallee, D., Gordon, S., & Harvey, J. H. (1998) Account-making: A model for understanding and resolving distressful reactions to retirement from sport. *The Sport Psychologist, 12,* 52–67.

Humphrey, J. H., Yow, D. A., & Bowden, W. W. (2000) *Stress in College Athletics: Causes, Consequences, Coping.* Binghamton, NY: Haworth Half-Court Press.

Jordan, J. M., & Denson, E. L. (1990) Student services for athletes: A model for enhancing student athletes' experiences. *Journal of Counseling and Development, 69,* 95–97.

Lavallee, D. (2005) The effect of a life development intervention on sports career transition adjustment. *The Sport Psychologist, 19,* 193–202.

Lee, C. C. (1983) An investigation of the athletic career expectations of high school student athletes. *The Personnel and Guidance Journal, 61(9),* 544–547.

Murphy, G. M., Petitpas, A. J., & Brewer, B. W. (1996) Identity foreclosure, athletic identity, and career maturity in intercollegiate athletes. *The Sport Psychologist, 10(3),* 239–246.

Papanikolaou, Z., Nikolaidis, D., Patsiaouras, A., & Alexopoulos, P. (2003) The freshman experience: High stress-low grades. *Athletic Insight: The On-line Journal of Sport*

Psychology, 5(4). Retrieved December 20, 2013 from http://www.athleticinsight.com/Vol5Iss4/Commentary.htm.

Pearson, R., & Petitpas, A. (1990) Transitions of athletes: Pitfalls and prevention. *Journal of Counseling and Development, 69,* 7–10.

Pinkerton, R., Hinz, L., & Barrow, J., (1989) The college student athlete: Psychological considerations and interventions. *Journal of American Health, 37,* 218–226.

Ridpath, B. (2002) *NCAA Division I Athlete Characteristics as Indicators of Academic Achievement and Graduation from College.* Ann Arbor, MI: Pro Quest.

Ridpath, B. (2008) Can the faculty reform intercollegiate athletics? A past, present, and future perspective. *Journal of Issues in Intercollegiate Athletics, 1,* 11–25.

Simiyu, N. W. W. (2010) Individual and institutional challenges facing student athletes on U.S. college campuses. *Journal of Physical Education and Sports Management, 1(2),* 16–24.

Simon, H. D., Bosworth, C., Fujita, S., & Jensen, M. (2007) The athlete stigma in higher education. *College Student Journal, 41(2),* 251–273.

Strum, J. E., Feltz, D. L., & Gilson, T. A. (2011) A comparison of athlete and student identity for Division I and Division III athletes. *Journal of Sport Behavior, 34(3),* 295–306.

Thomas, E. (2008) A college perspective on academics and the student athlete. *Coach & Athletics Director, 77(8),* 29–36.

Watt, S. K., & Moore III, J. L. (2001) Who are student athletes? *New Directions for Student Services, 93,* 7–18.

Wooten, Jr., H. R. (1994) Cutting losses for student athletes in transition: An integrative transition model. *Journal of Employment Counseling, 31,* 2–9.

12 Personal and Social Issues for the Student Athlete

Playing sports and engaging in athletics have long been associated with many social and emotional benefits during adolescence and young adulthood for various types of students. Though the pressure of athletic competition can sometimes place significant stress and demands on some student athletes (Abrahamsen, Roberts, & Pensgaard, 2008; Grossbard, Cumming, Standage, Smith, & Smoll, 2007; Magyar & Feltz, 2003), the social relationships and mentoring bonds that sometimes occur are largely viewed as helpful characteristics of what sports can add to a student athlete's development (Carter & Hart, 2010; Conniff, 1998; Dixon, Warner, & Bruening, 2008; Hanson, 2007; Smith, Balaguer, & Duda, 2006). There are various reasons why some student athletes handle personal and social issues in ways that can be helpful or harmful, and involve many different coping mechanisms and/or lack thereof. The school counselor may not be the sole individual to provide assistance to student athletes who struggle with these issues, but considering some of the more prominent matters that many student athletes face under the personal/social domain of the American School Counselor Association's (ASCA, 2012) National Model can provide further insight as to how such a professional can helpfully align with other systems involved with struggling student athletes dealing with said issues. Also, taking into account other counseling-related and sport-related organizations provides further evidence as to why the school counselor can further assist personal/social matters that can present challenges to the student athletes and the stakeholders involved with their support and success.

The American School Counselor Association (ASCA, 2012) has Student Standards for the personal/social domain. Though these standards are geared toward the entire school population, the variety and scope that they provide align well with other missions and objectives that professional organizations involved with athletics also have regarding personal-social development.

The National Athletic Trainers' Association (NATA) mainly defines personal-social issues through its mission statement, which is "to enhance the quality of health care provided by certified athletic trainers and to advance the athletic training profession." The Association for Applied Sports Psychology (AASP) makes specific delineations for working with student athletes who present with personal-social issues, especially when clinically significant. When dealing with personal-social issues "AASP members do not solicit testimonials from current psychotherapy clients or patients or other persons who because of their particular circumstances are vulnerable to undue influence." The American Psychological Association's (APA) Division 47 – Exercise and Sport Psychology addresses personal-social issues within its proficiency address, where it emphasizes "training in the development and use of psychological skills for optimal performance of athletes, in the well-being of athletes, in the systemic issues associated with sports settings and organizations and in developmental and social aspects of sports participation." There are also prominent training models that counseling professionals follow which specifically emphasize personal-social issues and clearly demonstrate the benefit of counseling services to student athletes.

The Council of Accreditation for Counseling and Related Educational Programs (CACREP) addresses personal-social issues within its standards regarding human growth and development. The National Collegiate Athletic Association (NCAA, 2011) provides a helpful guide related to mood disorders, anxiety disorders, eating disorders and disordered eating behaviors, and substance-related disorders that is helpful to professionals at the college level, and supports the idea that many personal-social issues—both directly and indirectly related to those mentioned—are important to address at the pre-collegiate level. Thus, when working with student athletes who face issues related to matters of mental health and well-being, conflict (such as bullying and hazing issues), substance use/abuse, body image, and sexual risk taking, counseling professionals are significant links to resources and support networks. Certainly, there are limitations as to what issues and interventions can be used by school counselors to address each of these issues, since they depend on district rules and policies as well as standards of care and protocols that vary from institution to institution. It is hoped that an overview of these issues, along with supporting research for intervention and approach, will assist school counselors with strategies and prevention efforts when working with their specific student athlete populations.

Conflict (Bullying and Hazing)

Adolescents experience conflict from various sources and in various ways. A tremendous amount of research exists regarding how conflict relates to forms of bullying behaviors that are often linked to perceived control and dominance as well as belongingness needs that peers must have as they progress through the social nature of schools (Espelage, Bosworth, & Simon, 2000; Magen, 1998; Olewus, 1993). Certainly, there are many other theories and factors behind why acts of bullying are performed and what form they take, and recent literature heavily suggests that such behaviors are not simply school-based or school-related (Powell & Ladd, 2010), and that they are not easily forgotten once childhood and adolescence pass (Malaby, 2009). However, student athletes are often in situations where their performance and evaluations are sometimes hard not to view without a sense of competition or personal take (Greenwood & Kanters, 2009; Horn, Glenn, & Wentzell, 1993). Adding to the mix are social media forums, such as Twitter, where performance and evaluation can be exposed to a world beyond the playing field and school campus, and these personal and professional comparisons can become even more emotionally charged (Pegoraro, 2010). The comparisons that are made and the identifications that student athletes form regarding these details can sometimes lead to forms of aggression between groups or within groups. Pokhrel, Sussman, Black, and Sun (2010) compared groups of students identified as high-risk with respect to relational and physical aggression over a one-year period. The groups were *Elites/Socials* (which included jocks and athletes), *Regulars*, and *Others* (which included academics). Elites/Socials and Others were not found to display physical aggression after one year had passed, but Elites/Socials were found to display higher levels of relational aggression. Though female Elites/Socials were not found to be more relationally aggressive after a year, Pokhrel et al.'s study does present some corroboration of past research that shows how bullying and aggression can manifest within groups that have a strong need for identification and inclusion among popular crowds (Eccles, Wigfield, Flanagan, Miller, Reuman, & Yee, 1989). Another issue that relates to this phenomenon is hazing.

Hazing can be similar to bullying in that the behavior can involve abuse, but also involves aspects of degradation and humiliation in order to become part of a group. Rosner and Crow (2002) provide an extensive review of high school and college level cases involving hazing activities within sport and sport culture. The Fourth and Fourteenth Amendments to the Constitution along with provisions included from Title IX are specifically cited as reasons as to why institutions are liable when such cases arise, and are also why a majority of U.S. states have passed anti-hazing laws to protect the rights of individuals victimized by such acts. Within campuses, coaches, athletic directors, and other school stakeholders are also responsible for ensuring the health and safety of others regarding such practices. Professional organizations such as the NCAA also provide very specific rules and guidelines for establishing such practices. The main issue, however, is that sometimes such individuals can be disconnected from the student athletes and not take active steps toward reducing or preventing hazing behaviors. Kowalski and Waldron specifically noted that:

> If the coach overconforms to the sport ethic, he or she may choose not to act in fear of disrupting team chemistry, or if the team is winning, success. But, if the coach is not approachable regarding hazing, there may be unnecessary pain and sacrifice by the athletes involved in the hazing.
>
> (Kowalski and Waldron, 2010, p. 98)

Some coaches and athletic stakeholders have such an investment in team chemistry and morale, they are unwilling to see the effects that hazing can have, despite research indicating hazing behaviors have negative effects on a student athlete's perception of team cohesion (Waldron & Kowalski, 2009; Waldron & Krane, 2005). Some student athletes have such an investment in team cohesion that it does not allow them to decide to avoid participation in events where acts of bullying and hazing take place (Jacobson, 2010). Taken to violent levels, conflicts can have numerous dire consequences for student athletes, school, sport, and community systems. Sport participation has been correlated with tendencies for students to carry weapons and physically fight at both middle school and high school levels (Garry & Morrissey, 2000; Miller, Melnick, Farrell, Sabo, & Barnes, 2006). However, there are encouraging signs that this phenomenon is weakening. In a comprehensive review of data from the Centers for Disease Control and Prevention's Youth Risk Behavior Surveys spanning an eight-year period, Taliaferro, Rienzo, and Donovan (2010) detected a negative correlation between male sport participation and carrying weapons and no correlation between female sport participation and carrying weapons. However, there were significant findings that Hispanic, African American and Other male athletes were more likely to engage in physical fights at school as compared to non-athletes; also, White female athletes were less likely than non-athletes to engage in physical fights at school (Taliaferro et al., 2010), suggesting that conflicts and tensions among certain school climates and student groups still need attention. All of these possibilities are why team approaches are recommended when it comes to addressing hazing and bullying matters for student athletes and athletic programs, and the school counselor is an important resource for guiding this process along.

School counselors are often ones who oversee violence prevention programs and the use of peer facilitation approaches when conflicts arise between students (Hermann & Finn, 2002). They also work with several forms of bullying and hazing behaviors, from direct physical to relational aggression and cyberbullying (Chibbaro, 2007). In most cases, their indirect connection to sport programs also allows them to interact with coaches and student athletes in a way that allows these aspects of behavior to be aired in a novel and unfiltered way, because the counselors are not direct overseers of sport team cohesion and athletic programs' performance(s). Thus, having a team meeting with coaching staff, parents, athletic stakeholders and the school counselor can at least provide some transparency and clarity about what behaviors are to be expected and what consequences are possible for those who engage in bullying and/or hazing behaviors. Though clearly not a solution for all possible incidents, the collaborative efforts of the school counselor can assist with the establishment of a safe and respectful team climate that can hopefully serve as a primary prevention method for bullying and hazing practices within and among student athlete populations, and at least encourage those with concerns about on-going behaviors to seek out further resources if such problems persist (Cole, Cornell, & Sheras, 2006; Jacobsen & Bauman, 2007). It also allows a balance between disciplinary action and counseling support to be struck, since collaboration between athletic staff and counseling staff can provide student athletes with prosocial messages and positive expectations, allowing a secure climate to surface (as opposed to a policing and search-and-seizure method for locating those who are likely to aggress) (McAdams & Schmidt, 2007). If individual counseling is to be a form of intervention regarding an aggressor, narrative approaches that focus on the student athlete's perception of "best self" appear to be effective in allowing personal issues regarding the bullying, taunting and aggression to surface, encouraging the individual to make proactive goals toward changing behaviors (Ghaye, Lee, Shaw, & Chesterfield, 2009). Regardless of what rules are in place, a proactive open forum for discussing hazing and bullying issues appears to make a greater impact than a crisis-based reactive response to incidents that have already occurred.

Sexual Risk Taking

The data regarding student athletes and sexual risk taking behaviors is mixed in many ways. Miller, Sabo, Farrell, Barnes, & Melnick (1999) found within a national sample of almost 9,000 high school students that female sport participants reported lower rates of sexual activity and experience, pregnancy (both past and present), and sexual partners, as well as higher rates of contraceptive use and later ages of first experience of intercourse than females who did not play sports. Male athletes reported higher rates of contraceptive use as well, but also reported higher levels of sexual activity and experience and partners as opposed to those who did not play sports (Miller et al., 1999). Miller et al. (2002) also compared differences between strenuous exercise(s) versus athletic participation regarding sexual risk behaviors on a nationally representative sample of over 16,000 high school students. Though both forms of physical activity were found to reduce sexual risk for girls, strenuous exercise was found to increase sexual risk for boys. Additionally, White male students who participated in sports reported lowered levels of sexual risk behaviors, while Black male students who participated in sports reported greater levels. Race, gender, and ethnicity effects have also been examined in recent research with respect to sexual risk taking behaviors.

Habel, Dittus, De Rosa, Chung, and Kerndt (2010) studied over 10,000 middle and high school students in the Los Angeles area, with over one third of these individuals reporting daily participation in sports. A clear majority of these students were female and Latino(a) and, though it is difficult to generalize such findings to all students and school systems, the overall sample displayed greater likelihood of having sexual intercourse and/or oral sex than those who did not play sports. Though daily sport participants also reported greater likelihood of condom use, there were also greater sexual risk behaviors reported by middle school students who played sports than high school students who played sports. Taliaferro et al.'s (2010) study, which contained a much larger nationally representative sample, corroborated the finding(s) of Miller et al. (1999) regarding higher levels of contraceptive use for male and female student athletes, and that female athletes reported lower levels of sexual activity/experience and multiple partners than non-athletes. However, Hispanic and Other male athletes were more likely to report having sexual intercourse over the past three months as opposed to non-athletes, while White female athletes were less likely to report this in their lifetime. Thus, regardless of exact findings, it is clear that student athletes can be susceptible to sexual pressures and risks and may need the support of counseling and health professionals in order to make informed decisions. Assisting with sexual education programs, when available and supported through the school district and community agencies, and enabling collaboration with athletic staff and stakeholders are the main and major ways that school counselors are recommended to engage with many students regarding sexual issues. Adherence to informed consent and confidentiality protocols are critical when such matters are discussed privately (Brown, Dahlbeck, & Sparkman-Barnes, 2006). Also, considering some of the benefits that mentors have for some student athletes (especially minority and female student athletes) (Carter & Hart, 2010; Grant, 2000), the school counselor may also serve a useful role by encouraging such relationships to occur, as well as when it comes to finding role models and sounding boards for some of these life issues.

Anxiety and Depression

Though a school counselor is not in a position to diagnose mood disorders, it is not uncommon for student and professional athletes to exhibit symptoms of depression and/or anxiety, regardless of clinical significance (Kamm, 2008). Sport psychiatrists and other mental health professionals can be highly valuable resources when therapeutic intervention is necessary (Brown et al., 2006; Kamm, 2008). However, the degree of hesitancy and/or reluctance of a student athlete to seek out a counselor or other psychological professionals to address such issues can be significant (Glick & Horsfall, 2001; Maniar, Curry, Sommers-Flanagan, & Walsh, 2001). Recent news events, such as the suicide of former professional football player Junior Seau, as well as other data about college-level and adolescent athletes regarding their experiences and suicidal ideations, has shed important light on the need for more support for individuals dealing with the pressures of sport and mental wellness (Epstein, 2012; Markser, 2011). Even elite athletes are susceptible to performance and nonperformance-related worry, which can last into adulthood (Backmand, Kaprio, Kujala, & Sarna, 2003). Abrahamsen, Roberts, and Pensgaard (2008) found that female athletes were more likely than male athletes to experience somatic anxiety due to perceptions and expectations associated with sport climate and personal goals. Storch and colleagues (2005) found that, within a sample of nearly 400 undergraduate students, female athletes tended to score higher on tests designed to measure social anxiety and depression levels than male athletes and female non-athletes; these athletes also reported lower levels of social support. Yang and colleagues (2007) reported similar findings in their study of undergraduate student athletes; more specifically, that athletes who were female, freshmen, or with self-reported physical pain were more likely to experience depression. Also, freshmen student athletes had greater probability of experiencing depression than senior students (Yang et al., 2007), which provides further evidence that such symptoms are likely to exist within high school student athlete populations. A study of 320 boys and girls between the ages of 13 and 14 involved in youth sport indicated that students with low perceptions of their personal competence in sport were likely to exhibit negative emotional symptoms in sport climates that emphasized strong performance expectations and levels of competition (Bortoli, Bertolio, Comani, & Robazza, 2011). While it is clear that student athletes can struggle with emotional issues and reactions, there are resources that can be provided to assist with their emotional needs and temper such reactions, so that extreme overreactions and behaviors are avoided.

Some of the most interesting resources that can assist student athletes are sports activities themselves. Sabo, Miller, Melnick, Farrell, and Barnes (2005) found that high school sport participation significantly reduced both boys' and girls' chances of considering suicide, and reduced girls' chances of planning suicide attempts. Taliaferro et al. (2010) discovered a negative correlation between suicide attempts and sport participation in males, and White female athletes were significantly less likely to both consider and attempt suicide than non-athletes. Thus, given the appropriate climate and culture within which teams are formed and sports are played, the social networks and interpersonal bonds that are formed between students and among authority figures can be extremely valuable tools by which depressive and anxious emotions can be processed and handled. They also align well with Auger's (2005) recommended guidelines for intervention by school counselors with K-12 students who have depressive disorders. Specifically, school-based interventions designed to effectively treat students with depression and depressive symptoms are based on networks of support, collaboration with various staff members, physicians and mental health professionals, and concrete evidence showing how individuals are making improvements, among other variables (Auger, 2005). Coaches and sport stakeholders can address these factors effectively, but the link between behavior and emotion does not always become clear to the student athlete, because of the context within which sports are teamwork are used. Individual attention from a counseling professional allows the ecological perspective to take precedence, and can provide a deeper insight into how moods and emotional matters might be impacting the student/student athlete (Abrams, Theberge, & Karan, 2005), while the confidential guidelines followed within the professional relationship can still allow the student athlete to appropriately balance boundaries between and within his/her systems (Glick & Horsfall, 2001). In other words, though coaches and family members can be sources of support and encouragement for many student athletes, the pressure and need to succeed in their eyes can actually have an inverse effect on student athletes being able to open up about personal matters that can tarnish the successful image that is believed to be so strongly coveted. The relative neutrality of the school counselor with respect to these systems can enable these student athletes to more realistically open up about their personal struggles and, when coupled with solution-focused activities and narrative approaches designed to have individuals focus on future planning and success, depression and anxiety can be better handled by the student athlete (Kamm 2008; Vallaire-Thomas, Hicks, & Growe, 2011). These preventive measures can also assist student athletes with avoiding some pitfalls with substance abuse that sometimes occur when depression and anxiety are taken to broader levels.

Substance Abuse and Performance Enhancement

Unfortunately, the use of substances and performance enhancement drugs is neither a new nor mild phenomenon within the world of sport. Many adolescents and young adults turn to drugs and alcohol due to family concerns, peer pressure, and various other bio-psychosocial reasons (Swan, Schwartz, Berg, Walker, Stephens, & Roffman, 2008). For student athletes who have a strong desire for social connection and acceptance, the need to physically perform, as well as peer pressure to conform with practices of teammates, can lead to such struggles (Grossman, Gieck, Fredman, & Fang, 1993; Waldron & Krane, 2005). Family pressures and personal perception issues can also lead some student athletes to turn to these devices (Buchholz, Mack, McVey, Feder, & Barrowman, 2008; Elliot, Moe, Goldberg, DeFrancesco, Durham, & Hix-Small, 2006). There have been no consistent direct links found within literature between sport participation and substance abuse (Swan et al., 2008; Taliaferro et al., 2010), but the ranges of treatment options and prevention programs that are used out of need to address students who abuse alcohol, substances and performance enhancing drugs strongly suggest that such issues are noticeably present within the student athlete population (Dodge & Jaccard, 2006; Swan et al., 2008; Tobler, Roona, Ochshorn, Marshall, Streke, & Stackpole, 2000).

Taliaferro et al. (2010) found that male high school athletes were more likely than non-athletes to use alcohol and chewing tobacco across all years and races/ethnicities within their nationally representative sample, and less likely to smoke cigarettes. There were also some differences when racial/ethnic components were analyzed. White male athletes were found to be less likely to use marijuana and cocaine than non-athletes. White female athletes were found to use cigarettes, cocaine, and steroids less than non-athletes; White female athletes also reported less likelihood of using marijuana and other illegal drugs (Taliaferro et al., 2010). Within a nationally representative sample of 15,000 adolescents, Dodge and Jaccard (2006) found that using legal performance enhancing substances (PES) was more common than the use of anabolic steroids, but that males were more likely to use these substances than females. They also found that sport participation during adolescence increased the likelihood that boys and girls would use these substances as young adults. However, when drawing from a sample of female athletes only, Fralinger and colleagues (2007) found that the use of performance enhancers was explained through needs to deal with the pressure to win from sources such as themselves, coaches, peers, teammates and school stakeholders. More specifically, students cited pressure to win as the greatest reason for PES use within schools that had top athletic rankings, while other students at the lesser-ranked schools cited teammate pressures, body image concerns, and competition levels as the major reasons. These latter responses also varied from sport to sport and school to school, where swimmers tended to cite body image and level of competition as the most important factors more than other sport participants (Fralinger et al., 2007). These findings suggest that, although substance abuse and the use of illegal performance enhancers are not necessarily a widespread epidemic within youth sport and school athletics, the issues behind why some student athletes use them necessitate the work of a school counselor to design and implement appropriate interventions.

One of the more explicit models found to address issues of substance abuse by student athletes at the college level is the Athletic Prevention Programming and Leadership Education (APPLE) model (Grossman et al., 1993). With its specific design toward educating its participants about the effects of alcohol and other drugs, APPLE takes a seven-element approach toward engaging its intervention process. There is first emphasis placed on *expectations and attitudes* regarding the athletic and academic responsibilities of student athletes when they join the program (Grossman et al., 1993), similar to ways in which a K-12 school denotes the mission statements and objectives of its system and supported programs for its students and related stakeholders (Stone & Dahir, 2006). The second, but most important, feature is the provision of *education and programs* about legal and health-related ramifications of alcohol and substance abuse (Grossman et al., 1993). This information is often delivered via educators, counselors, and also through peer mentors and coaching staff, in much the same way that mainstream programs within K-12 take systemic approaches to dealing with issues of physical and emotional abuse that also relate to alcohol and substance abuse behaviors (Lambie & Sias, 2005). It is not simply a discussion of warning signs used to see if someone has been abusing a substance, but rather a comprehensive discussion with emphasis on federal, state, district and local rules that establish why alcohol and substances must be dealt with and the various resources available to those who have problems. The third element is the development of appropriate *policies* that align the athletic department's approaches to these issues with that of the campus community, along with the fourth element of *drug testing* which must conform to NCAA guidelines. Though such policies and procedures may not be available within K-12 systems, the knowledge of available resources and referral agencies by which abusing student athletes can be connected when in need is highly appropriate and necessary for the school counselor to have and educate athletic stakeholders about. The final two elements, *discipline* and *referral and counseling*, are based on effective integration between athletic training practices and clinical/psychological practices. One practice should not overrule the other but, when violations occur, the consequences must match the level of behavioral violation in a uniform fashion for all players and sports. In K-12 settings, adherence to appropriate confidentiality and informed/parental consent guidelines can go a long way toward fulfilling these goals (Elliot et al., 2006; Lambie & Sias, 2005; Stone & Dahir, 2006). The school counselor is best thought of as the liaison between the disciplinary and therapeutic process within this type of program, but there are also curriculum-based approaches that allow him/her to take a more active classroom role toward addressing student athletes who struggle with drug, alcohol, and substance abuse issues.

The Athletes Training and Learning to Avoid Steroids (ATLAS) program for boys (Elliot et al., 2006) and BodySense for girls (Buchholz et al., 2008) are two examples of curriculum-based approaches that tackle the significance of drug use and substance abuse within high school populations. Both are similar to the APPLE model in that they involve group approaches to educating and establishing the facts about substance use, and are best implemented by way of counseling, educational, and athletic professionals. However, their emphases on group processing and discussion-oriented dynamics add an element of normalizing and peer support which focus on emotional aspects of abuse, as well as physical and behavioral consequences; it is this link that helps participants deal with the social pressures associated with their abusing behaviors without tuning out the educational and factual aspects that the program(s) also deliver. It also empowers the participants to self-assess and monitor their progress, which serves as an appropriate source of motivation to deal with substance abuse issues in other mainstream school-based programs dealing with similar issues, such as marijuana and alcohol use (Swan et al., 2008). In other words, these curriculum-based approaches synthesize educational information about substance abuse with reflective assessments and exercises. By engaging in such an approach, not only do student athletes feel supported and more able to understand what changes are necessary to better deal with the issue, but also counseling, educational and athletic staff members parallel this process by learning about the social/emotional, cognitive/academic, and behavioral/physical aspects that each agent has primary responsibility for when working with student athletes. Thus, individual follow-ups are possible with student athletes who recognize the particular rapport and connection(s) they form with peers and school stakeholders during this process, which can ultimately enable him/her to cope with athletic, social and academic pressures that will, hopefully, not perpetuate continued abuse. Similar approaches are also recommended for student athletes who struggle with body image and disordered eating behaviors.

Body Image and Disordered Eating Behaviors

Anorexia, bulimia, and distorted body image perceptions are significant issues within adolescent and adult populations; student athletes not only deal with these issues, but also have additional stressors that can increase their susceptibility to such issues. It is obvious that student athletes are often under considerable pressure to be physically fit and maintain appropriate weights for many sports that they play. Many sports that favor thin body design or lower weight proportions, such as gymnastics and running, require athletes to diet and maintain this regimen in a way that can often be strict and frequent (NCAA, 2011). At the college level, because of transitions that are often being made by student athletes and their families, eating disorders and disordered eating practices can become more likely. However, recognizing differences between clinically significant body image disorders and eating behaviors, versus disciplined practices designed to maintain an appropriate orientation to sport(s), are often very difficult for coaches, athletic staff, counselors, peers, family members, and educators to identify (Baum, 2006; Sherman & Thompson, 2001). This can also explain why research studies have not consistently been able to link sport participation with such disorders and practices but, as is the case for substance abuse issues, there are enough known trends and treatments to strongly suggest that it is important to address these matters with adolescent and college-level student athletes.

Within a sample of 1,445 college student athletes, Johnson and colleagues (2004) noted that White female athletes expressed significantly lower levels of self-esteem than Black female, Black male, and White male athletes. Also, White female athletes reported higher levels of body dissatisfaction, drives to be thinner, and disturbed eating practices than all male athletes and Black female athletes within the same study, while Black female athletes reported the same levels of self-esteem than all of the male athletes (Johnson et al., 2004). However, when studying a sample of male college student athletes only, Galli and colleagues (2011) discovered that these individuals cited pressure associated with weight expectations from their coaches and teammates, and pressure to maintain a particular weight for individuals with whom they socialize outside of the sport system (including personal friends, community and family members) as the most significant factors as to why certain eating and dieting practices are followed. Though none of the athletes in this study were found to display clinically significant eating disorders, coach and teammate pressures were found to be the main factor(s) that correlated with symptoms of eating disorders such as bulimia. There were valid findings that also showed that these male athletes experienced lower self-esteem levels when they displayed higher levels of appearance pressure(s); also, similar to Johnson et al.'s findings, weight pressure also varied from sport to sport. Specifically, power sports such as running/track appeared to have specific correlations with body shape and size that carry more intense criticism than would normally be the case for endurance sports such as soccer and baseball (Galli et al., 2011). Unlike Johnson et al.'s findings, however, White male athletes did not express different levels of weight pressure than any other racially/ethnically different athletes (Galli et al., 2011). These behaviors and issues appear to have some roots during pre-collegiate years.

Taliaferro et al. (2010) discovered that high school male athletes at all age and grade levels and racial/ethnic groups were less likely to attempt losing weight, but were more likely to use laxatives, pills, and vomiting practices than non-athletes. Female high school athletes were only found to be more likely to attempt losing weight, but no other significant relationships were found with respect to methods or behaviors associated with weight loss. White, African American, and Hispanic female athletes at all age and grade levels were less likely to report weight loss attempts than non-athletes (Taliaferro et al., 2010). While sports may have something of a balancing effect on adolescents' potential for developing body image and eating disorders, it is still clear that these issues exist within school climates, and that homogenous sample studies provide some insight as to why.

Leone and colleagues (2011) conducted a study on male adolescents, 85% of which reported sport participation of some kind, and discovered factors related to Body Image Disorder (BID) among these participants. Several social factors such as the inability to cope with criticism from family members, aspiring to media images of an "ideal" body, having few friends and a limited social network, and enduring taunts and teasing during points of physical growth appeared to moderately or strongly correlate with BID, and to a certain but small extent, thoughts about using androgenic-anabolic steroids (AAS) (Leone et al., 2011). Elliot et al. (2006) found very similar social issues related to body image, disordered eating and the use of body-shaping drugs when studying female samples of middle and high school students. The effects of low self-esteem, media perceptions of men and women, peer and family pressures related to appearance and success, and a lack of teammate/peer bonding were found to be some of the strongest predictors of these disordered behaviors (Elliot et al., 2006). It seems that, without the ability to process and discuss personal feelings and perceptions regarding body image and health practices, symptoms of disorders are more likely to manifest and intensify. Thus, school counselors are helpful resources for student athletes when it comes to facilitating the emotional dialogue(s) and social connections necessary to prevent some of these issues from developing into greater disorders. While coaches and teachers can be available to student athletes for such purposes, their tendency to focus on performance and outcome can sometimes not connect with these deeper-level issues that can relieve some of the pressures that student athletes face regarding their perceptions and beliefs about their appearance. Fortunately, some effective school-based programs exist to bridge this gap between stakeholders and between emotional and behavioral matters associated with BID and related health behaviors.

One specific curriculum designed to address disordered eating and the use of body-shaping drugs among male high school students is the Athletes Training and Learning to Avoid Steroids (ATLAS) program (introduced above) and, for female student athletes, the Athletes Targeting Healthy Exercise and Nutrition Alternatives (ATHENA) program (both Elliot et al., 2006). A combination of reflective exercises and education about healthy behaviors are used to encourage participants to elaborate on their beliefs regarding their bodies, why they feel particular ways about themselves as the result of their appearance(s), and what plans they can make to develop healthier behaviors. Though these programs are often led by coaches and team captain peers, they link to social and emotional issues that often require the involvement of the school counselor, nurse and/or psychologist. It is because of the curriculum's emphasis on fact-based discussions about personal health practices within their small group lesson plans, and supplementary use of interpersonal change agents for further discussion, that these programs have been viewed as largely successful tools by which student athletes can address BID and weight issues (Elliot et al., 2006). However, when seeking more individualized treatment, school counselors are recommended to provide particular forms of assistance for these students.

In respect of school-based counseling approaches to eating disorders and body image, much of the research supports the use of narrative approaches, solution-focused planning, and cognitive behavioral theory (Abood & Black, 2000; Bardick, Bernes, McCulloch, Witko, Spriddle, Roest, 2004; Buchholtz et al., 2008; Choate, 2007). The narrative approach greatly assists during the initial phases of counseling, because it allows the student athlete to openly describe his/her concerns about who (s)he is and what his/her behaviors regarding health and image are like (Bardick et al., 2004). Presenting information about health risk factors and essentially lecturing the student athlete at this point in the counseling relationship is not likely to establish a climate of trust and comfort, and will not likely appear to the client to be anything different from what coaches and athletic staff normally speak about with respect to sport performance. Even in cases where the student athlete may not initially feel comfortable discussing his/her own issues with eating and/or body image, other documented narratives can be shared with him/her to help normalize the fact that what (s)he is going through is not an isolated case; there are materials that exist for boys and girls, as well as athletes and non-athletes that can assist with this process (Brooks-Reese, 2007; Grant, 2000). Student athletes will often work with coaches and athletic professionals to assist with more physical matters such as dietary and weight maintenance, but the school counselor can provide some strategies and exercises that can assist with their motivation to continue with these practices once they are established; this is where solution-focused approaches such as scaling questions, miracle questions, and the use of exceptions often help (Bardick et al., 2004; Choate, 2007; Vallaire-Thomas et al., 2011). Also, since the student athlete is likely to be prone to progress and setbacks along the way, cognitive behavioral approaches that require him/her to focus on the antecedents, behaviors, and consequences of the actions (s)he takes enable him/her to create strategies that can best prevent setbacks from derailing the entire improvement process (Bardick et al., 2004; Choate, 2007). Being able to reflect on media images which trigger particular reactions is one method by which the student athlete can be mindful of such antecedents. Keeping a personal journal that documents the events and reactions that (s)he encounters along the way of the sport season, and the counseling process, can also be an effective way by which student athletes can mentally focus on these issues, and, when shared with trusted others within their family and/or school support network, can lead to greater feelings of security and efficacy which further reinforce the process of change (Baum, 2006; Choate, 2007). Journaling also helps to uncover strengths and personal assets that may not otherwise be concrete enough for the performing student athlete to fully credit to him/herself. Thus, using the journal to document such strengths also provides the student athlete with alternative strategies to combat the difficulties (s)he may encounter as a result of attempting to make changes. Ideally, the counseling process can also enable the establishment of support networks and groups to be established for student athletes who struggle with these issues, but school counselors must also be mindful of how they are to publicize these resources and recruit participants, so as not to compromise confidentiality and the need to have certain levels of privacy exist within the otherwise transparent climate that can be a school campus (Stone & Dahir, 2006). However, in the end, these approaches are likely to be valued and appreciated by the student athlete and athletic staff, because the difficult balance they must keep between the performance-based evaluations they must provide and personally focused issue(s) that may not be their area of expertise within the context of sport culture and sporting seasons.

Summary

This chapter presented a brief overview of various personal-social issues that student athletes can encounter during their K-12 years. It should be more than obvious that these issues are more complex and intricate for every individual athlete than any large-scale research study can ever provide, but recent studies have indicated that the particular issues cited in this chapter remain significant for school counselors to explore and collaborate with other school and community-based professionals when addressing them with student athletes they may encounter. Although coaches and athletic staff are usually well-connected with student athletes in terms of schedules and practices, they are not always aware of the emotional and personal facets behind some of the behaviors their players exhibit. The expertise they often have regarding motivation and sport performance can sometimes be an obstacle for student athletes who struggle with personal-social issues to feel a sense of connection, especially with ascribed roles of evaluative power also complicating the relationship. The school counselor can help reduce much of this burden by collaborating with coaches, parents, teachers, and athletic staff during early points in the sport season, providing some classroom guidance and informational materials regarding bullying/hazing, anxiety/depression, alcohol/substance abuse, and body image/disordered eating, so that these topics are not covert issues that are only dealt with after they have reached levels of crisis. These collaborations can help messages of punishment and consequence remain within the systems expected to enforce such actions, and not compromise the therapeutic and supportive nature of the roles that counseling and psychological staff are expected to have. They can also make each party more aware of warning signs and symptoms that can assist with the identification and treatment of future student athletes who may be struggling with similar issues, which establishes a climate of prevention-mindedness instead of judgmental scrutiny when it comes to assisting those who have personal-social matters affecting their performance(s). Regardless of whether a group approach, curriculum-based presentation, or individual session delivery is employed, the school counselor is recommended to start with a narrative style that enables the student athlete to present him/her self as a person experiencing a problem, as opposed to a person defined by the problem (s)he has. This way, future plans and goals can be perceived as more approachable and able to be worked through when setbacks occur. With the appropriate use of confidentiality and informed/parental consent, the student athlete can also be encouraged to seek out other forms of personal/social support that can be available as the sport season continues and stress levels increase. In the end, however, the use of teamwork can help combat the personal feelings of frustration and uncertainty that may be correlated with the competitive nature of sports, and allow the proper balance between personal and professional growth for the student athlete to occur.

Questions for Discussion

1. What are the appropriate ways for a school counselor to promote personal-social groups for student athletes? What are the advantages and disadvantages of approaching personal-social issues in heterogeneous groups? Homogenous groups?
2. What level of involvement should the school counselor have with respect to hazing and bullying behaviors of student athletes? How can this role best be defined and related to athletic staff?
3. What conditions are best for school-based counseling approaches regarding alcohol/substance abuse? Body image and disordered eating behaviors?

References

Abood, D. A., & Black, D. R. (2000) Health education prevention for eating disorders among college female athletes. *American Journal of Health Behavior, 24(3)*, 209–219.

Abrahamsen, F. E., Roberts, G. C., & Pensgaard, A. M. (2008) Achievement goals and gender effects on multidimensional anxiety in national elite sport. *Psychology of Sport and Exercise, 9*, 449–464.

Abrams, K., Theberge, S. K., & Karan, O. C. (2005) Children who are depressed: An ecological approach. *Professional School Counseling, 8(3),* 284–292.

ASCA (American School Counselor Association) (2012) *The ASCA National Model: A Framework for School Counseling Programs* (3rd ed.). Alexandria, VA: Author.

Auger, R. W. (2005) School-based interventions for students with depressive disorders. *Professional School Counseling, 8(4),* 344–352.

Backmand, H., Kaprio, J., Kujala, U., & Sarna, S. (2003) Influence of physical activity on depression and anxiety of former elite athletes. *International Journal of Sports Medicine, 24,* 609–619.

Bardick, A. D., Bernes, K. B., McCulloch, A. R. M., Witko, K. D., Spriddle, J. W., & Roest, A. R. (2004) Eating disorder intervention, prevention, and treatment: Recommendations for school counselors. *Professional School Counseling, 8(2),* 168–175.

Baum, A. (2006) Eating disorders in the male athlete. *Sports Medicine, 36(1),* 1–6.

Bortoli, L., Bertollo, M., Comani, S., & Robazza, C. (2011) Competence, achievement goals, motivational climate, and pleasant biopsychosocial states in youth sport. *Journal of Sports Sciences, 29(2),* 171–180.

Brooks-Reese, K. E. (2007) Skinny boy: A young man's battle and triumph over anorexia. *School Library Journal, 53(12),* 162.

Brown, C., Dahlbeck, D. T., & Sparkman-Barnes, L. (2006) Collaborative relationships: School counselors and non-school mental health professionals working together to improve the mental health needs of students. *Professional School Counseling, 9(4),* 332–335.

Buchholz, A., Mack, H., McVey, G., Feder, S., & Barrowman, N. (2008) BodySense: An evaluation of a positive body image intervention on sport climate for female athletes. *Eating Disorders, 16,* 308–321.

Carter, A. R., & Hart, A. (2010) Perspectives of mentoring: The Black female student-athlete. *Sport Management Review, 13,* 382–394.

Chibbaro, J. S. (2007) School counselors and the cyberbully: Interventions and implications. *Professional School Counseling, 11(1),* 65–68.

Choate, L. H. (2007) Counseling adolescent girls for body image resilience: Strategies for school counselors. *Professional School Counseling, 10(3),* 317–323.

Cole, J. C. M., Cornell, D. G., & Sheras, P. (2006) Identification of school bullies by survey methods. *Professional School Counseling, 9(4),* 305–313.

Conniff, R. (1998) The joy of women's sports: A whole generation of girls knows it's not how a body looks, it's what it can do. *The Nation, 10(17),* 26–30.

Dixon, M. A., Warner, S. M., & Bruening, J. E. (2008) More than just letting them play: Parental influence on women's lifetime sport involvement. *Sociology of Sport Journal, 25,* 538–559.

Dodge, T. L., & Jaccard, J. J. (2006) The effect of high school sports participation on the use of performance-enhancing substances in young adulthood. *Journal of Adolescent Health, 39,* 367–373.

Eccles, J., Wigfield, A., Flanagan, C., Miller, C., Rueman, D., & Yee, D. (1989) Self-concepts, domain values, and self-esteem: Relations and changes at early adolescence. *Journal of Personality, 57,* 283–310.

Elliot, D. L., Moe, E. L., Goldberg, L., DeFrancesco, C. A., Durham, M. B., & Hix-Small, H. (2006) Definition and outcome of a curriculum to prevent disordered eating and body-shaping drug use. *Journal of School Health, 76(2),* 67–73.

Epstein, D. (2012) Depression and football: Uncertain connections. *Sports Illustrated, 116(20),* 46–47.

Espelage, D. L., Bosworth, K., & Simon, T. R. (2000) Examining the social context of bullying behaviors in early adolescence. *Journal of Counseling and Development, 78,* 326–333.

Fralinger, B. K., Pinto-Zipp, G., Olson, V., & Simpkins, S. (2007) Female athletes and performance-enhancer usage. *Journal of College Teaching and Learning, 4(12),* 33–44.

Galli, N., Reel, J. J., Petrie, T., Greenleaf, C., & Carter, J. (2011) Preliminary development of the weight pressures in sport scale for male athletes. *Journal of Sport Behavior, 34(1),* 47–68.

Garry, J., & Morrissey, S. (2000) Team sports participation and risk taking behaviors among a biracial middle school population. *Clinical Journal of Sports Medicine, 10,* 185–190.

Ghaye, T., Lee, S., Shaw, D. J., & Chesterfield, G. (2009) When winning is not enough: Learning through reflections on the "best self". *Reflective Practice, 10(3),* 385–401.

Glick, I. D., & Horsfall, J. L. (2001) Psychiatric conditions in sports: Diagnosis, treatment, and quality of life. *The Physician and Sports Medicine, 29(8),* 45–50.

Grant, D. F. (2000) The journey through college of seven gifted females: Influences on their career related decisions. *Roeper Review, 22(4),* 251–261.

Greenwood, P. B., & Kanters, M. A. (2009) Talented male athletes: Exemplary character or questionable characters? *Journal of Sport Behavior, 32(3),* 298–324.

Grossbard, J. R., Cumming, S. P., Standage, M., Smith, R. E., & Smoll, F. L. (2007) Social desirability and relations between goal orientations and competitive trait anxiety in young athletes. *Psychology of Sport and Exercise, 8,* 491–505.

Grossman, S. J., Gieck, J., Freedman, A., & Fang, W. L. (1993) The Athletic Prevention Programming and Leadership Education (APPLE) model: Developing substance abuse prevention programs. *Journal of Athletic Training, 28(2),* 137–144.

Habel, M. A., Dittus, P. J., De Rosa, C. J., Chung, E. Q., & Kerndt, P. R. (2010) Daily participation in sports and students' sexual activity. *Perspectives on Sexual and Reproductive Health, 42(4),* 244–250.

Hanson, S. L. (2007) Young women, sports, and science. *Theory into Practice, 46(2),* 155–161.

Hermann, M. A., & Finn, A. (2002) An ethical and legal perspective on the role of school counselors in preventing violence in schools. *Professional School Counseling, 6(1),* 46–54.

Horn, T. S., Glenn, S. D., & Wentzell, A. B. (1993) Sources of information underlying personal ability judgments in high school athletes. *Pediatric Exercise Science, 5,* 263–274.

Jacobsen, K. E., & Bauman, S. (2007) Bullying in schools: School counselors' responses to three types of bullying incidents. *Professional School Counseling, 11(1),* 1–9.

Jacobson, R. B. (2010) On bullshit and bullying: Taking seriously those we educate. *Journal of Moral Education, 39(4),* 437–448.

Johnson, C., Crosby, R., Engel, S., Mitchell, J., Powers, P., Wittrock, D., & Wonderlich, S. (2004) Gender, ethnicity, self-esteem, and disordered eating among college athletes. *Eating Behaviors, 5,* 147–156.

Kamm, R. L. (2008) Diagnosing emotional disorders in athletes: A sport psychiatrist's perspective. *Journal of Clinical Sport Psychology, 2,* 178–201.

Kowalski, C., & Waldron, J. (2010) Looking the other way: Athletes' perceptions of coaches responses to hazing. *International Journal of Sports Science & Coaching, 5(1),* 87–100.

Lambie, G. W., & Sias, S. M. (2005) Children of alcoholics: Implication for professional school counseling. *Professional School Counseling, 8(3),* 266–274.

Leone, J. E., Fetro, J. V., Kittleson, M., Welshimer, K. J., Partridge, J. A., & Robertson, S. L. (2011) Predictors of adolescent male body image dissatisfaction: Implications for negative health practices and consequences for school health form a regionally representative sample. *Journal of School Health, 81(4)*, 174–184.

McAdams, C. R., & Schmidt, C. D. (2007) How to help a bully: Recommendations for counseling the proactive aggressor. *Professional School Counseling, 11(2)*, 120–128.

Magen, Z. (1998) *Exploring Adolescent Happiness: Commitment, Purpose and Fulfillment.* Thousand Oaks, CA: Sage.

Magyar, T. M., & Feltz, D. J. (2003) The influence of dispositional and situational tendencies on adolescent girls' sport confidence sources. *Psychology of Sport and Exercise, 4*, 175–190.

Malaby, M. (2009) Public and secret agents: Personal power and reflective agency in male memories of childhood violence and bullying. *Gender and Education, 21(4)*, 371–386.

Maniar, S. D., Curry, L. A., Sommers-Flanagan, J., & Walsh, J. A. (2001) Student athlete preferences in seeking help when confronted with sport performance problems. *The Sport Psychologist, 15*, 205–223.

Markser, V. Z. (2011) Sport psychiatry and psychotherapy. Mental strains and disorders in professional sports. Challenge and answer to societal changes. *European Archives of Psychiatry and Clinical Neuroscience, 261*, S182–S185.

Miller, K. E., Melnick, M. J., Farrell, M. P., Sabo, D. F., & Barnes, G. M. (2006) Jocks, gender, binge drinking, and adolescent violence. *Journal of Interpersonal Violence, 21*, 105–120.

Miller, K. E., Sabo, D. F., Farrell, M. P., Barnes, G. M., & Melnick, M. J. (1999) Sports, sexual behavior, contraceptive use, and pregnancy among female and male high school students: Testing cultural resource theory. *Sociology of Sport Journal, 16*, 366–387.

NCAA (National Collegiate Athletic Association) (2011) *Managing Student Athletes' Mental Health Issues.* Bloomington, IN: Author.

Olweus, D. (1993) *Bullying at School: What We Know and What We Can Do.* Cambridge, MA: Blackwell.

Pegoraro, A. (2010) Look who's talking – Athletes on Twitter: A case study. *International Journal of Sport Communication, 3*, 501–514.

Pokhrel, P., Sussman, S., Black, D., & Sun, P. (2010) Peer group self-identification as a predictor of relational and physical aggression among high school students. *Journal of School Health, 80(5)*, 249–258.

Powell, M. D., & Ladd, L. D. (2010) Bullying: A review of the literature and implications for family therapists. *The American Journal of Family Therapy, 38*, 189–206.

Rosner, S. R., & Crow, R. B. (2002) Institutional liability for hazing in interscholastic sports. *Houston Law Review, 39*, 275–305.

Sabo, D., Miller, K. E., Melnick, M. J., Farrell, M. P., & Barnes, G. M. (2005) High school athletic participation and adolescent suicide. *International Review for the Sociology of Sport, 40(1)*, 5–23.

Sherman, R. T., & Thompson, R. A. (2001) Athletes and disordered eating: Four major issues for the professional psychologist. *Professional Psychology: Research and Practice, 32(1)*, 27–33.

Smith, A. L., Balaguer, I., & Duda. J. L. (2006) Goal orientation profile differences on perceived motivational climate, perceived peer relationships, and motivation-related responses of youth athletes. *Journal of Sports Sciences, 24(12)*, 1315–1327.

Stone, C. B., & Dahir, C. A. (2006) *The Transformed School Counselor.* Boston: Lahaska Press.

Storch, E. A., Storch, J. B., Killiany, E. M., & Roberti, J. W. (2005) Self-reported psychopathology in athletes: A comparison of intercollegiate student athletes and non-athletes. *Journal of Sport Behavior, 28(1),* 86–98.

Swan, M., Schwartz, S., Berg, B., Walker, D., Stephens, R., & Roffman, R. (2008) The teen marijuana check-up: In school protocol for eliciting voluntary self-assessment of marijuana use. *Journal of Social Work Practice in the Addictions, 8(3),* 284–302.

Taliaferro, L. A., Rienzo, B. A., & Donovan, K. A. (2010) Relationships between youth sport participation and selected health risk behaviors from 1999 to 2007. *Journal of School Health, 80(8),* 399–410.

Tobler, N. S., Roona, M. R., Ochshorn, P., Marshall, D. G., Streke, A. V., & Stackpole, K. M. (2000) School-based adolescent drug prevention programs: 1998 meta-analysis. *Journal of Primary Prevention, 20(4),* 275–336.

Vallaire-Thomas, L., Hicks, J., & Growe, R. (2011) Solution-focused brief therapy: An interventional approach to improving negative student behaviors. *Journal of Instructional Psychology, 38(4),* 224–234.

Waldron, J. J., & Kowalski, C. L. (2009) Crossing the line: Rites of passage, team aspects, and ambiguity of hazing. *Research Quarterly for Exercise and Sport, 80(2),* 291–302.

Waldron, J. J., & Krane, V. (2005) Whatever it takes: Health compromising behaviors in female athletes. *Quest, 57,* 315–329.

Vallaire-Thomas, L., Hicks, J., & Growe, R. (2011) Solution-focused brief therapy: An interventional approach to improving negative student behaviors. *Journal of Instructional Psychology, 38(4),* 224–234.

Yang, J., Peek-Asia, C., Corlette, J. D., Cheng, G., Foster, D. T., & Allbright, J. (2007) Prevalence of and risk factors associated with symptoms of depression in competitive collegiate student athletes. *Clinical Journal of Sport Medicine, 17(6),* 481–487.

13 The Transitional Student Athlete
Movement Away from Sport

Carmen Wandel and Adam Zagelbaum

The National Collegiate Athletic Association has had a campaign for many years that stresses there are many student athletes who become professionals in fields other than sports. Certainly, the known statistics of becoming a professional athlete suggest that student athletes must be prepared on some level to encounter the possibility of needing to have such a plan. However, the reasons for a transition away from sport may not always follow a plan, a free-willed decision path, or a clear-cut pattern for which the student athlete can always be prepared. The process by which the student athlete transitions away from sport may not always take a slow, predictable pace that permits solid adjustments to life outside of athletic participation. For example, in Chapter 2, The Mobilization Model (Stambulova, 2011) was presented as a way to inform readers about approaches that can assist a student athlete who is encountering a crisis and/or making a transition away from a sporting career. Though the decision can be made, it does not mean that the student athlete can simply act on the decision, as if it were a practiced move constructed during the course of scrimmage games that now can be enacted on the playing field. Movement away from sport can, for many, involve a change of identity, lifestyle, and culture, that requires gradual adjustment and careful social and emotional support. This support needs to allow highs and lows to surface and be met with proper reactions and resources that a transitioning student athlete can use, because they are perceived as being available and accessible from a source of encouragement and empowerment, and not solely from a need to show pity or grief over what could have been. In this chapter, we examine ways the school counselor can serve as a role model for this purpose, and/or facilitate a response from others close to the transitional student athlete that help to achieve such a goal. The reasons behind the transition are also presented as ways to help readers frame the different responses and approaches that student athletes may encounter as they move away from sport.

Identifying Issues, Relationships, and Stakeholders

Many circumstances result in student athletes moving away from or exiting sports participation. Reasons range from academic ineligibility, performance peak, injury or other health issues, to the conscious or unconscious decision to end participation. This latter may be due to lack of interest, underlying fear, desire to avoid commitment and pressure, rebellion, cultural pressures, or new and expanding interests in other areas. In these ways, student athletes are forced out of sport, or choose to opt out, deciding not to proceed to the collegiate or professional levels.

It is important to work collaboratively with all stakeholders, including the student athlete's family, teachers, coaches, and other health care professionals when counseling student athletes who are leaving sports. This process of collaboration may involve gathering and providing information, providing solutions, providing recommendations about what needs to happen next, building consensus among stakeholders, and improving communication between individuals through the modeling of deep respect for all participants with an investment in the outcome (Dougherty, 2009). Working with all of the interested parties in this way will help uncover the nuances of the student athlete's situation.

When a student athlete goes through the process of giving up future potential and dreams attached to collegiate- and professional-level sports, a practical level of consideration needs to be addressed as well as the emotional and social aspects. The student athlete may go through a process which mirrors aspects of grief, as there can be a loss of relationships formed through team belongingness and relationships to adults who support the student athlete (Mankad & Gordon, 2010). That closeness is often given to a student athlete only with continued participation in sport. The recognition and prestige afforded to athletes is associated with the positive and pleasant feelings of being unique and exceptional (Stephan & Brewer, 2007). The loss of perceived prestige associated with being a part of team sports can trigger sadness or anger, and deserves acknowledgment and support. All this comes at a time when Erikson (1968) asserts in his Psychosocial Development Theory, that teens are undergoing the developmental stage of Identity vs. Role Confusion and discovering the task of creating a sense of an independent self. The independence component makes teens particularly vulnerable to a wide range of stressors. This is a time when teens are known to pull away from parental influences to establish a separate identity and are building stronger peer relationships, yet the peer group may not have the experience or the skill-set to be supportive (Thomas, 2011) and parents are still legally and morally bound to protect and care for their child even when their authority and caring is actively being rebuked.

There may also be a loss of a sense of self that needs to be reestablished through the counseling relationship with student athletes as they begin to find other ways to express their interests and talents. Participating in sports often requires a single focus, and student athletes may need support in expanding other options available to them. Student athletes may only understand themselves within the context of sport and team dynamics. Helping student athletes extract personal values, strengths, and specific qualities which contributed to sports performance and team dynamics—and expanding perspectives on how those values and unique qualities translate to new interests and options—will allow for a smoother transition out of sports. The transition is impacted by various factors with regard to the extent and degree of specialty within a sport, and the relative degree of personal identity that has been built around sports participation. Soukup, Henrich and Barton-Weston (2010) found that athletes who participate in sports "seemed to have developed and internalized stronger exercise identities through their sport participation than the students that took physical education" (p. 35). Stronger exercise identities are formed, in part, through the positive association of extra time spent alongside like-minded teammates. Supervision and direction of coaches who may serve as positive role models can also contribute to a stronger exercise identity. Recognition of sports accomplishment from parents and siblings may encourage a student athlete's continual growth of sports identity. These factors all give meaning and context to the primary positive motivating force for a student athlete, and con-tribute to the overall impact of his/her transition away from sport.

It will be important for the school counselor to help a student athlete discover additional strengths and find ways to link the motivations originat-ing from sports participation and identity to motivations and identity outside of sport. Applying overarching values, strengths, and qualities to personal, academic, and career interests and strengths may be beneficial to student athletes making the transition from sports. It is important for the school counselor to maintain and emphasize a broader view of the student athlete. Motivated by the current social and financial rewards given to professional athletes, the high level of role identity within sports can devalue the pursuit of quality education or detract from the necessary developmental progress of adolescence (Miron, 2010).

Career Identity Exploration and Expansion

Strong identity around sport is associated with a delay specifically with regard to career development, because of the strong emphasis on sports and sport performance from coaches and student athletes (Miron, 2010). During the adolescent years, career identity and exploration of career aptitude is in an expansion phase. Helping a student athlete identify and apply self-awareness and self-concept developed by participation in sports will help student athletes along the path to a career. Exit from sport gives the school counselor an oppor-tunity to help build a student athlete's awareness of the life-long process of expanding awareness of self, applying and integrating information gained from participation in sport for use in making decisions in the world of work beyond school. The school counselor can also make use of the similarities between success in sport and finding success in future employment. Troutman (2003) highlighted the key elements in sports which prepare student athletes for the world of work. These include decision-making ability, commitment, learning the rules and elements of the specific job or overall workplace, skill, strategy, visualization, matching interests and experience with job requirements, communicating strengths related to the job in resumes and cover letters, networking, and concentration. Therefore, the school counselor becomes an important resource for a transitioning student athlete in helping to reframe skills and strategies once used in the sporting pursuit to ones that are critical for a career path that may or may not be directly related to sport. However, such transitions are also impacted by other social influences, like friends and family, and working with these individuals may also be part of the counseling process.

Family: Importance and Impact

Feelings of loss and stress may be evident even when student athletes make the choice to opt out of sports participation, such as when they are acting in rebellion against family pressures. Perceptions regarding levels of support and pressure within the family dynamics can differ between the student athlete and their parent(s). With good intentions, parents may encourage their children to participate in sports in support of overall social and emotional growth. Over the years parents may invest a great deal of time and money in providing the opportunity for their child to participate in sports—sports equipment, uniforms, private coaching, summer sports camps, specialty trainings, transportation fees, registration fees, and even the potential cost of time spent away from work to transport, watch, and cheer for their child. Kanters, Bocarro, and Casper (2008) found that while perceptions of skill level are not significantly different between parent and child, their measures showed children report significantly higher scores for pressure and parents report significantly higher scores for measures of support, creating a discrepancy between the parent and child experiences of sport. This discrepancy allows the disconnection to continue between parents and their children. If parents are not able to acknowledge their increasing degree of involvement in their child's sport, it may result in additional stress rather than feelings of support for their child. A student athlete may make the choice to leave sport and the school counselor can be a valuable resource during the transition process at school and within the family. Being an advocate for the student athlete who has decided to leave against the wishes of others is an important role for the school counselor. The school counselor can facilitate a meeting with the interested parties to provide physical and moral support for a student athlete ready to make disclosures to a resistant family. A counselor can provide an opportunity for role-play, so the student athlete can practice responses to family forces. Sharing the desires of the student athlete with regard to terminating sports, and a call for acceptance and support from family members or others with contrary opinion, can also be a way for a counselor to offer support and service when a student athlete feels too overwhelmed to deal directly with family members or coaches. For student athletes with extreme external resistance in their exit from sports participation, providing on-going encouragement, and linking them to their internal strengths as well as community resources, is often necessary. Unfortunately, the decision to end sports participation can create division, rather than the bonding that can sometimes occur with shared grief. Giving up part or all of a dream may mean sorting through the expectations that the family—as well as respected and revered coaches—hold for a student athlete. Making the decision to end participation in sports requires consideration of those abandoned dreams, whether belonging to the student athlete, the family member, or coach. It is important to get a clear sense from student athletes those they feel are impacted by their decision, and help them differentiate their own desires and interests from the desires and interests of others.

For some student athletes, the pressure to compete and excel comes from the hope and promise of financial relief or academic opportunity that an athletic career or full-ride scholarship might provide. Medic, Mack, Wilson, and Starkes (2007) found that, especially among male student athletes, full athletic scholarships often carry pressure and factors associated with guilt and anxiety. This kind of pressure can sometimes result in the student athlete opting out of sport altogether, to avoid the possibility of disappointment and the discomfort of so much pressure. Even for non-scholarship athletes, the mere possibility of obtaining a full athletic scholarship placed enough pressure on the student athlete to diminish internal motivation with regard to participation in athletics and accomplishment (Medic et al., 2007). For both scholarship and non-scholarship athletes, the influence of athletic scholarship's potential was shown to exert significant pressure to change perceptions and behaviors of student athletes. Using an awareness of these dynamics, school counselors can be sensitive to the pressures felt by student athletes, and help them evaluate the potentially conflicting internal and external demands of athletic scholarships. Consider the case of Claire:

> Claire was a first time member of the Track and Field team in her freshman year of high school. She had previously participated in local recreational soccer, beginning at age 8 and playing in the recreational league until joining with the high school junior varsity soccer team. By the end of her first season she won the school and league records for junior varsity. Her coaches were excited at her potential, giving her a lot of attention, support and encouragement, while recommending additional training, strength building activities and exercises to increase her natural talent and ability. They were already discussing, with confidence, that she would be scouted by universities and even started mentioning the possibility for full-ride scholarships. Her mother was very excited about the possibility of assistance with college costs and for her daughter to have the prestige of a full-ride sports scholarship. Her mother paid for a weeklong pole-vaulting training camp with an internationally known pole-vaulting champion and coach. Claire sustained an injury to her iliotibial (IT) band during

her sophomore year. The coaches continued to work with her, recognizing her talent even with the injury limiting her full potential. Claire eventually opted out of Track and Field in her junior year stating, "I don't want to go to college and have pole-vaulting take up my entire life." She also shared that she did not want the constant pressure to perform or loose her continued financial support through scholarship. She is now in her freshman year attending college on academic scholarship and utilizing student loans. She recently remarked that she misses pole-vaulting and would like to return to the sport.

Injury: Temporary and Permanent Considerations

In cases of physical injury, the grief and feeling of loss is physical as well as emotional. By understanding the physically necessary restrictions of the student athlete, and working in conjunction with recommendations of physicians, a school counselor can help redirect the student athlete in maintaining a healthy level of activity. If injuries are temporary, advocating for the student athlete with coaches to allow the student athlete to remain a part of the team, even if not on the official roster, can keep those bonds and maintain the strength and motivation to return as soon as the student athlete is capable. When continued athletic participation is not an option, encouraging student athletes to become part of the spectator group, to build ties through school and team spirit, can help build new relationships and a sense of belonging for student athletes as they transition from sports. Consider the case of Cora:

> Cora was a member of the girl's varsity soccer team in her junior year when, early in the season, she tore her anterior cruciate ligament (ACL, a small ligament in the knee). It is an extremely painful injury and in Cora's case required surgery. Though hopeful of a full recovery, she could not to continue her participation in soccer for the remainder of the season and possibly into her senior year. With combined approval from the athletic director and coach, as well as support from her teammates and parents, Cora continued to attend every practice and every game, even riding the bus to away games, cheering from the sideline bench with teammates, offering positive feedback and support for her team. In this way she was able to maintain her social connections even though physically she could not play on the field. Following her doctor's guidelines, adhering to her physical therapy timelines, and implementing a positive mental imagery component, Cora was able to fully return to the varsity soccer team in her senior year.

Additionally, sports exit may simply be a transition from one sport to another. When a student athlete is forced out of one sport and is willing and able to shift to a new, less familiar one, the counselor is a valuable resource in facilitating that transitional process. For example, injury may make a student athlete unable to participate in the sport around which (s)he has built a strong identity. When a student athlete has sustained physical injury as a result of a contact sport like football, it is possible to help facilitate the exit from one sport and the development of a new identity within a new sport that does not place the student athlete at risk of re-injury. This information becomes critical in this day and age, especially considering the recent issues of concussion-based lawsuits and concerns expressed about how football leagues are handling the care of players exposed to this type of injury (Associated Press, 2013). Even with a shift like this, the counselor can serve a student athlete in forming new identity and growth. Consider the case of Grant:

> From ages 7 to 13, Grant played football with the local youth football league, during which time he suffered several concussions ranging from mild to severe. His doctors urged his mother to discontinue his participation in all contact sports, including baseball, his other favorite youth sport. Upon entering high school he wanted to resume participation in football. His prior history of brain trauma from the concussions was still of concern to doctors and to his mother. She consequently allowed Grant to make the decision himself—whether to participate in football or not—saying the consequence of any further injury would ultimately rest with him. Grant considered wrestling, another contact sport, and finally decided to move out of his comfort zone and became a member of the swimming team. He was ultimately able to transfer some of his successful experiences with prior sports participation (such as working hard, asking for and accepting technique coaching), and was moved up quickly from the junior varsity to the varsity team, expanding his identity within his new sport.

It is also important to realize that life event stress does not always come after an injury; rather, it can be a contributor to the injury in the first place (Nippert & Smith, 2008). Nippert and Smith (2008) encourage medical professionals to be aware of the influence of stressful life events when working with young athletes. Counselors working in collaboration with medical professionals can be the bridge between the physical cause and treatment for injury, and the identification and support for emotional factors associated with stressful events occurring in the student athlete's life.

For student athletes with very strong sport identities, the motivation to continue training through injury often leads to premature return to sport. Early return to sports creates additional concern, as it can often lead to immediate re-injury or, in some cases, permanent pain and limited movement (Nippert & Smith, 2008). A counselor can be valuable in expressing the concerns of all athletic stakeholders in a way that communicates caring and advocates long-term health and well being, especially when the athletic stakeholders hold differing opinions on what is best overall for the student athlete. Through the use of goal setting, relaxation tools, mental imagery, and positive self-talk, a counselor can provide support as the student athlete transitions away from sport as a result of injury (Nippert & Smith, 2008).

It is important to be aware that sports participation also comes with the ultimate and tragic risks of permanent brain injury, permanent spinal cord injury, heat stroke via exertion that results in brain injury and death, and sudden cardiac arrest. The National Center for Catastrophic Sports Injury Research (NCCSIR) was established in 1982 to expand research on catastrophic injuries sustained in all high school and college sports in an attempt to bring increased safety to sports participation. Mueller and Cantu (2011) identify catastrophic injury "as any severe injury incurred during participation in a school/college sponsored sport." (p. 2). They further divide catastrophic injury into three parts: fatality (death), non-fatal, and serious. *Non-fatal* is defined as resulting in permanent, severe functional disability, while *serious* is defined as an injury resulting in no permanent functional disability but still a severe injury (such as a fractured cervical vertebra with no paralysis). Additionally, sports injury is categorized as direct or indirect. *Direct* injuries result from direct participation in the skills of the sport. *Indirect* injuries are caused as a result of exertion while participating in a sport activity or a complication that was secondary to a non-fatal injury (Mueller & Cantu, 2011). The resulting data from 29 years of NCCSIR research from 1982–2011 show a combined catastrophic rate for high school participants of 0.91 per 100,000, meaning approximately one high school athlete out of every 100,000 participating would receive some kind of catastrophic injury (Mueller & Cantu, 2011). The fatality rate taken separately would be 0.39 per 100,000 and non-fatal 0.27 per 100,000 (Mueller & Cantu, 2011). It is also important to note that these catastrophic injuries are sustained across all sports, including cheer, swimming, football, soccer, wrestling, basketball, baseball, softball, and track. Here are just a few cases from the Twenty-Ninth Annual Report (Mueller and Cantu, 2011, pp. 38–41, 43) highlighting the very real and severe nature of the risk of sports participation:

- An 18-year-old high school swimmer completed a 220-yard freestyle relay in a meet and collapsed on the pool deck after the race. He died of cardiac arrest.
- A high school female athlete suffered a traumatic brain injury during a basketball game after hitting her head on the floor after a rebound. There was no sign of a fracture or brain bleed, but she has memory loss and her recovery is incomplete.
- A female high school cheerleader was paralyzed from the chest down after attempting a back flip off the back of another cheerleader.

The Youth Sports Safety Alliance created the National Action Plan for Sports Safety (YSSA, 2013) to help minimize or eliminate risk and adverse outcomes. Among the general recommended actions (such as requiring all schools to have a comprehensive athletic health care administration program and an athletic health care team comprised of a physician, athletic trainer, school nurse, or other health care professional and the athletic director), they also suggest that all schools have a place for confidential conversations with athletes and parents about medical issues. A school counselor can aptly fill this role. Should such a tragic event happen, a school counselor should be ready to implement the School Crisis Response Plan to identify community resources for staff and students, determine the extent of counseling services needed, call on community resources, and oversee the mental health services provided to students (Schonfeld & Newgass, 2003). Follow-up and on-going observation will allow the school counselor to recognize common needs of students and staff that can be addressed by establishing support groups in the school (Schonfeld & Newgass, 2003).

Benefits of Movement and Activity Outside of Sports Participation

Even when the decision to leave sports is not due to injury or risk of injury, helping a student athlete find a way to shift from intense training to more moderate ways of maintaining activity levels will help support the former student athlete. Movement for the benefit of academic focus, emotional wellbeing, body image, and overall health and fitness are important aspects to consider. The United States Department of Health and Human Services (USDHHS, 2008) has published recommendations based on research findings, asserting strong evidence of benefits for children and adolescents in improved cardio-respiratory endurance and muscular fitness, favorable body composition, improved bone health, improved cardiovascular and metabolic health biomarkers, as well as moderate evidence for reduced symptoms of anxiety and depression. The USDHHS (2008) also states the importance of encouraging "youth to participate in physical activities that are appropriate for their age and ability, that are enjoyable, and that offer variety" (p. vii). The school counselor can help a student athlete explore and expand the vision of those possibilities. Petosa and Hortz (2009) address the benefits of physical activity and how it can enhance the overall health of adolescents in their evaluation of a 10-week program, Planning to be Active (P2BA). The P2BA program was designed to increase regular exercise in both active and sedentary adolescents. Because school sports usually operate from a more competitive structure, as school counselors helping a student athlete transition from sports, we can help ease the process by utilizing the tenets of the program which rely on "behavioral goal setting, lifestyle planning, self-monitoring, and self-reflection" in developing a regular exercise routine (Petosa & Hortz, 2009, p. 416). In having an understanding of the wellness benefits of physical activity and educating the student athlete about the wellness benefits of physical activity in a non-competitive and skill-independent environment, school counselors can help by maintaining a positive outlook for a student athlete.

Exploring other modalities for movement, such as yoga, stretching, walking, or medically modified movement as necessary, may ease the potential for increased limits on mobility and loss of physical strength resulting from newfound inactivity or relative inactivity. The Physical Activity Guidelines for Americans Midcourse Report Subcommittee of the President's Council on Fitness, Sports & Nutrition (USDHHS, 2012) gives guidelines for activity levels for children ages 6 to 17, recommending 60 minutes of activity in any combination that will contribute aerobic, muscle and bone strengthening components to aid in overall life-long physical and mental health. The CDC (2011) additionally confirms that the consistent use of regular physical activity (such as aerobic or a mix of aerobic and muscle-strengthening activities three to five times a week for 30 to 60 minutes) can impart physical and mental health benefits, including helping to keep mental processes sharp, reducing risk of depression, and may help with better sleep. Moraes et al. (2011) further suggest that even 20 minutes of exercise can produce significant effects on mood and specifically lessen feelings of anger.

It is also important to consider that, while lessening physical activity levels can affect body image in a negative way, ending sports participation can also give relief to a student athlete. By exiting sports participation, a student athlete may no longer feel the pressure to measure up to a sport-specific ideal with regard to weight standards for divisional sports, such as wrestling. While young women are not the only ones affected by body image concerns, female athletes more often suffer from the dual pressures from sport and societal images in maintaining a perfect body (Nippert & Smith, 2008). The confusion and pressure from competing images may cause female athletes to develop unhealthy eating behaviors, and a counselor can act as a resource in getting help for student athletes who may be practicing binging, purging, and fasting to control weight and other stressful life events (Nippert & Smith, 2008).

Physical Limits of Performance Peak

If the termination of sports participation results from true performance peak (where student athletes simply will not move on to college level athletics because of their ability), counseling can provide a student athlete with an effective way to process the feelings of disappointment and anger. Counseling and collaboration with athletic stakeholders can also help a student athlete determine if there is a less intense way to participate in the sport that might still have some satisfaction for them, even though the collegiate and professional levels may no longer be a viable option. Providing support and expanding options available to a student athlete outside the limits of sports participation can help ease the transition and help them be ready to see a wider range of possibilities. For example, being a volunteer coach or mentor for younger athletes may provide a continued link to a sport that a student athlete really loves and does not want to give up entirely. Sharing knowledge with others is a great way for a student athlete to maintain a sports identity,

provided they are willing to adopt the new role of coach rather than participant (Bullen, Farruggia, Gomez, Hebaishi, & Mahmood, 2010).

Academic Ineligibility

In cases of academic ineligibility, there can be a drive to restore eligibility, and
the student athlete's frustration may be felt and expressed through anger and acting out in academic and social settings. By addressing the student athlete's
frustration first from a Rogerian approach, establishing a genuine connection,
creating a climate of acceptance, and offering empathy, along with expressing
belief in the student athlete's abilities and strengths, the student athlete is
primed to make the changes from self-reserves of creative resources and is able
to self-direct the process of personal and academic learning (Rogers, 1979).
The counselor may need to work collaboratively with—or even act as mediator
between—coaches and teachers to arrive at reasonable expectations and limits
for participation. Engaging in a collaborative process to utilize the investment
and expertise of all stakeholders may result in additional motivation for setting
new academic goals, accepting academic support, and implementing academic
improvement interventions.

Alcohol and Drug Use or Abuse Counseling and Collaboration

Another unwilling exit from sport arises from alcohol and drug use or abuse
as the cause for eviction from sports participation. Linking student athletes
with community resources and assessing the degree of parental support to
overcome substance use or abuse is in the overall best interest of the student
athlete. Substance use or abuse may also be a secondary risk of dropping out
of sports, as drug use can be a substitute for the adrenaline rush provided
through the physiology of sports participation and provide some of the
charge of the developmental risk-taking behavior practiced by teens.
Additionally, while there is a common perception that participation in
sports is linked with reduced drug and alcohol use, studies show differing
results; some show that student athletes may actually have higher incidences
of drug and alcohol use (Geisner, 2012), while other studies show no significant difference between athlete and non-athlete use of alcohol, smokeless
tobacco, and marijuana (Naylor, Gardner & Zaichkowsky, 2001). Operating
under the veil of positive perception of student athletes with regard to substance use, substance abuses may only come to light when a student athlete
has actually been caught in the act. Counselors can provide resources for
drug and alcohol prevention or rehabilitation in collaboration with school
administrators who must carry out the district policies and disciplinary
actions concerning substance use at school or school-related events. Having
a list of community resources and keeping an awareness of the possibility of
drug-related concerns enables a quicker response to the needs of the student
athlete. The counselor can further be an advocate in schools to enlist the

support of prevention specialists in providing training to coaches and student athletes on alcohol and drug prevention.

Teen Pregnancy and Title IX

Teen pregnancy poses another sensitive concern related to exit from sports. Title IX of the Education Amendments of 1972, Discrimination Against Pregnant Students, Section 106.40, conveys federal law and requires counselors to appropriately advocate for the female student athlete regarding sports participation and pregnancy:

• Schools are prohibited from discriminating against pregnant students based upon their marital status and cannot discriminate against a student because of childbirth, false pregnancy, or recovery from these conditions.

• A school is permitted to require a doctor's certificate from a pregnant student only if the school imposes the same requirement upon all other students with physical or emotional conditions requiring a physician's care.

• Participation in special schools or programs reserved or designed for pregnant or parenting students must be completely voluntary on the part of the student. Such programs or schools must be comparable to programs and schools offered to non-pregnant students.

• Schools must treat pregnancy as they treat other medical conditions. Health plans, medical benefits, and related services are to be provided to pregnant students in the same manner as services are provided to students with other temporary disabilities.

• A pregnant student may be granted a leave of absence for as long as it is deemed medically necessary and at the conclusion of her leave must be allowed to resume the status she held when the leave began.

(California Department of Education, 2012)

Recent events highlight the need for counselors to advocate for pregnant student athletes who may choose to continue with school athletics, as well as the need to collaborate with medical professionals, coaches, and parents in helping a student athlete make the decision to stay with or exit sport participation. A 2009 civil rights complaint from a pregnant volleyball player filed against her high school was denied after federal officials found insufficient evidence of discrimination. Even though the school district was not held responsible for the missed potential college scholarships, the school district was involved in a costly and time-intensive investigation, and the student athlete felt her opportunities had been limited as a result of not being allowed to play (Hayton, 2010).

In collaboration with athletic stakeholders, counselors can help the student athlete address the extreme body and lifestyle changes that are part of being pregnant, as well as the additional stigma that comes with being pregnant as a teen. When medically necessary, helping a pregnant student athlete transition healthfully from sports has twice the importance when looking toward the impact on the unborn child. The counselor can help a pregnant student athlete establish new priorities, beginning with the care of her changing body and the physical demands of pregnancy. In some ways, a student athlete may have an advantage: being familiar with what is required to fuel excellence in sports performance, she can apply healthy choices during pregnancy. A counselor can help a pregnant teen strengthen her bonds with individuals she can rely on to help her through the overall shift, initially in her exit from sports, and in developing relationships that will support her decisions with regard to the changes in her overall lifestyle and into motherhood.

Suicide Risk and Assessment

Another issue with potentially more significance to female athletes—but certainly relevant to all student athletes exiting sport—is suicide risk and assessment. From a national sample of 9–12 graders in 2011, the CDC (2012) found that the overall prevalence of several risk factors were reported as being higher among female students than for male students. Such risk factors included: feeling sad or hopeless (females 35.9% versus males 21.5%), having seriously considered attempting suicide (females 19.3% versus males 12.5%), having made a suicide plan (females 15% versus males 10%), and making a suicide attempt (females 9.8% versus males 5.8%) (p. 10–12). In a Leading Cause of Death Report generated for 2010, national results show suicide as the second leading cause of death for 13- to 18-year-olds (CDC, 2010). Taliaferro, Rienzo, Miller, Pigg, and Dodd (2008) found participation in sports "was significantly associated with reduced odds of hopelessness and suicidal behavior among both genders" (p. 549). The protective factors of athletic participation disappeared even when just decreased to moderate levels of participation (Sabo, Miller, Melnick, Farrell, & Barnes, 2005). Taking into account the variables of age, race/ethnicity, parental education, and locale, both males and females with high levels of participation in athletics showed reduced odds of seriously considering suicide over their non-athletic counterparts (Sabo et al., 2005). Because participation in sports is a protective factor for both females and males, when participation in sports is terminated, no matter the reason, follow-up suicide risk assessment is an important component of counseling a student athlete leaving sport. The school counselor's efforts in this area are clearly necessary considering 13% of students taking a Columbia Suicide Screen self-assessment were otherwise overlooked in results of the self-assessment measure, and were identified as at risk of suicide only by the efforts and attention of school professionals (Scott et al., 2009).

Transitions Throughout Life

The role of the school counselor is multi-leveled and includes educating student athletes on the very personal nature of grief as well as acknowledging that it applies to the loss of sports participation—chosen or imposed. In the collaborative role, school counselors can provide education on how to be supportive during times of grieving and loss to all stakeholders involved in athletics, as well as expanding to include the school community as a whole (Thomas, 2011). This will help student athletes become aware of their own individual processes and will allow them to identify the type of help and support they may need at any time during the process of grieving and healing, specifically with regard to sports exit, and translating to other life events involving loss (Wooten, 2005). Mankad and Gordon (2010) also discuss grief within the context of sport-injury. Giving student athletes the space to grieve and share their loss has the potential to not only ease the disappointment and devastation around leaving sport, but can also yield greater capacity to mentally regroup and find new motivation and enthusiasm for peer interaction as well as actively reach out to social supports (Mankad & Gordon, 2010). Helping student athletes understand the nature and flow of continual life transitions at this early stage in their development will equip them with varied and practiced tools they can use as they leave high school, enter college, begin careers, and start their families.

Summary

We began this chapter with the notion that student athletes often become professionals in areas other than sports. However, the reasons as to why this process unfolds can be as diverse and unique as the student athletes involved. Some reasons, such as academic ineligibility and not qualifying for professional level, are not necessarily career-ending ones as serious physical injury and illness can be. This does not mean that the transition is any easier for a student athlete to make, because there are situational and motivational factors that must be considered in order to help a student athlete take appropriate actions. School counselors can often be in one of the best positions to assist with movement away from sport, because of specific career and personal/social resources that can tangibly and concretely be given to a transitional student athlete, allowing a dialogue centered on taking action to occur. The grief process, along with identity changes, that can impact student athletes and those around them are still allowed to occur, but the notion of setting new goals and following-up on these transitional plans becomes an important element of many models of transition support for student athletes who encounter such issues (Stambulova, 2011; Mankad & Gordon, 2010; Nippert & Smith, 2008). Another way that the school counselor can assist with this process is to engage with other stakeholders who are connected to the transitioning student athlete, so that extra-curricular and community-based resources can also be part of the transition plan. Some moves away from sport can provide opportunities for student athletes to serve as coaches, assistants, and mentors for future generations. Some moves may have student athletes disengage from the field of athletics altogether, but the use of a support network may still be crucial to provide for such individuals who may revisit feelings of depression and grief from time to time. Regardless of what moves are to be made, the school counselor is encouraged to actively engage with the transitional student athlete so that plans are not only made, but also attempted, because change is not always an easy process.

Questions for Discussion

1. For each case (Claire, Cora, and Grant):

   - Who are the important stakeholders in this case study?
   - How would you collaborate with each of the stakeholders for the benefit of the student athlete?

2. What are your local resources for youth drug and alcohol prevention and education?
3. How will you address suicide risk assessment with student athletes exiting sport?

   - What assessment tools do you have to assist you in making risk assessments?
   - Who would you involve in evaluating suicide risk factors for each of the cases?

4. What special concerns do you have for pregnant teens exiting sports?
5. In what way would your approach with a student athlete who is frustrated and angered by academic ineligibility compare/contrast to working with a student who wants to quit and is frustrated by external pressure from parents to continue with sport?

References

Associated Press. (2013) Four ex-NFL players file new concussion lawsuit against league. *NFL.com*. Retrieved September 4, 2013 from http://www.nfl.com/news/story/0ap1000000237961/article/four-exnfl-players-file-new-concussion-lawsuit-against-league.

Bullen, P., Farruggia, S. P., Gomez, C., Hebaishi, G., & Mahmood, M. (2010) Meeting the graduating teacher standards: The added benefits for undergraduate university students who mentor youth. *Educational Horizons, 89(1)*, 47–61.

California Department of Education (2012) *Title IX of the Education Amendments of 1972* [Fact sheet]. (October 11, 2012). Sacramento, CA: Author. Retrieved June 7, 2013 from http://www.cde.ca.gov/ls/cg/pp/titlenine.asp.

CDC (Centers for Disease Control and Prevention) (2010) *Web-based Injury Statistics Query and Reporting System (WISQARS)* [online]. Atlanta, GA: Author. Retrieved June 6, 2013 from www.cdc.gov/injury/wisqars/index.html.

CDC (Centers for Disease Control and Prevention) (2011) *Physical Activity and Health: The Benefits of Physical Activity* [Fact sheet]. (February 16, 2011). Atlanta, GA: Author. Retrieved June 7, 2013 from: http://www.cdc.gov/physicalactivity/everyone/health/index.html.

CDC (Centers for Disease Control and Prevention) (2012) Youth Risk Behavior Surveillance – United States, 2011. *MMWR Morbidity and Mortality Weekly Report 2012,* 61(4), 1–168. Retrieved November 8, 2013 from http://www.cdc.gov/mmwr/pdf/ss/ss6104.pdf.

Dougherty, A. M. (2009) *Psychological Consultation and Collaboration in School and Community Settings* (5th ed.). Belmont, CA: Brooks/Cole, Cengage Learning.

Erikson, E. (1968) *Identity: Youth and Crisis.* New York: Norton.

Geisner, I. (2012) Differences between athletes and non-athletes in risk and health behaviors in graduating high school seniors. *Journal of Child & Adolescent Substance Abuse, 21(2),* 156–166.

Hayton, T. (2010) Feds deny pregnant volleyball player's complaint against Fort Worth school. *The Dallas Morning News,* April 21. Retrieved June 7, 2013 from http://www.dallasnews.com/news/education/headlines/20100421-Feds-deny-pregnant-volley-ball-player-s-6522.ece.

Kanters, M. A., Bocarro, J., & Casper, J. (2008) Supported or pressured? An examination of agreement among parents and children on parent's role in youth sports. *Journal of Sport Behavior, 31(1),* 64–80.

Mankad, A., & Gordon, S. (2010) Psycholinguistic changes in athletes' grief response to injury after written emotional disclosure. *Journal of Sport Rehabilitation, 19(3),* 328–342.

Medic, N., Mack, D. E., Wilson, P. M., & Starkes, J. L. (2007) The effects of athletic scholarships on motivation in sport. *Journal of Sport Behavior, 30(3),* 292–306.

Miron, P. (2010) Role identity and its implications in the athlete's personal development. *Timisoara Physical Education & Rehabilitation Journal, 3(5),* 7–12.

Moraes, H., Deslandes, A., Silveira, H., Ribeiro, P., Cagy, M., Piedade, R., & Laks, J. (2011) The effect of acute effort on EEG in healthy young and elderly subjects. *European Journal of Applied Physiology, 111(1),* 67–75.

Mueller, F. O., & Cantu, R. C. (2011) Catastrophic sports injury research: Twenty-ninth annual report, Fall 1982–Spring 2011. Retrieved August 31, 2013 from http://www.unc.edu/depts/nccsi/2011Allsport.pdf

Naylor, A. H., Gardner, D., & Zaichkowsky, L. (2001) Drug use patterns among high school athletes and nonathletes. *Adolescence, 36(144),* 627–639.

Nippert, A. H., & Smith, A. M. (2008) Psychological stress related to injury and impact on sport performance. *Physical Medicine and Rehabilitation Clinics of North America, 19,* 399–418. http://dx.doi.org/10.1016/j.pmr.2007.12.003.

Petosa, R. L., & Hortz, B. V. (2009) Wholistic wellness and exercise among adolescents. In R. Gilman, E. S. Huebner, & M. J. Furlong (Eds.), *Handbook of Positive Psychology* (pp. 409–422). New York, Routledge.

Rogers, C. R. (1979) The foundations of the person centered approach. *Education, 100(2),* 98.

Sabo, D., Miller, K. E., Melnick, M. J., Farrell, M. P., & Barnes, G. M. (2005) High school athletic participation and adolescent suicide: A nationwide US study. *International Review for the Sociology of Sport, 40(5).* doi: 10.1177/1012690205052160.

Schonfeld, D. J., & Newgass, S. (2003) School crisis response initiative [PDF]. *OVC Bulletin*, 1–8. Retrieved November 8, 2013 from http://www.ojp.usdoj.gov/ovc/publications/bulletins/schoolcrisis/ncj197832.pdf.

Scott, M. A., Wilcox, H. C., Schonfeld, I., Davies, M., Hicks, R. C., Turner, J., & Shaffer, D. (2009) School-based screening to identify at-risk students not already known to school professionals: The Columbia suicide screen. *American Journal of Public Health*, *99(2)*, 324–329.

Soukup Sr., G. J., Henrich, T. W., & Barton-Weston, H. M. (2010) Differences in exercise identity between secondary physical education students and athletes. *ICHPER – SD Journal of Research in Health, Physical Education, Recreation, Sport & Dance*, *5(1)*, 33–36.

Stambulova, N. (2011) The Mobilization Model of counseling athletes in crisis-transitions: An educational intervention tool. *Journal of Sport Psychology in Action*, *2*, 156–170.

Stephan, Y., & Brewer, B. W. (2007) Perceived determinants of identification with the athlete role among elite competitors. *Journal of Applied Sport Psychology*, *19(1)*, 67–79. doi:10.1080/10413200600944090.

Taliaferro, L. A., Rienzo, B. A., Miller, M., Pigg Jr., R., & Dodd, V. J. (2008) High school youth and suicide risk: Exploring protection afforded through physical activity and sport participation. *Journal of School Health*, *78(10)*, 545–553. doi:10.1111/j.1746-1561.2008.00342.x.

Thomas, C. A. (2011) Supporting the grieving adolescent: An interview with a 21st century perspective. *Prevention Researcher*, *18(3)*, 14–16.

Troutman, K. (2003) *Looking for a New Sport that Pays Well? Consider the Game of Federal Job Search*. Retrieved November 8, 2013 from http://www.eric.ed.gov/PDFS/ED480514.pdf.

USDHHS (U. S. Department of Health and Human Services) (2008) *2008 Physical Activity Guidelines for Americans*. (ODPHP Publication No. U0036). Washington, DC: Author. Retrieved June 7, 2013 from http://www.health.gov/paguidelines/pdf/paguide.pdf.

USDHHS (U. S. Department of Health and Human Services) (2012) *Physical Activity Guidelines for Americans Midcourse Report: Strategies to Increase Physical Activity Among Youth*. Washington, DC: Author. Retrieved June 9, 2013 from http://www.health.gov/paguidelines/midcourse/pag-mid-course-report-final.pdf.

Wooten, H. (2005) Healing into life after sport: Dealing with student athlete loss, grief, and transition with EFT. *Journal of Creativity in Mental Health*, *1(3/4)*, 89–102. doi:10.1300/J456v01n03_06.

YSSA (Youth Sports Safety Alliance) (2013) *National action plan for sports safety: Protecting America's student athletes*. Retrieved August 31, 2013 from http://youth-sportssafetyalliance.org/sites/default/files/docs/National-Action-Plan.pdf.

14 The Future of Student Athletics and School-based Counseling Services

To conclude our journey through the world of student athletics with respect to school counseling, we examine some of the issues that appear to be looming on the horizon. Though it is difficult to completely predict the future, the topics included in this chapter appear to be gaining significant momentum because of prevalence, media attention, and existing research and theoretical writings which showcase the significance these matters have for current and potential student athletes. Athletic drives and motivation to play sports appear to be a strong part of many individuals' development, from elementary school on. Advances in technology and growth in the amount of sports available have created a larger field and more diverse athletic pool than ever before. It is because of this larger field that counseling professionals will likely be required to address the needs of more student athletes as time marches on. Counselors are recommended to have specific training and resources designed to recognize these needs and to assist other school stakeholders in addressing them.

Training Programs

One of the best ways to understand the future of student athletes and school-based counseling services is to recognize the current state of training counseling professionals regarding the needs of this field and population. Currently, there is only one certification program in the United States, which is an online sequence of courses from California University of Pennsylvania (Tinsley, 2008). The essentials of its mission statement read as follows:

> Sports counseling is a process that assists individuals in maximizing their personal, academic, and athletic potential. Sports counseling is accomplished through a proactive, growth-oriented, approach that incorporates the principles of counseling, career development, movement science, psychology, and lifespan human development.

The more specific details regarding the program overview, application process and related information can be accessed via the Internet through the following link:

www.calu.edu/academics/online-programs/sports-counseling/index.htm

The main curriculum components of this program, rooted in Counselor Education approaches, center on professional ethics and legal issues, record keeping, NCAA guidelines, and working as part of an interdisciplinary team or as a consultant with individual athletes, teams and athletic organizations. Many of the issues covered center around the three main areas of: (1) motivation and life skill development; (2) psychosocial development; and (3) career maturity. It is also noteworthy that the program involves youth sport, high school, college and professional levels of athletics, so that it prepares counseling professionals for the needs of various populations and organizational work.

Springfield College of Massachusetts also has a program within its Psychology Department for Athletic Counseling. According to its overall description: "The goal of the Athletic Counseling Program is to provide graduate students with preparation in counseling, psychology, and the sport sciences that will enable them to provide support services to athletes in a variety of settings." This program has a thesis requirement, along with various other elements that allow philosophies of psychology and counselor education to drive the training mechanism behind which a master's degree is ultimately obtained (Petitpas & Buntrock, 1995). Though its contact information is listed at the end of this chapter, the program's World Wide Web page can be accessed directly through the following link:

www.spfldcol.edu/homepage/dept.nsf/04E52AE2BE212E4245256
BD80029D783/3AF57063397739B845256C68003F681B

Individuals who pursue this degree are also able to seek a research option that allows them to further their careers at the doctoral level—most likely within a Sports Psychology program.

It important for counseling professionals to distinguish between Athletic Counseling and other areas of study, such as Sport Psychology, because of the confusion that can arise. Though Sport Psychology also centers around athletics, it is a multi-disciplinary field spanning psychology, sport science and medicine. Also, Sport Psychology is not a specialty area within the American Psychological Association, but rather an area of proficiency. The day may come when Sport Psychology needs to be extended to a specialty area—with increased interest in sports and sport-related fields, such as management and consultation, this is highly likely.

Regardless of whether or not sports counseling becomes more specialized, it is still important to note that many student athletes are still initially reluctant or unlikely to seek counseling from school counselors and related professionals. Many reasons are due to the strong relationships they have with coaches, teammates, and peers, which are often the networks by which student athletes seek initial support. There are also reports that indicate social stigma associated with seeking the help of a counselor may initially deter student athletes from seeking his/her services, but such findings are not as prominent as they used to be (Watson, 2006). Perhaps greater attention to professional athletes, who are publicly discussing their issues with mental health and wellness, is serving as a modeling approach for some student athletes to avoid similar struggles (Epstein, 2012); perhaps the rise in collaborative and comprehensive school-wide programs are also contributing to climate shifts that allow greater accessibility and contact with school counselors to be made (Dollarhide & Saginak, 2012; Stone & Dahir, 2006). It appears that issues of time management and responsibilities to academic and athletic schedules are usually the more prominent reasons as to why school counseling is not always the avenue by which student athletes turn for help (Watson, 2006). It is neither wise nor fair to assume that student athletes do not turn to school counselors, or that their initial support systems are always their first option(s). Recent reports regarding college-level student athletes are also showing that levels of depression and suicidal factors among this population are providing some need for counseling and psychological assistance (Miller & Hoffman, 2009). There are plenty of connections that allow student athletes and school counselors to establish effective rapport and significant bonds; it certainly seems that establishing effective bonds with coaches and parents serves as a significant foundation upon which these connections develop (Goldberg & Chandler, 1995).

Boundary Issues

Unfortunately, there are issues that indicate how blurry and concerning the boundaries between coaches and student athletes can sometimes be. Clearly, the most significant and egregious violation of these boundaries came in the form of the sexual abuse cases confirmed to have been committed by former Penn State University Assistant Football Coach Jerry Sandusky. There is no way to fully and accurately encompass the issues related to this scandal, but it has definitely cast a significant light on how deep and inappropriate some personal boundaries can be. For example, at the high school level, former Head Basketball Coach of Hinsdale Central High School (Chicago, IL) Robert Muller was found guilty of having sexual relationships with two female students and is serving a 32-year prison sentence as a result (Drehs, 2011). One student was a manager of the basketball team, while the other was a student athlete. Also, an interim girls' basketball coach, Marquita Adley, at West Broward High School (Miami, FL), was charged with three counts of sexual battery against a minor when she was reported to have had sexual relations with a 16-year-old female athlete who was a participant on the traveling team; this team is not directly affiliated with the school's team. Adley did admit to engaging in certain inappropriate sexual acts according to police (NBCUniversal, 2012). All of these cases are certainly not a characterization of all coaches who exist within K-12 and collegiate-level athletics. However, it is important to note that there are individuals within student athletics who exercise questionable judgment at times regarding the boundaries between professional and personal issues associated with student athletes.

Coaches can sometimes engage in other types of questionable decision-making involving academic matters. A recent case involved a former assistant football coach and head softball coach from Forest Hill High School (Palm Beach County, FL), who also served as a math teacher. Michael Stephen Dudeck was charged with two felony counts of falsifying documents and receiving unlawful compensation which involved the construction of false summer school transcripts which were given to the school's guidance office in order to allow students to play sports. Investigators questioned teachers who were listed on some of the paperwork for the students in question, and at least two teachers stated they had not met particular students nor instructed them (Greer, 2012). While it remains to be seen what type of process(es) led to the decisions that were made, from both the student and coach perspective, this situation serves as an important reminder to school counselors and guidance program employees that familiarity with documentation and student tracking are variables that also impact the growth and development of student athletes.

There has always been debate as to whether or not school counselors should be primarily responsible for scheduling classes and tracking transcript information (Dollarhide & Saginak, 2012; Stone & Dahir, 2006). The need to balance face-to-face time with students along with case and file management is a very difficult task. In cases where it is not possible for a comprehensive and full-time staff to assist with managing records, it may be necessary for a school counselor to spend a significant portion of his/her time engaged in such a task. Computer-assisted organizational systems may help manage some of the time that may otherwise be required for such responsibility but, with the sheer numbers of student-to-counselor ratios often being well in excess of 250:1 as recommended by American School Counselor Association (ASCA), it becomes critical that teacher and counselor collaborations be used to help with this duty. It should not be assumed that documents are false when submitted for credit, but teachers, coaches and counselors should be in direct communication as much as possible about a student athlete's academic progress, credit deficiencies, and class performance in order to limit the opportunity for inaccurate tracking and turbulent matriculation to occur. In so having these communications, counselors, teachers and coaches are held to greater levels of accountability, which reduces the risk that boundary violations will occur.

It seems that boundary violations—at least the ones that are reported with immediacy and urgency—are not limited by age, gender, race/ethnicity, or school. While the school counselor is not meant to serve in the role of police officer or school administrator, (s)he may be in a position to receive information about particular dilemmas regarding boundary issues. Knowing the district and school system policies regarding protocol and standards of care are essential when navigating through these types of issues. However, in terms of prevention efforts, school districts are often recommended to create a climate that enables issues of boundary not to be viewed as a taboo or secretive issue among staff, and that setting a professional example is important for adults to convey to all students. There will always be debates about where such lines between personal and professional connections exist, but striking the balance between these two concepts is important for adults to model for youngsters, especially ones who value many of the authority figures in their lives, like many student athletes.

Social Media

Also, with respect to the notion of modeling, comes the phenomenon of social media. There are more outlets by which sports are covered within contemporary society, more constant news-feeds and exposure to elements of the personal as well as professional sides of sports than ever before. Professional athletes are followed on the field, off the field, during training camps, while drafting and trading periods are taking place, and during the latter/termination stages of their careers. While it seems this has always existed within the world of sports and field of journalism, the use of Internet technology and broadcasting networks that are focused on all aspects of the industry has made such coverage more accessible and more frequent to the viewing public. Certainly, there are pros to this availability and its abundance. Given that sports can already be a chance for social capital and bonding to occur among many groups—especially adolescents—more exposure to more sides of the field can be more engaging to those who follow these aspects (Perks, 2007; Ward, Jr., 2008). There are peer networks and public relations that can be built from the visibility of athletics and the popularity that draws people to view the sports. There is also a chance for fans to connect to players, and vice-versa, through the use of social media that can inspire, motivate, and reinforce passions and pursuits of athletic and personal goals (Pegoraro, 2010). However, since much of this communication is in a virtual forum, there can be many pitfalls with this level of raw and frequent exposure.

Because much of this technology (such as social networking sites like Twitter and Facebook) continues to evolve and increase in scale, it can be very difficult to establish consistent rules and forms of etiquette by which people interact. Some individuals do not understand the fact that what they place online can resurface in ways that can be detrimental to personal and professional development. To assume a message is always private and confidential when it becomes tweeted, blogged, emailed, or broadcast is tremendously naïve, considering the amount of press and news coverage given—on what seems to be a daily basis—to professionals who have been fined or terminated from positions due to inappropriate or offensive disclosures of information through electronic media. Just recently, 23-year-old Voula Papachristou, an Olympic hopeful from Greece, was banned from the 2012 Olympic Games within a matter of days of sending a "tweet" deemed to be racist toward

African Americans. Though she apologized for this remark and called it a "joke in bad taste" (Reuters, 2012), it provides yet another example of how the Internet is not a confidential forum and that the visibility an athlete has within the virtual and real world does not permit limited coverage to exist when it comes to the personal and professional experiences one shares through the media. There have been many other cases like this which have led to fines, terminations and suspensions; many National Football League and National Basketball Association players, owners, and coaches have created situations that have resulted in these outcomes (Klemko, 2011; Pegoraro, 2012). Some cases are starting to occur at the high school level, such as that of Yuri Wright who, though he managed to successfully land a position on a college football team, was expelled from his high school for sexually graphic and racist Twitter posts (Jones, 2012). It is difficult to determine what kind of precedent this can set; only time may be able to accurately tell for certain.

What appears to be clear about these matters is that more training and discussion about the role and purpose social media has within the world of student athletics is needed. The school counselor is in an appropriate position to at least collaborate with coaches and athletic directors in discussing this issue, primarily because of incidents of cyberbullying and harassment that often require him/her to work with victims and perpetrators (Chibarro, 2007). Though coaches and athletic staff may address with their players how to communicate with media and the press, as well as what it means to represent school pride and sportsmanship, the world of social media is not limited to the parameters of sporting events and local news coverage. Some reports have also indicated that individuals (such as athletic trainers, who are also influential in the lives of student athletes) do not feel adequately prepared to counsel student athletes regarding some of these matters within the personal/social domain (Misasi, Davis Jr., Morin, & Stockman, 1996). The work of school counselors regarding the responsibilities of social media can serve as an effective complement to sportsmanship discussions, and will likely be a necessary resource as student athletics and the phenomenon of social media continue to develop over the next few years.

Redshirting the Children

Another interesting phenomenon that is gaining more publicity regarding athletics and education is the practice of "redshirting" children at the kindergarten level (CBS News, 2012). The concept (which refers to the practice of holding children back from starting kindergarten in order to have them begin at age 6) is on the rise because of beliefs that it gives children certain competitive edges regarding social skills, academic skill development, and sport eligibility. Data and studies are still being analyzed to discern how specific and significant the advantages of this practice are, but some experts point to the fact that starting later, beyond age 5, appears to enhance a child's self-regulatory behaviors (Gentry, 2010). These behaviors are often thought to give competitive edges to students who can focus on educational and cognitive stimuli, as well as handle frustrations associated with social interactions that can be difficult to grasp at earlier ages, such as sharing, cooperation, and patience. Gladwell (2008) has been able to report that the majority of children who have become Canadian Junior All-Stars are starting school when they are age 6, and appear to have received a fair amount of attention from both teachers and coaches because of their larger size and perceived competence levels. Many parents are taking notice of these types of results within the United States as well. It is interesting to note that, while this may be a form of assisting children enter school with the identity of not being the youngest, smallest, or slowest to learn and adapt to the social surround, it can be grounds for a new form of competition and expectation that parents are placing on their children at younger ages than ever before. There are numerous questions that are raised by this practice from a nature versus nurture standpoint, as well as how long term the effects of redshirting practices can be beyond the scope of K-12 schooling. Though the school counselor is ultimately not the one who makes the determination to redshirt, it seems somewhat likely that (s)he may be consulted more regarding this option as more parents turn to the practice. It also remains to be seen how the expectations of parents are affected by engaging in this practice: will it lead to more pressure for students to perform? Who is primarily responsible if a redshirted child does not accomplish these advancements? Considering these matters will be important for school counselors and related support staff in years to come.

The "Meaning" of Student Athletics

There has also been a suggestion that the term *student athlete* may be better thought of as *student who participates in athletics* (Goldberg & Chandler, 1995). Such a shift in actual terminology may be difficult to achieve without significant buy-in from parents, coaches, administrators, educators, and various other stakeholders. Some schools and communities have such a prominent and dominant sport culture that vernacular and common parlance would be nearly impossible for such terminology to take full form. It appears that the student athlete label is likely to remain intact, and this does not need to be equated with negative biases or perceptions about what roles and/or identities such a student has within the context of a school. However, with proper attention and emphasis placed on the academic and service-learning components of education, it can also be argued that student athletes can be viewed in the frame of students who participate in athletics. The use of the student athlete title can at times be confused almost as if it were a job or career title. Student-volunteers and student organizations appear to be part of commonly shared terms and parlance throughout the nation, and denote a less commercially skewed angle than can be the case with student athletics. As was discussed previously, even students who are recognized as being "mathletes" may be using this as an endearing form of flattery, or perhaps a sarcastic moniker that imitates the competitive energy of athletics within a scholastically focused pursuit. The educational role of student athletes may not always be seen by everyone, even though there are plenty of student athletes who are highly capable scholars. The ability to play sports and attend school can be appreciated by campus and community members in similar ways that do not necessarily imbalance one accomplishment in lieu of the other. This means calling attention to accomplishments (such as scholarship attainment, hours served within the community for philanthropic purposes), and participation in clubs and groups outside of athletic teams (such as peer mediation programs, tutoring services, and involvement in local boys' and girls' clubs). In doing this, students who do not participate in sports may also feel less of a social comparison effect with those who do, because of the tendency to emphasize collective efforts that serve others (Magen, 1998) and not outcome-driven results, such as winning an athletic competition. Certainly, athletic accomplishments are not supposed to be disregarded or erased from consciousness. It is simply a matter of recognizing off-the-field accomplishments when off the field, and encouraging the support and motivation for success on the field when on it. Naturally, it is not a task that can be perfectly performed, but even the recent ad campaigns of the National Collegiate Athletic Association suggest that it is possible. One of its more recent tag lines stresses that, though there are numerous student athletes, "most of us will go pro in something other than sports". Ratings and statistics indicate that the campaign is popular, but further research may be needed to determine how believable or significant the message is when it comes to conveying the balance between academic and athletic identity. Nevertheless, helping student athletes necessitates an understanding of both roles, and the professional school counselor can be supportive of both and provide resources that assist with the development of each.

Again, it cannot be overstated how valuable student athletics and sports are when it comes to the personal, mental, physical, social, and psychological development of individuals during their K-12 years. The world of professional athletics can be an opportunity that not only provides significant financial resource, but tremendous shared and personal accomplishments that can inspire individuals, towns, communities, and various other audiences on as great a level as a worldwide stage. The reasons that students do and do not play are numerous and varied as much as the types of sports and individuals who support them. Whether or not a student athlete continues onto a professional level is ultimately not in the hands of a school counselor, but the approaches (s)he takes toward assisting a student athlete to address needs that (s)he encounters along the way can make a tremendous difference: one that may not necessarily happen if left to athletic and/or educational staff and faculty. It is hoped that the future of student athletics and the future of school counseling become more closely supplemental to one another, so that every student athlete—or student who desires to become one—can be effectively addressed and prepared for whatever personal and professional goals they wish to achieve.

Available Resources

Like all professionals who work within school systems, it is highly recommended that counselors keep a list of available resources handy for consultative and informational purposes. Though certain athletic programs vary from school to school, district to district, and state to state, the following organizations provide valuable information at the national level and can certainly assist with further resources that can guide the counseling professional to more localized resources when attempting to address the academic, career, and personal/social needs of student athletes. Just like many sports, it takes a team effort for some of the best results to be gained in full, so do consider what strengths and complements these resources provide, and recognize that using them all will likely yield a better outcome for all stakeholders who may have specific needs for assisting student athletes. There is no "I" in "team", and there is no "one" in "resources".

In terms of eligibility requirements, scholarship application, and college guidelines, the following resources are particularly useful:

National Collegiate Athletic Association (NCAA)

NCAA

700 W. Washington St.

P.O. Box 6222

Indianapolis, IN 46206-6222

(317) 917-6222

www.ncaa.org

National Association of Intercollegiate Athletics (NAIA)

NAIA

1200 Grand Blvd.

Kansas City, MO 64106

(816) 595-8180

www.naia.org

National Junior College Athletic Association (NJCAA)

NJCAA

1631 Mesa Ave Suite B

Colorado Springs, CO 80906

(719) 590-9788

www.njcaa.org

College Board

College Board National Office

45 Columbus Avenue

New York, NY 10023-6917

Phone: 212-713-8000

www.collegeboard.org

In terms of social-emotional, ethical, and curriculum-based topics that impact the development of student athletes, the following organizations may be of particular interest:

American School Counselor Association (ASCA)

ASCA

1101 King St., Suite 625

Alexandria, VA 22314

(703) 683-ASCA

(800) 306-4722

www.schoolcounselor.org

Council for Accreditation of Counseling and Related Educational Programs (CACREP)

CACREP

1001 North Fairfax Street, Suite 510

Alexandria, VA 22314

(703) 535-5990

www.cacrep.org

American Psychological Association Division 47: Exercise and Sports Psychology

Division 47 Administrative Office

American Psychological Association

750 First St, NE

Washington, DC 20002-4242

(202) 336-6121

www.apadivisions.org/division-47/index.aspx

Sports Counseling Interest Network (Approved March 2006 by American Counseling Association)

American Counseling Association

5999 Stevenson Ave. Alexandria, VA 22304

(800) 347-6647

www.counseling.org

Association for Applied Sport Psychology

AASP

8365 Keystone Crossing, Suite 107

Indianapolis, IN 46240

Phone: (317) 205-9225

www.appliedsportpsych.org

National Athletic Trainers Association (NATA)

NATA

2952 Stemmons Freeway #200

Dallas, TX 75247

(214) 637-6282

www.nata.org

California University of Pennsylvania – Graduate Certificate in Sports Counseling

California University of Pennsylvania

250 University Avenue

California, PA 15419

(724) 938-4000

Springfield College – Master of Science in Athletic Counseling

Department of Psychology

Springfield College

263 Alden Street

Springfield, MA 01109

(413) 748-3388

Questions for Discussion

1. What is your view of the title of *student athlete*? How would the terminology *student who participates in athletics* impact school climate? How would this affect community perception? Can and/or should it be done?
2. Considering the role that social media and broadcasting play in the current state of athletics, how can school counselors assist with issues related to media communication? Online etiquette? Sportsmanship?
3. What role should the school counselor have when addressing issues of academic ineligibility? What steps can and/or should be taken to best inform invested parties?

References

CBS News (2012) Redshirting: Holding kids back from kindergarten. *CBS News* (March 4). Retrieved July 23, 2012 from http://www.cbsnews.com/8301-18560_162-57459888/redshirting-holding-kids-back-from-kindergarten/.

Chibbaro, J. S. (2007) School counselors and the cyberbully: Interventions and implications. *Professional School Counseling, 11(1)*, 65–68.

Dollarhide, C. T., & Saginak, K. A. (2012) *Comprehensive School Counseling Programs: K-12 Delivery Systems in Action.* Upper Saddle River, NJ: Pearson.

Drehs, W. (2011) Not my coach, Not my Town, Not anymore. *ESPN the Magazine, December 26, 2011*, 42–47.

Epstein, D. (2012) Depression and football: Uncertain connections. *Sports Illustrated, 116(20)*, 46–47.

Gentry, J. R. (2010) Kindergarten – Ready or not? Should you redshirt next year? *Psychology Today* (November 18). Retrieved July 23, 2012 from http://www.psychologytoday.com/blog/raising-readers-writers-and-spellers/201011/kindergarten-ready-or-not-should-you-redshirt-next-.

Gladwell, M. (2008) *Outliers: The Story of Success.* New York: Little, Brown.

Goldberg, A. D., & Chandler, T. (1995) Sports counseling: Enhancing the development of the high school student athlete. *Journal of Counseling and Development, 74*, 39–44.

Greer, J. (2012) Former Forest Hill Assistant Football Coach Arrested for Falsifying Transcripts. *The Palm Beach Post* (July 24). Retrieved July 26, 2012 from http://blogs.

palmbeachpost.com/highschoolbuzz/2012/07/24/former-forest-hill-assistant-football-coach-arrested-for-falsifying-transcripts/.

Jones, L. H. (2012) Prep football star Yuri Wright bringing baggage to CU Buffs. *The Denver Post* (February 1). Retrieved July 27, 2012 from http://www.denverpost.com/colleges/ci_19865056.

Klemko, R. (2011) Gilbert Arenas, athletes still causing Twitter headaches. *USA Today* (June 9). Retrieved July 27, 2012 from http://www.usatoday.com/sports/2011-06-08-regrettable-tweets-gilbert-arenas_n.htm.

Magen, Z. (1998) *Exploring adolescent happiness: Commitment, purpose, and fulfillment.* Thousand Oaks, CA: Sage.

Miller, K. E., & Hoffman, J. H. (2009) Mental well-being and sport-related identities in college students. *Sociology of Sport Journal, 26*, 335–356.

Misasi, S. P., Davis Jr., C. F., Morin, G. E., & Stockman, D. (1996) Academic preparation of athletic trainers as counselors. *Journal of Athletic Training, 31(1)*, 39–42.

NBCUniversal (2012) Female Basketball Coach Arrested for Having Sex with Girl Under 18. July 5. Retrieved July 25, 2012 from http://www.nbcmiami.com/news/local/Female-Basketball-Coach-Arrested-For-Having-Sex-With-Girl-Under-18-Report-161341095.html.

Pegoraro, A. (2010) Look who's talking – Athletes on Twitter: A case study. *International Journal of Sport Communication, 3*, 501–514.

Perks, T. (2007) Does sport foster social capital? The contribution of sport to lifestyle of community participation. *Sociology of Sport Journal, 24*, 378–401.

Petitpas, A. J., & Buntrock, C. L. (1995) Counseling athletes: A new specialty in counselor education. *Counselor Education & Supervision, 34*, 212–220.

Reuters (2012) London 2012: Greek athlete 'very bitter and upset' over racism ban. *The Guardian* (July 26). Retrieved July 27, 2012 from http://www.guardian.co.uk/sport/2012/jul/26/london-2012-greek-upset-racism-ban?CMP=twt_gu.

Stone, C. B., & Dahir, C. A. (2006) *The Transformed School Counselor.* Boston: Lahaska Press.

Tinsley, T. M. (2008) Advising and counseling high school student athletes. In A. Leslie Toogood & E. Gill (Eds.), *Advising Student Athletes: A Collaborative Approach to Success.* Monograph Series Number 18. Manhattan, KS: NACADA.

Ward, Jr. (2008) Athletic expenditures and the academic mission of American schools: A group-level analysis. *Sociology of Sport Journal, 25*, 560–578.

Watson, J. C. (2006) Student athletes and counseling: Factors influencing the decision to seek counseling services. *College Student Journal, 40(1)*, 35–42.

Index

Auger, R. W. 158
autonomy supportive/democratic
    style 104

Bandura, A. 43
Barnes, G. M. 130–1, 156, 158
Barnett, N. P. 118–19
Barrow, J. 147
Barton-Weston, H. M. 173
Beale, A. 62
Beamon, K. K. 74
Belaguer, I. 132–3
beliefs 46–7
Benford, R. D. 30, 138
BID 163
Black, D. 116, 154
Bocarro, J. 174
body image 33, 162–5, 180
Body Image Disorder (BID) 163
BodySense 161
Boland, P. 79
boundary issues 190–2
Bowden, W. W. 145
"boy crisis" 73
Brackenridge, C. 78
Brewer, B. W. 146
bullying 69–70, 153–6
Burdsey, D. 75
Burnes, T. 81
bystander effect 69

California University of Pennsylvania
    188–9, 198
Canadian Junior All-Stars 194
Cantu, R. C. 178
career: planning ahead 62–3
career identity 173–4
career issues 141
career maturity 146
Carroll, K. 81
case and file management 191
Casper, J. 174
Castillo, I. 132–3
"catching them being good" 8, 121
Catlett, B. 69
CBT *see* Cognitive Behavioral Therapy
CDC 180, 183
Centers for Disease Control and
    Prevention: Youth Risk Behavior
    Surveys 155
Chandler, T. 8, 68, 101, 130
change: as inevitable 20; model of 17

Channel One 32
Chao, R. 74–5
Chao, S. 76
cheating 135
Chesir-Teran, D. 78
Chicago Bulls 37
Choice Theory 48–51; strengths and
    limitations 50–1
Christensen, M. K. 43
Chung, C. Y. 76
Chung, E. Q. 71, 156
"Claire" (Track and Field athlete) 175–6
classroom behaviors: improvement 52
Clayton, B. 71
club sports: school sports vs. 60
coaches as consultees: autonomy
    supportive/democratic style 104;
    controlling/autocratic style 104; types
    103–4
cognitive behavioral approaches 64, 65,
    164–5
Cognitive Behavioral Therapy (CBT)
    46–8, 147; strengths and limitations
    47–8
cognitive exhaustion 68
collaboration: with community 114,
    136; with stakeholders 172; use of
    104–5, 136
collaborative approach 122, 136–7
collaborative learning approach 45
College Board 6–7, 197
college issues 141–9; athletic stigma
    147–8; choice of school 142; identity
    issues 145–7; intercollegiate athletic
    organizations 142–4; student athlete
    transitions beyond college 148–9; time
    constraints 144–5; *see also* transitional
    student athlete
"color-blind ideology" 75
Columbia Suicide Screen 183
commercialism 27–38; in schools 31–3;
    in sports 30–1; stopping mixed
    messages 35–7; technology changes
    and 33–5
communication: between home and
    school 114; skills in approaching
    parents 120
community: collaboration with 114, 136
confidentiality: ability to maintain 102;
    ethical codes and 99, 100; protocols/
    guidelines 157, 158, 161
confirmation bias 92